Joining the Choir

Joining the Choir

*Religious Membership and
Social Trust among
Transnational Ghanaians*

NICOLETTE D.
MANGLOS-WEBER

OXFORD
UNIVERSITY PRESS

OXFORD
UNIVERSITY PRESS

Oxford University Press is a department of the University of Oxford. It furthers
the University's objective of excellence in research, scholarship, and education
by publishing worldwide. Oxford is a registered trade mark of Oxford University
Press in the UK and certain other countries.

Published in the United States of America by Oxford University Press
198 Madison Avenue, New York, NY 10016, United States of America.

© Oxford University Press 2018

All rights reserved. No part of this publication may be reproduced, stored in
a retrieval system, or transmitted, in any form or by any means, without the
prior permission in writing of Oxford University Press, or as expressly permitted
by law, by license, or under terms agreed with the appropriate reproduction
rights organization. Inquiries concerning reproduction outside the scope of the
above should be sent to the Rights Department, Oxford University Press, at the
address above.

You must not circulate this work in any other form
and you must impose this same condition on any acquirer.

Library of Congress Cataloging-in-Publication Data
Names: Manglos-Weber, Nicolette D., 1983– author.
Title: Joining the choir: religious membership and social trust among
transnational Ghanaians / Nicolette D. Manglos-Weber.
Description: New York, NY, United States of America: Oxford University Press, [2018] |
Includes bibliographical references and index. |
Identifiers: LCCN 2017028644 (print) | LCCN 2018002107 (ebook) | ISBN 9780190841058 (updf) |
ISBN 9780190841065 (epub) | ISBN 9780190841072 (online content) |
ISBN 9780190841041 (cloth)
Subjects: LCSH: Christianity—Ghana. | Ghanaian
Americans—Religion—Illinois—Chicago.
Classification: LCC BR1463.G5 (ebook) | LCC BR1463.G5 M36 2018 (print) |
DDC 305.6/700899667—dc23
LC record available at https://lccn.loc.gov/2017028644

3 5 7 9 8 6 4 2

Printed by Sheridan Books, Inc., United States of America

Contents

Acknowledgments — vii
Central Characters — ix

1. Introduction — 1
2. The Setting: Migration, Social Trust, and Religion — 12
3. The Sources of Risk: Inequality, the Racial Order, and Group Competition — 36
4. The Draw of Religion: Accessibility, Portability, and Promise — 66
5. The Culture of Connection: Practices and Principles — 90
6. The Shape of Identity: Visions, Revisions, and Negotiations — 131
7. The Nature of Faith: Between Believing and Belonging — 155
8. Conclusion: Religious Bases of Trust and Integration — 180

Research Methodology — 187
Notes — 195
References — 205
Index — 219

Acknowledgments

WRITERS ARE OF many types. Some make linear progress, fixed on a clear vision of what they want to communicate and steadily moving toward it; others travel more irregularly, never certain of the path or its endpoint, but driven by an intuition that there is *something* to be seen and said if one keeps at it long enough. I am most certainly one of the latter.

This makes me especially indebted to everyone who encouraged me to listen to my intuition, or to go back down the path and reassess when necessary. During the early phases of research, Javier Auyero, Alexander Weinreb, Maya Charrad, Thomas Tweed, and Mark Regnerus played this role. Their doors were always open to me and they always trusted my abilities, even when I did not. Later on, Christian Smith and Mary Ellen Konieczny read and gave very helpful feedback on portions of the manuscript. Theo Calderara saw the value in the work when it was far from complete and steadily guided me through the review process. He was exactly the kind of editor this particular book and this particular writer needed. Tom Tweed has been a faithful guide through the ups and downs of life as a junior academic. He has been ever supportive even as his standards of excellence and empathy are unwavering.

There are many others who in smaller ways contributed to this project, either in the form of professional support or conceptual insight. Those include Ann Swidler, Jenny Trinitapoli, Margarita Mooney, Tricia Bruce, Steve Warner, Phil Gorski, Rhys Williams, and Hank Allen. Sarah Nun Moeri provided excellent copy editing with an eye to translating jargon into normal language. The students of the Spring 2015 session of Global Religion at Notre Dame University read a test draft and were kind enough to say they liked it.

Several organizations funded this project, including the University of Texas-Austin Population Research Center (UT-Austin PRC), the Society for the Scientific Study of Religion, and the Social Science Research Council. Much of the research was done while in graduate traineeship at the UT-Austin PRC, funded by the National Institutes of Child and Human Development (NICHD grant #HD007081-32). The Regional Institute for Population Studies (RIPS) was my hosting institution in Ghana, and its director F. Nii-Amoo Dodoo provided gracious assistance during that phase of research.

I would never have gotten this far without my own personal trust network: my fellow artists and thinkers, Jess, B. Sterling, Betsy, Holly, Rachel, and Sarah; my dear family, particularly Kurt, Carol, Chris, Ben, Alicia, Jane, Mike, Eric, and Jessica; and those friends I made while researching this book, particularly those I call Ama, Evangeline, Anna, Timothy, Samantha, Benjamin, Daniel, David, Amanda, Elijah, Catherine, and Alinea. I am honored you shared your stories with me and I hope you like the result.

This book is dedicated to my father, Stephen Manglos. Most of what I need to do this kind of work, I got from him.

Central Characters

In Chicago, Evangel Ministries Congregation

Elijah and Catherine—Married couple, pastors of Evangel Ministries, long-time residents of United States, one child

Benjamin—Single (later married) man, member of Evangel Ministries, recent arrival in United States, no children

Gift—Single man, member of Evangel Ministries, recent arrival in the United States, no children

Sandra—Married woman, husband living in Ghana, member of Evangel Ministries, recent arrival in United States, one child (and one on the way)

Anna and Timothy—Married couple, members of Evangel Ministries, long-time residents of United States, two children

Evangeline—Married woman, member and choir director of Evangel Ministries (later left to start new Charismatic church with husband), recent arrival in United States, two children

David—Married man, wife living in another state, choir director after Evangeline, no children

In Chicago, Other or No Religious Congregation

Sylvia—Married woman, member of American Evangelical congregation, long-time resident of United States, no children

Franklin—Single man, not a congregation member, recent arrival in United States, no children

Jeremiah—Married man, leader of Ghanaian Catholic congregation, long-time resident of United States, two children, wife and children living in Ghana

Jonathan—Single man, not a congregation member, university student, no children

In Accra, Ghana

Stephen—Single man, member of Evangel Ministries, no children
Annie—Single woman, member of Anglican congregation, no children
Ama—Single woman, member of Evangel Ministries, no children
Daniel—Soon-to-be-married man, aspiring to start new Charismatic Evangelical church, no children
Mary—Single woman, member of Evangel Ministries, no children

All proper names of people and religious organizations are pseudonyms unless otherwise noted.

I

Introduction

ON A SUMMER afternoon in downtown Chicago, within view of the Lake Michigan shoreline and Grant Park, I talked over sandwiches with Benjamin, a young man who moved from Ghana to the United States just a few years before. We met at his church, Evangel Ministries, where I had also been participating for about a month, and where we both sang with the choir each week. He told me about his privileged life back in Ghana, his hopes for obtaining his Ph.D. in the United States, and his setbacks since arriving. He couldn't pay his college tuition and so was currently out of school, working as a taxi driver. While telling his story he made a revealing comment.

"I am telling you the truth," he said, "because you are my colleague at church."

Initially I paid this statement little attention. I was more interested in how his life in Chicago had failed to meet his expectations, and in how he ended up stuck between his dreams and the reality of being an African migrant in America. Yet after more weeks and months at Evangel and more such conversations I started to realize its significance. Benjamin had said something important about how he navigated his relationships with others since his migration and how he dealt with the problem of trust.

As a foreigner having big dreams and facing big disappointments, there were many challenges to trusting others in his life, and to being trusted by them in turn. He had a lot on the line and could not afford to rely on the wrong people, whether family members, strangers, or new acquaintances. He was also often treated with suspicion or ignorance. Strangers presumed he was poor and uneducated and were hesitant to extend trust, whether in the form of an apartment lease, a job, or a friendly interaction in a grocery store. Even other Ghanaians like himself expressed distrust in him as a newcomer who might ask them for money or help down the line. Yet in spite of this he felt he could trust his church "colleagues," the people he worshiped with every Sunday and increasingly counted as friends. Because he and I were part of this church, he decided he could trust me with the truth about his failures, frustrations, and anxieties about the future.

This book is about migrants like Benjamin who face challenges in finding trusting and trustworthy relationships, and who seek out and discover a basis of social trust in religion. Immigrant religion is often depicted as an expression of ethnic solidarity, or studied in terms of how well existing religious associations help migrants access helpful resources. Yet these stories of Ghanaians in Chicago reveal that today's migrants also make choices about where and with whom to worship; and the desire for close, personal bonds of social trust is a major concern as they do so. In turn, this process draws many of them into new or deeper commitments to religious life after migration. Their new church-based trust networks shape how they revise their goals and negotiate their identities, thus having a direct impact on their professional and personal lives.

Historically, the United States has received regular waves of newcomers. The number crossing our borders today is often portrayed as unprecedented and alarming, yet there have been earlier phases of our history with similarly high numbers of people moving into the United States. One key thing has changed, however: migrant diversity. In earlier immigration peaks, most newcomers came from Europe, and with some exceptions they were white, working-class laborers looking to escape poverty, war, or religious persecution.[1] During our current peak, however—in which about 13.1 percent of the population is foreign-born—migrants have come from all parts of Asia, Africa, and Latin America, with a wide array of backgrounds, aspirations, and expectations for their lives in the United States.[2] This new, more diverse migrant wave is often called the post-1965 immigration, following landmark legislation in that year that focused on attracting skilled labor, established family reunification as a major priority for allowing entry into the country, and opened new doors to larger numbers of migrants from Asia, Africa, and Latin America.[3]

In the 1960s, people from African countries made up a very small portion of the migrant population. Yet since then, their numbers have grown quickly. In each decade since the 1970s, the African-born population in the United States has roughly doubled, and today it is close to 2 million.[4] This group also has some unique characteristics. Although many of them are indeed refugees, fleeing conflicts in places like Somalia and Sudan, many others are educated, English-speaking, middle- and upper-class denizens of countries with growing economies such as Ghana and Nigeria, with an intense demand for jobs and college degrees. They come with big aspirations and many social and economic resources, as compared to other migrant groups.[5] They also tend to come from contexts where going abroad to the United States or Europe is very common, as in the Ghanaian and Nigerian urban centers of Accra and Lagos. For example, in the 2000s, it was estimated that about 8 percent of Ghanaian university students were studying abroad; 12 percent of the Ghanaian population lived abroad; and just over half of all doctors trained in Ghana were working abroad.[6]

In American society we tend to highlight the successes of such migrants while ignoring or downplaying the obstacles they face. In 2014, many news outlets ran a story about Kwasi, a high-school student accepted into all eight Ivy League schools.[7] Kwasi is Ghanaian. In each photograph he wore a suit and was often posed with his violin—he is an accomplished musician, as well as a stellar student. In one news outlet he was pictured with his parents, who were both born in Ghana and had worked as nurses in Brooklyn hospitals after coming to the United States. His ambition was to go to medical school. He was a modern example of the rags-to-riches, foreigner-to-model-American kind of story we love to tell.

Yet the media's celebration of Kwasi's accomplishments masks the challenges Ghanaians face in the United States and the complexity of their social and relational experiences. Being black and foreign at Harvard or Yale is not easy,[8] and through his college years Kwasi will have to decide whether he is "mainstream" American, African American, or African in America.[9] His dedicated parents likely struggled to establish themselves as black foreigners. They also had to decide whether and how much to instill in their children a sense of connection to that "dark" place across the ocean where they were born—a nation Americans are often unable to place accurately on a map, let alone on their mental landscape.[10]

Thus while African blacks seem better positioned than many other migrant groups to succeed in America, and some like Kwasi do reach impressive heights, there is a gap between what they hope for and the reality. They often do not see commensurate returns to their education in terms of earnings.[11] The rising cost of higher education forces many to step off their intended professional tracks and take up working-class jobs, like driving taxis, working in hair salons, and cleaning houses. They are often miscategorized as poor, uneducated, or part of the "immigrant threat," which affects their ability to compete with native-born Americans for good jobs. Their families back home expect much from them, and that pressure can often feel paralyzing.

Many of these migrants initially view their moves abroad as strategies for achieving upward mobility rather than final resettlements. Some would rather not leave Ghana in the first place, but they feel they have no choice if they want to pursue certain professions. Many of them purchase businesses and homes in Ghana while living abroad, as an anchor in the homeland and a reassurance of their eventual return. Although sometimes those dreams of return are delayed or never achieved, particularly if they end up raising children in the United States, they still almost always desire and intend to return.

Throughout this book, therefore, I refer to my interviewees as aspirational migrants rather than immigrants, to define them in terms of their primary reasons for migration and to avoid prematurely presuming they will settle permanently. I also often use the terminology of "transnational Ghanaians," to identify them as people who are native to Ghana but live between two, or sometimes multiple, nations. What they have in common is that they were born in Ghana, they are actively seeking to improve their life chances, they have moved abroad to do so, and they are simultaneously connected to people and places on either side of the Atlantic.

Certainly, difficulties in the initial migration process and dreams of eventual return are not unique to this group. Today's second-, third-, and fourth-generation Irish, Germans, and Italians are descendants of yesterday's new migrants, who also often hoped to go back to the homeland once they made their fortune. Immigrant assimilation has usually been a trans-generational process, and it is too soon to know whether these aspirational migrants will follow a similar path, eventually settling in the United States and seeing their children and grandchildren integrate into American life.

Yet there are also reasons to expect diverse integration trajectories among migrants in the current era. Based on a growing body of evidence, prominent migration scholars Alejandro Portes and Ruben Rumbaut (2014, 2001) have shown how integration into U.S. society is segmented, meaning that it looks very different for migrants of different ethnicities and nationalities.[12] It can often be stalled or reversed, and it can involve an array of positive or very negative outcomes. It can also mean that migrants experience high degrees of economic and professional integration while still holding onto a strong sense of cultural distinctiveness.

Furthermore, the advance of rapid global travel and communications technologies makes it easier than ever for new migrants to live truly transnational lives, where they are simultaneously deeply connected to both the host and the home communities (Levitt and Glick Schiller 2004; Levitt 2001). This increasingly common in-between, "both and" existence further complicates the process of integration. Indeed, transnational migrants with more resources may be less likely to intend to settle permanently or to pursue citizenship in their host country (Massey and Akresh 2006). So, while the integration of past waves of immigrants may not have always been as uniform or as inevitable as it looks in retrospect, there is reason to expect even more variability, diversity, and even reversal in the process of integration among the post-1965 migrants.

For aspirational, transnational Ghanaians, religious identities and memberships are closely tied to these questions about integration, as has been historically the case for many North American immigrants. Since the early years of Protestant settlement in the New World, the growth of the United States has been bound up with the free practice of religion, and inclusion in American life has often been a matter of joining a church, temple, or synagogue. Each wave of immigrants has added to the vibrancy of American religious associations in turn, which is part of why the United States remains uniquely religious among North American and Western European countries.[13]

Over a century ago, Max Weber (1946 [1904]) observed that German immigrants in America were more invested in religious congregations than were their counterparts in the homeland. In business transactions and social life generally, he noted, strangers would commonly ask each other, "To what church do you belong?" Although America had formal church–state separation, the social significance of churchgoing appeared to be much greater in the New World than in the European countries from which most immigrants came. Fifty years later, Will Herberg (1983 [1955]) made a similar observation: "To have a name and an identity, one must belong somewhere; and more and more one 'belongs' in America by belonging to a religious community, which tells one *what* he is" (53).

American disestablishment of religion has also allowed grassroots movements and localized communities to determine the nature of religious membership. The local congregation, in particular, is a central institution in American life. Local congregations are voluntary and functionally diffuse, meaning they combine explicitly religious ritual with many social and even political functions (Ammerman 2005, 51ff; Warner 1994). Although usually connected to larger, bureaucratic religious organizations, they are also highly responsive to local needs and interests, often taking on distinct cultures that reflect the people who attend them and their immediate context. Increasingly, their active members are motivated by their commitment to the specific, localized community rather than to a larger organization or affiliation. Within this model, religious Americans congregate to worship, but also to have fun, build relationships, and serve their wider communities; and in so doing they create local religious associations with distinct cultures.

This model often serves new immigrants well, allowing them to meet diverse social needs in religious congregations. Many immigrant groups have therefore been drawn toward religious membership even if they weren't very religious before migrating, and even if the traditions of their homelands, like Buddhism, Hinduism, or Islam, didn't historically follow a congregational model. In the United States, people of many faiths and traditions have adopted the model of congregation-based membership. This has been shown in case studies across groups from East and South Asia, Latin America, and Africa.[14]

Yet again, post-1965 immigrants exhibit increasing diversity in this area. Like the wider U.S. population, they increasingly view religious membership as a matter of choice rather than a fixed identity. They are less concerned to find a congregation of a particular faith or denomination, and more interested in discovering a congregation that meets their social needs. They also increasingly make a distinction between ethnic and religious identity, in which the two become decoupled and distinct (Kurien 2012). As a result, they seem less tied to the idea of worshiping with others of their own ethnic or national background, and may not even attend "immigrant churches" at all. This pattern is particularly visible among African groups.[15] According to a congregation-based study done in Washington, D.C. (Foley and Hoge 2007), many African migrants attend congregations where their own nationality is not the majority.

Still, there is much to learn about why certain migrants experience religious renewal or change; why in particular some migrants gravitate toward diverse, nonmigrant congregations while others worship with those of their own ethnic or national background; and how their religious transformations in turn affect how they see themselves in relation to the new society and what they want for the future. To this point there have been few attempts to analyze diverse trajectories of religious memberships within a single migrant group, or to understand how such diverse trajectories may influence other aspects of group members' lives. This study, therefore, was designed to answer the following questions: (1) How do Christian aspirational migrants from Ghana choose a church upon arrival in the United States?; and (2) How do their church choices and resulting memberships affect the development of their identities and goals for their migrations?

My goal in asking these questions was to get at the larger issues of integration from the perspective of migrants' own experiences, desires, and choices, as expressed in their religious lives. Put simply, I wanted to know what Christian migrants from Ghana *want* out of their migrations to the United States and from their churches, and how the two intersect. In southern Ghana, where many transnational migrants move from, organized religion is a central institution, and Christians make up the majority. In the area around Accra, for example, 83 percent are Christians, and 74 percent are either active members or leaders of a religious group.[16] This makes churchgoing a particularly good arena in which to study desires and choices that impact integration.

To answer these questions I collected stories and observations that were transnational, diverse, and spread out over time. I went to both southern Ghana and Chicago, to get a sense of the sending country and one host community; I interviewed Christian Ghanaians who attended a variety of churches or who didn't attend at all, in order to see whether they were more different or more similar in what they were looking for; and I got to know members of one church, Evangel Ministries, very well, so that I was able to learn their stories in depth and witness changes in their lives over a period of years. In particular, by becoming a choir member in this congregation, I was able to more fully engage in the behind-the-scenes work of the community, experience the embodied and emotional rituals of public worship, and come to know the stories of members at a deeper level. Joining the choir ultimately became the main avenue for my own integration into the community, and a meaningful symbol of racial and ethnic integration more generally.

What I found in these stories was that Ghanaian migrants often wanted to find new relations they could rely on after migration. They evaluated different religious options based on their "social feel," and how well suited they seem to be for finding new connections. Importantly, and perhaps surprisingly, they often stated they preferred to attend with groups other than fellow migrants; but they also often had trouble finding the kind of social feel they wanted in American congregations.

When they did invest in a religious congregation, they often built new close ties with other members, and those ties expressed the characteristics of personal trust. Over time, those ties often led to a deepening religious commitment, which in turn shaped how they negotiated their identities and goals for the future. Thus I use their stories in this book to examine religion as a basis of social trust, and develop a theory of social trust as an *imaginative and symbolic activity*.

I conclude that the relationship between religious membership and immigrant integration at least partly depends on the dynamics of social trust: where and how it is formed, when it erodes, and how it shapes aspirations and identities. Religious congregations are voluntary social spaces in which such processes take place, and they can thus be particularly important integrative spaces for those who move across borders and are motivated to seek new trust networks. Ghanaian migrants are often attuned to these dynamics and want to build new ties across social divisions of race and nationality through religious association. Yet congregations can only support this pathway to integration to the extent that they truly facilitate personal trust across such boundaries. They can only bridge such divides if they are indeed able to join members in bonds of trust.

Joining the Choir

Becoming a "colleague" of Benjamin at Evangel Ministries was an experience that stretched my own imagination. It was not initially comfortable. I spent hundreds of hours in unknown settings, eating unfamiliar (and very spicy) foods, interacting with people of different backgrounds, and learning the ropes within an organization that had its own rituals, rules, and norms of behavior. My journey was awkward and anxiety inducing as often as it was exhilarating and enlightening; and yet my own reactions and fears were perhaps the best teachers of the lessons of trust and distrust. I learned in the experience how much race and foreignness shape my own perceptions of people, and how the work of collective ritual and imagination can overcome some of these biases.

I began my research in 2009 as a foreign visitor to Accra, Ghana's coastal capital city of over 2 million people. My visit was the culmination of an interest in the new Evangelical churches of Africa, which began during several research experiences among Charismatic and Pentecostal churches in Malawi, East Africa.[17] In reading about the movement I learned that some of its biggest growth—and its most prominent leaders and congregations—were in the urban centers of West Africa. If I was going to understand this major shift toward Evangelicalism in so many parts of the continent, I decided Accra was a good place to start.

It was impossible to spend much time in Accra without hearing about Evangel Ministries. It was one of several Charismatic Evangelical churches that attracted thousands of devoted participants and curious spectators to its central meeting hall every Sunday morning. Posters advertising its midweek prayer events and new books and audiovisual media lined the walls of bus stations and public buildings. Driving through the countryside outside of Accra, I spotted signs directing people to its satellite branches in homes, down alleyways, and in small rented storefronts. On Sunday mornings, smaller branches met in the hostels— dormitory-like residences—on the campus of the University of Ghana where I was staying.

Two things were apparent to me about Evangel Ministries when I first walked in the door: it is a young church and it is a global church. The music pouring out of its windows on Sunday mornings is heavy on the bass and drums. The preaching deals with subjects like dating, future goals, and getting along with parents. And because so many of Ghana's youth now have friends and family abroad, and think about emigrating as a route to a bright future of their own, Evangel Ministries reflects their transnational awareness. The leadership regularly reports on the growth of the organization's many branches of the church around the world, and discusses in depth the political and social issues that extend beyond Ghana. Aspects of global youth culture, including styles of dress and the use of technology, are everywhere in the church space.

That summer I attended midweek and Sunday services at Evangel Ministries and interviewed some of its members, asking questions about their views on religion in Ghana and what brought them to this particular church in the first place. I kept noticing how, as described later in chapter 4, their experiences at Evangel shaped their social networks and their goals for the future. I also became curious about how Evangel's branches abroad, particularly in the United States, function in a setting where they are no longer associated with a mainstream organization but, rather, with a foreign country like Ghana. I wanted to know what these overseas branches looked, sounded, and acted like.

The following summer I went to Chicago to answer this question. I chose Chicago because Evangel Ministries has a branch there and I had also lived there in the past. I had old friends in the city and at least one personal connection to a Ghanaian friend, which guaranteed me a couch to sleep on and at least one phone number to call upon arrival. The Chicago Evangel Ministries branch was just a few years old at the time and was still small—there were about twenty consistent members and sometimes thirty to forty people present on Sunday. They mostly ranged in age from the 20s to 40s. Some were successful professionals—many worked as nurses or doctors—and others like Benjamin were still trying to find their footing. The members were almost all Ghanaian migrants to the United States, and for the time I participated there I was the only white and native-born American.

Formally, it was easy to show up and start participating. Sunday services within Protestant Evangelical Christian traditions are by nature free and open to the public. Yet even though initial entry was fairly easy, there were subtler personal barriers that I had to overcome throughout my participation. Growing up in racialized America, I had been socialized to see race as a significant marker of difference between people; and I was accustomed to being in the racial majority in most social settings. All of my knowledge and training on the variable, constructed nature of race as an idea could not eliminate the awkwardness I felt at consistently being the only white person in the room. More than anything else, I felt conspicuous, as if anything I said or did would be noted, remembered, and remarked upon. At the same time, since I put myself in the situation with the goal of research, it was hard not to worry about making mistakes and giving the other participations reasons not to trust me, which would hinder the progress of my study.

Joining the choir helped me overcome some of these obstacles. This was a group that came to the stage in the first half of every Sunday morning service and led the congregation in collective singing. Week to week, the choir ranged in size from three to ten people, usually the younger and heavily committed members of the group. One day while making small talk I revealed that I had some experience with singing, and I was soon after invited to come to a choir rehearsal and see if it was a good fit. I did, and it stuck. I spent the rest of that summer and the next singing with the choir.

We met on Saturday afternoons, in Benjamin's high-rise apartment building or in the church's rented meeting space. The rehearsals often involved meals together, and lots of down time while waiting for someone to show up, or just lingering after our work was done. Several times choir members would surprise me with a helping of *waakye,* one of my favorite Ghanaian dishes. These meetings were my first and best informal times with Evangel's members, where I learned the best jokes and each person's small quirks. And on Sunday mornings, when we came together on the stage in our suits and dresses, and guided the rest of the congregation through the songs we had picked for that week, I felt the awkwardness and anxieties of being a stranger slip away.

I wrote this book in large part to understand and share that experience: coming in as a stranger, struggling to trust and wondering if I would be trusted, and then moving past it to a place of solidarity in spite of the wide gulfs between me and the rest of the group. I also wrote it to explore whether this experience, so personally valuable to me as a researcher, could be promoted and shared more broadly between native- and foreign-born Americans and between whites and blacks. Of course, I cannot pretend that my experience is identical to that of Ghanaian newcomers to the United States, who spend every moment of their new lives as strangers, working to avoid being perceived as a threat. Yet I do believe my experience, along with the many stories and observations I collected, taught me more general truths about how social dynamics operate and how religion intervenes in this process, and it is those ideas I mean this book to convey.

Each of the chapters that follow deals with some aspect of social trust and distrust in the experience of Ghanaians at home and abroad, and how religion functions as a portable, voluntary basis of such trust. The second chapter provides the background to the study by describing how Ghanaian migration to the United States fits within the history of Ghana's relationship to the wider world, and presenting the theoretical resources I used to understand trust and religion. The next two chapters focus on the challenges to trust in the black migrant experience and the appeal of collective religious practice, setting up the context for the relationships formed at Evangel Ministries. The fifth chapter focuses on the specifics of how trust is formed, using examples and stories to analyze the culture of connection that supports the building of personal trust networks at Evangel Ministries and churches like it. The sixth and seventh chapters deal with the impact of religious-based trust in their lives: how it helps these migrants navigate questions of identity and faith, and how this process often involves a renewal or deepening of religious commitment. Finally, the conclusion summarizes the main themes of the book and revisits the argument about the relationship between religion, as a basis of personal trust, and integration.

Everyone's story is different. But the more stories we hear and tell, the more themes start to emerge and teach us both what we have in common and what distinguishes us. My purpose in writing this book is to convey and analyze the stories

I heard, focusing on those that often go untold. I hope my readers will feel just a bit of what I've felt in response to these stories, and as a consequence greet black Africans in America with respect and compassion. I also hope in this small way to repay those at Evangel Ministries who, time and again, trusted me. They made me feel as if I did belong, despite the differences between us. In my journey I learned about sadness, disappointment, and misunderstanding; but I also learned about the nature of generosity, and about trust extended as a gift. I can never thank them enough. All I can do to invite others to see that, for African newcomers and all of us, such trust is real, possible, and indeed necessary.

2

The Setting

MIGRATION, SOCIAL TRUST, AND RELIGION

ALTHOUGH ASPIRATIONAL GHANAIANS are a relatively new migrant group in North America, their migrations are part of a long history of interaction and exchange with foreign societies. In this chapter I give context to the current trend of Ghanaian out-migration, and I explain the factors that draw transnational Ghanaians away from home. I also address the conceptual issues involved in studying social trust and religion, present a working definition of "personal trust" as a distinct type of social trust, and describe the religious landscape of Chicago and how it presents and precludes certain options for these Christian aspirational migrants.

Ghana in the World

The geographic area that is now Ghana is located along two historically important avenues of global trade: the maritime routes connecting West Africa to Europe and the Americas, and the overland routes running along the southern edge of the Saharan Desert connecting West Africa to the Middle East and Asia. It is also an area with a long history of human civilization. Archeological evidence suggests the area was inhabited by 10,000 B.C.E.; and one of the area's predominant local people groups, the Akans, settled in the area by the fifth century B.C.E.

During the westward expansion of the Muslim world that began in the 600s C.E., during which the cultures and economies of increasingly far-flung societies were connected, the Akan states and their neighbors began to interact extensively with Islamic civilization. They exported gold and kola nuts, among other valuable goods, and hosted foreigners from North Africa and the Middle East in their cities and towns. This early period of West African exchange with the outside world resulted in the Islamization of many local populations; and this heritage is still observable in the predominantly Muslim northern parts of Ghana. The rise in commerce during this period also resulted in an increase in economic production and political centralization among those kingdoms best situated to take advantage of such trade, such as the Akans.[1]

A second major period of exchange followed the expansion of trade throughout the Atlantic World in the Age of Sail. Historian Jonathan Thornton (1998) chronicles the rise of the Atlantic World as an increasingly integrated economic and cultural region, following innovations in sea transportation. Before the fifteenth century, maritime expeditions connecting Europe, Africa, and the Americas were rare and hazardous to undertake. After that point, though, it became more feasible to reliably transport commodities around the Atlantic World by sea. Such commodities included the natural riches coming from West Africa. Gold, silver, cocoa, and the woven textiles of the Akans were particularly valued. In fact, so much gold from the area was traded abroad that by the mid-sixteenth century most of the currency in the Netherlands was fabricated from it.[2]

In the late 1600s, a powerful kingdom arose and established itself over the area, the Asante Empire. The kingdom began as a clan-based Akan community that was consolidated into a major military and economic power by one king, Osei Tutu. He extended his rule outward over other Akan groups and their neighbors, and for several hundred years the empire was the dominant political force in the area. The empire developed a sophisticated central government that built upon and reinforced the clan-based, matrilineal social structure of the Akans, and was a major trading partner of the Europeans. As European trade and imperialism expanded throughout the Atlantic, the Asante Empire also provided large numbers of slaves—usually the soldiers of rival state armies captured in war—to the growing demand for bonded labor.[3] English, Dutch, Portuguese, and Swedish traders built many coastal forts that served as hubs for the trade in and imprisoning of slaves, such as the still-pristine Cape Coast Castle (figure 2.1), northwest of Accra.

During this time, each of the ethno-linguistic groups in the area upheld its own local religious traditions, closely tied to the institutions of chieftaincy and ancestral lineage. For example, the Akans believed in a system of deities personifying elements in the natural world, they had one supreme god, and they considered chiefs to be divinely appointed. As mentioned, Islam had come into the area in the seventh century, and over time came to be practiced alongside local traditions, particularly in northern parts of the area. Christianity came later with the European trade, and did not have a significant local presence until the late nineteenth century. Conversion to Christianity was then widespread in the south—particularly among the Akan, Ga, and Ewe groups—while the northern regions retained their Islamic character. Through much of this period, the people

FIGURE 2.1 Cape Coast Castle.

continued to practice the local traditions in conjunction with Christianity and Islam.[4]

In the mid- and late-1800s, the relatively equal trade relationship between the Europeans and the local kingdoms of West Africa shifted. The slave trade was formally abolished, but the colonization of Africa became a core strategy in the global competition between the European powers. This was part of the imperial scramble for Africa, a process that in a relatively short period resulted in the divvying up of the continent among French, British, Belgian, Portuguese, and German holdings. At the Berlin Conference of 1884–85, hosted by Otto von Bismarck of Germany, a new map of Africa was drawn that gave the various powers a collective mandate to establish imperial control in their designated areas. This story is vividly explained by Adam Hochschild (1999) as the end product of Europe's growing military dominance, strategic moves by various kings and presidents to enhance their geopolitical positions, and a developing image of Africans as pagan, brutish, and uncivilized.[5]

At the Berlin Conference, areas including and surrounding the Asante Empire were allocated to the British, who were by that time the Asantes' most active European trading partners. Although the Asante Empire had enjoyed military dominance in the area for several centuries, and thus were not easy to subjugate, ultimately the superiority of British guns and a growing internal dissatisfaction with the administration of the reigning Asante monarch caused the empire to crumble. In 1896, the British conquered the Asantes, took control of their outer provinces and tributaries, and established the Gold Coast colony, ruled from their own center of government on the southern coast (the area that is now Accra, Ghana's capital).[6]

The colony was governed by British expatriates, who relied on local elites—both those of the Akans and of their neighboring groups, the Ewes and Gas—to administer systems of governance modeled after British conventions. This strategy, known as indirect rule, relied on a steady flow of graduates from schools founded by Christian missionaries. German Presbyterians, Portuguese and French Catholics, and Anglicans from Britain had been doing missionary work in the area throughout the 1800s. One of their main objectives was to set up schools that could teach basic literacy in European languages so that new converts could read the Bible. Once colonial rule was established, the graduates of such schools also formed a pool of civil servants with the required literacy skills to learn British-style bureaucracy.

Formal education thus became both a new pathway to enhanced social status and an engine of inculturation into Western religious, economic, and political frameworks. As an example of this, the first institution of higher education in Ghana was Achimota College, established in the mid-1920s as a prep school for entry into the University of London. Even after the University College of the Gold Coast was established as a formally independent university in 1948, it was awarding University of London degrees until 1961.[7]

The elite classes produced by this system of education and indirect rule were conversant across cultures, in more ways than one. They spoke the language of the colonizers and the language of the villages in which they were raised. Many of them lived and traveled extensively abroad, and obtained British university degrees. Not surprisingly, the first leaders of sovereign Ghana came from this group. After they achieved independence from the British in 1957, they sought to build a unified citizenry that transcended the differences among local ethnolinguistic groups (the Akans, Gas, Ewes, Mole-Dagbanis, and Hausa-Fulanis, among others), and the divide between rural agriculturalists and urban elites.

The achievement of this vision proved difficult, however. The years immediately after independence saw multiple military coups and shifts in power, and a period of economic stagnation and food scarcity in the 1980s. In the early 1990s, under pressure from international governments and nongovernmental agencies, the ruling elite took steps to institute multiparty democracy. Yet political and economic reform during these years was slow, given the continued divide between elite interests and public demands. For many years, Ghana's political leaders had little incentive to prioritize social welfare above their own accumulation of wealth; and even in the period during which they came under global pressure to democratize, many of their reforms were either misguided or too limited to make lasting improvements in the citizens' quality of life.[8]

Today there is more good news. Ghana exhibits steady economic growth, is relatively free from civil conflict, and consistently has experienced peaceful elections and transitions of power. Yet there are still in many ways two Ghanas: the Ghana of the educated, urban, and globally connected classes—geographically concentrated in the south, dominated by those of Akan, Ewe, and Ga descent, and proportionally more Christian—and the Ghana of the rural subsistence farmers and uneducated poor, concentrated in the northern regions, dominated by Mole-Dagbani and Hausa-Fulani groups and their neighbors, and proportionally more Muslim (see figure 2.2).

Trends in Emigration

In the earlier decades of the 1900s, out-migration was somewhat limited to the very wealthy. It was an option for those who could afford to send their children to European and North American schools, and those with the means to travel abroad. In the 1970s, however, emigration became more common among the wealthiest classes and was also increasingly pursued by middle- and working-class families as a strategy for upward mobility. This emigration was in part driven by political and economic instability at home, as well as the expansion of primary and secondary schools, which dramatically increased the demand for international higher education.

As it pertains to migration to the United States, the growth of Ghanaian migrants in the 1970s and the following decades was partly due to the post-1965 shifts in immigration policy mentioned in Chapter 1 that opened up new possibilities for those from non-European countries. The doors were opened even further by the institution of the diversity visa program in 1990, which awards residency visas to applicants from countries that have not traditionally sent large numbers of immigrants to the United States. Ghanaian migration was also partly driven by growth in the U.S. higher education system and its global visibility, and by the goals of colleges and universities to expand and diversify their student populations by bringing in more international students.

U.S. immigration policy has since shifted again, both prior to and following the September 11, 2001, attack on the World Trade Center. With the transfer of immigrant control procedures from the Immigration and Nationalization Service (INS) to the more ominously titled Immigration and Customs

FIGURE 2.2 Map of Ghana's ethno-linguistic groups by Census region.
Source: Ghana Demographic and Health Survey, 2008.

Enforcement (ICE) agency of the Department of Homeland Security (DHS), undocumented immigration has been criminalized to an unprecedented degree.[9] Although the same avenues for lawful entry exist, including student visas, diversity visas, and family reunification visas, the application process is perceived by most Ghanaians to be much more stringent and arbitrary than in the past. Deportation is now a real possibility that makes their position—or that of close friends and relatives—tenuous. Even for those with relatively more resources to navigate this system successfully, it communicates an anti-immigrant message that is hard to ignore.[10]

Yet there is little evidence that migration from Ghana to the United States has slowed significantly since the early 2000s. Changes at home, including an uptick in economic growth accompanied by deepening inequality, have given even more Ghanaians reason to move abroad. In a pattern repeated across modern-day Africa, Ghana's gross domestic product (GDP) has grown by between 4 and 14 percent each year since 2000, while its GINI coefficient—a standard measure of inequality— has also increased from 36 in the late 1980s to about 43 in the mid-2000s; as of 2005, 25 percent of the population was still earning less than $1.90 a day.[11] Thus, although prosperity is spreading more widely, the class divide is also deepening; and those on the wrong side of that divide have a daily struggle for survival. The aspirations to move forward and upward, expressed by each of the people mentioned in this book, are desires to avoid such economic insecurity and to firmly establish themselves and their children in a Ghana of regular employment, bank accounts, store-bought clothes, cars, computers, cellphones, and pristine homes.

Coming to Chicago

The experiences of the Ghanaians I met in Chicago were shaped by both these economic and historic factors in Ghana and the social context they entered upon arrival in the United States. As blacks in a major American urban center, they had to contend with the effects of a troubled racial history, embedded in the physical environment and in the minds and hearts of those with whom they shared that space.

Chicago is deeply segregated along color lines, exemplifying the urban American apartheid pattern described by sociologists Douglas Massey and Nancy Denton (1998). The mostly black neighborhoods west and south of the central business district have some of the highest crime and poverty rates in the country. They have been deprioritized over decades of city planning, as is obvious when one looks at the Chicago public transit map: large swaths of the predominantly black South Side remain inaccessible by train, as compared to the thick network of lines serving the North Side of the city. There is also deep antipathy between public officials and the black population, as illustrated in several high-profile cases of police violence in the 2010s. Chicago is thus a highly segregated and racially charged environment. These realities weigh on new black migrants when they think about where to live, where to work, where to send their kids to school, and with whom to associate.

There is currently limited data on the size, character, or origins of the Ghanaian community in Chicago. The population started growing in the 1970s, on a par with the growth in Ghanaian Americans elsewhere in the country. One local community organization, the Ghana National Council, began as a Ghanaian Student's Union in the 1960s, suggesting that by that time there were a number of Ghanaian students in the area seeking connection and representation. Estimates of the size of the population today vary widely. At the high end, Emmanuel Akyeampong (2000) has estimated the population of Ghanaians in Chicago at 30,000. At the far low end, 2013 data from the American Community Survey of the U.S. Census Bureau estimates the number of Ghanaians in the Chicago metropolitan area at just under 4,000, and the number of Ghanaians in the United States at about 92,000.[12] Given that immigrant populations are notoriously difficult to count in official censuses, the actual number is likely somewhere between these estimates.

In my own research I found the Ghanaian immigrant population in Chicago to have several distinct characteristics.[13] First, they are socioeconomically better off and more educated compared to many other immigrant groups in the area, and also relative to the Ghanaian population at home, although as the emigration trend in Ghana has grown, there is increasing class diversity among immigrants. Second, they are a rapidly growing group that only recently has gained visibility in public life. Because of these two factors, much of what has been written about this group has emphasized how well positioned they are to succeed in the United States and how different they are from American blacks, a point to which I will return later in this chapter. Articles in Chicago-area news outlets often give inspiring stories of Ghanaians succeeding as entrepreneurs and local business owners, for example, and chronicle their efforts to maintain a sense of their distinct ethnic heritage.[14]

Third, this group is heavily concentrated in certain professions that vary in occupational prestige. On the higher end of the prestige spectrum, Ghanaians tend to gravitate toward allied medical professions. They are commonly physicians, nurses, pharmacists, physicians' assistants, and x-ray technicians, for example. To a somewhat lesser extent, they move into business and financial sector careers. These are largely the idealized professions within the community, in part because they are seen as stable and portable. There is always a demand for doctors and nurses, for example, and it is a good job to have whether one wants to stay in the United States or return to Ghana.

On the lower end of the prestige spectrum, many take jobs that are appealing for different reasons. Common jobs include taxi driving, food service work, and cosmetology. Those who work in such jobs are often employed as freelance or contract workers rather than regular salaried employees, which can be useful for setting their own hours (and thus balancing multiple sources of income around continuing education, for example), and helps them avoid scrutiny into their legal status. Because of the high numbers of West Africans in these less prestigious professions, it is now common for new migrants to work for West African–owned taxi companies, restaurants, or salons, which are unlikely to report them for visa violations.

Fourth, and related, the legal status of Ghanaian migrants can at times be complicated. As I will discuss in Chapter 3, many come to the United States with valid documentation, such as student or visitor's visas. It is not common for them enter the country illegally. Nonetheless, there are many cases in which unexpected setbacks, as well as processing delays in the immigration system, channel them into a kind of legal limbo, where they are best described as "partially undocumented." Common examples include those who come with student visas but are forced to drop out for financial reasons, and are thus staying and working in the country illegally; or those who come on visitor's visas, sponsored by relatives, and then stay and find jobs while waiting—often for long periods of time—for their applications for legal permanent residency to be approved. That said, their ability to avoid or navigate such situations varies dramatically, particularly depending on social class. There are also many in the community who are properly documented legal permanent residents and thus do not worry about their immigration status.

Fifth, and finally, this group exhibits fairly diffuse residential and associational patterns. In other words, they do not on the whole tend to fit the model of the urban immigrant enclave, in terms of either where they live or with whom they associate. There is one urban neighborhood, Uptown, with a large number of Ghanaians and West Africans, and it has a cluster of Ghanaian grocery stores, salons, churches, and restaurants. Yet Ghanaians are also concentrated in Bolingbrook, a major suburb far to the southwest of the city center. Further, many Ghanaians, especially if they have been in the United States a bit longer and are more established, prefer not to live in those areas. In my study I found that only about one-third of those who attended the Evangel Ministries church lived in close proximity to other Ghanaians; and the church itself, although it changed locations several times during my research, never met in a known West African neighborhood.

This diffuseness is also reflected in where Ghanaian migrants live elsewhere in the country. While cities like New York, Chicago, Washington, D.C., and Boston certainly have the highest numbers of Ghanaians, it is also increasingly common for them to settle in small cities and towns across the country, where they may be one of only a few West African families. Given their tendency to move for education, they often go where the colleges and universities are. This could be the semi-rural Midwest or the metropolitan areas of the Northeast. Their pursuit of new and better job opportunities also often takes them to smaller cities and towns.

For example, a handful of the core members of Evangel Ministries moved to new locations during my time there—places like Nashville, Las Vegas, Sacramento, Dallas, and other spots apart from the familiar immigrant gateway cities. Others lived or had formerly lived in small college towns in Massachusetts, Connecticut, or Iowa. Some claimed they preferred the life there to the anonymity, complexity, and expense of the big city, even though there was more opportunity to interact with other Ghanaians in larger urban centers.

Such geographical dispersion was also reflected in where Evangel Ministries had branches throughout the region. At the regional meetings I attended, described in more detail in chapter 5, I met members from small branches in Minneapolis, Minnesota, Lexington, Kentucky, and Cleveland, Ohio, to name a few. Some of those members also lived in even smaller towns or outer suburban rims, and drove one or two hours to attend their Evangel Ministries branch.

In their group associations, there is a similar pattern of both concentration and dispersion. While there are numerous community organizations, there are also many who opt out of such associations. The most active community organization is the Ghana National Council (GNC), mentioned earlier. Their signature event is the Ghanafest, a yearly summer cultural festival in a Chicago city park, which I describe in more detail in chapter 3. The GNC also organizes events throughout the year and spreads information about important happenings within the community. They have about a dozen affiliated associations representing ethnic identities such as Akan and Ewe, regions such as the northern parts of Ghana, and professional identities such as nursing. A study of the Ewe Association in Chicago (Lehrer 1998), one of the GNC's associated organizations, found the group to be active in fundraising for members with financial needs and in organizing weddings and funerals.

However, in my study I talked to many Ghanaians in the area who had very little interaction with such groups. As I will discuss in Chapter 3, many at Evangel Ministries were completely uninvolved in any Ghanaian organization apart from their church; and some claimed such cultural organizations and activities were primarily appealing to Ghanaians who were older or less educated. Thus, while these organizations are clearly important sources of cultural continuity and social support for some—perhaps in very similar ways to church congregations—Ghanaians vary in whether and how much they are involved in such groups. The most common pattern among those I interviewed was to have some periodic involvement in the community by attending some weddings and funerals, going to Ghanafest each summer, and shopping from time to time in Ghanaian grocery stories, while grounding most of their social life in family or church-based relationships.

As the stories in the following chapters show, most of my Ghanaian interviewees viewed their moves to the United States in general and to Chicago specifically as avenues for achieving certain goals. They varied in the degree to which their upper-class status was already solidified. Some were the children of government ministers and business leaders, with extensive resources at their disposal, while others were the first in their families to leave the village, go to school, and get a paying job. Yet all of their stories demonstrate how important emigration has become to the culture and economy of Ghana today, and more broadly the embeddedness of Ghanaian society within global processes of exchange and interaction. Finally, their stories demonstrate the pervasive but tenuous condition of living in an urban, racially charged environment, while also balancing home and abroad, the familiar and the foreign, and aspiration and risk. In such a context, whom they associate with and why is not something they can leave to chance.

Why Social Trust Matters

Making an international move out of aspiration is an inherently risky endeavor, in which the ability to rely on certain trustworthy others is crucial for success. Yet it is also an acute case of a more general condition—the fact that most human activities require some degree of social trust. As social beings, we often depend on others to help and not to harm us, even though we cannot ever fully guarantee their cooperation.

In *The Evolution of Ethics* (2015), psychologist Blaine Fowers writes that cooperation involves two or more people acting in ways to produce shared benefits, and the impulse toward cooperation is an important evolutionary development in human life. Yet non-cooperators do at times exploit cooperators, accessing the benefits of cooperation without paying the costs. Trust is what allows cooperation in spite of the possibility of exploitation. It supports the expectation that another will act fairly, or in other words will act in line with our perceptions of how people *should* act in cooperation with each other. Social trust is thus a key concept for sociologists, particularly those who are interested in social capital—that is, the "benefits that inhere in relationships" (Small 2009, 6).[15] Such benefits, it is often argued, could not be enjoyed without some degree of social trust.

Social trust is also usually divided into two types, based on where it occurs and the nature of the relationship between the trusters. *Personal trust* occurs between people who have a more or less enduring social tie and some degree of knowledge of or experience with each other. This type of trust develops in relation to the specifics of the tie itself: how the two people know each other, their history of interactions, and how they come to feel toward each other. *Impersonal trust* occurs between strangers who are nevertheless part of some larger society or social grouping. This is the kind of trust we place in other drivers to follow the rules of the road, for example. This trust has little to do with what we know about that particular person, but rather is supported by the existence of legal institutions (i.e., violating traffic laws is punishable by the law), and by a sense of generally shared moral principles (i.e., the other driver has probably also been socialized in the value of cooperating with the law, and likewise wants to avoid an accident). Throughout this book, my concern is primarily with the nature of personal trust; while acknowledging that personal trust often builds from impersonal trust, and thus there is rarely a distinct boundary between the two types in practice.

Charles Tilly (2005, 2006, 2007, 2010) uses the term "trust network" to refer to important relations of personal trust. With this concept he moves beyond the dyad of two people to the realm of collective interaction and association. He notes,

> Trust sometimes connects larger numbers of people who are carrying on some weighty, high-risk, long-term collective enterprise . . . and [who are] placing the enterprise at risk of member's malfeasance, mistakes, or failure. When that happens, members can typically call on each other for aid on the simple basis of shared membership. (2010, 271)

Such clusters of relations are trust networks. They involve relatively high levels of risk and a sense of obligation based in co-membership. They are necessary for many of the most significant activities in social life, such as building families, establishing financial security, making meaning out of situations and experiences, and establishing moral principles of behavior. They are, in other words, the essential contexts in which people engage in such meaningful activities.

Personal Trust as an Imaginative and Symbolic Activity

Tilly wrote extensively about the impact of trust networks on democracy and the development of cities and states. Yet how and why such networks come into being are equally important questions. Tilly notes that many types of activities can provide a basis for trust networks, using examples such as "birth, common residence, sexual relations, mutual aid, religious practice, public ceremonies, and more" (2005, 57). He does not discuss in much depth, however, why people form trust networks with certain particular others among the diversity of strangers they interact with throughout life, or whether there is an element of choice involved in where and with whom people build those trust networks.

Georg Simmel's classic writings on trust help to fill in this gap, particularly where he discusses personal trust in relation to the monetary system (1990) and religious life (1955). Simmel vividly described trusting on a personal level as a "quasi-religious leap of faith" (1990, 179). A leap of faith is an act that is almost willful, resistant to contrary arguments or evidence, and based in the emotional power of deeply meaningful symbols. Other theorists of trust have elaborated on this imagery (Fredericksen 2012; Möllering 2001), outlining how such leaps of faith involve both subjective interpretations of available evidence and suspension of possible doubts, leading to a positive expectation of how the other will act.

Trusting a particular person in a particular situation thus requires that one interpret available information as "proof" of trustworthiness, even when one's actual knowledge or experience of the other is limited. In order to make such an interpretation, a person must read the intersubjective symbolic cues projected by the other—the person's self-presentation, habits, expressions, and so on—in a positive light, and imagine the other to be a trustworthy person on the basis of those symbols. In other words, the truster relies on symbolic indicators of trustworthiness and imaginatively interprets these to be good evidence for trusting the other. Emotion plays an important role in this process as well, since feelings are what give such symbols their power. We feel inclined to trust the other when the person can symbolically convey certain impressions (Barbalet 2009; Lewis and Wiegert 1985).[16] Collectively, these insights support a working definition of personal trust as an *imaginative and symbolic activity.*

This Simmelian view of trust is intriguing because in some ways it runs counter to both commonsense notions and other scholarly perspectives on trust. People often talk about trust as being earned, presumably through a history of positive interactions. Similarly, rational choice theorist James Coleman (1990, 175ff) argues that trust is based on "credit slips" built up through exchanges between person A and person B. Person A provides a good or service to person B, which functions as a guarantee that person B will then provide a comparable good or service to person A at some point in the future. Yet talk of trust as being earned or built on the basis of a credit-slip system implies that trusters are generally skeptical about the trustworthiness of others until they find identifiable reasons to trust. The trustee is guilty until proven innocent, so to speak. By contrast, in the imaginative and symbolic model, trusters are generally hopeful about the trustworthiness of others. Provided a solid symbolic basis, the trustee is innocent until proven guilty.

Mario Small (2009) demonstrates this inclination to trust in his study of mothers at a daycare center in New York. These mothers habitually trusted their children's care to other mothers associated with the daycare center, even if they didn't know much about those other mothers. Small notes their "willingness to trust other mothers with their children rarely required much information about the trustee" (109). This was particularly striking for their trust in acquaintances or distant friends, the types of relationships that sit between the very closest ties (family members, most intimate friends, etc.) and the very weakest ones (strangers or near strangers with whom they interacted).

Small argues that trust in such weak friendships relies in large part upon their shared connection to the daycare center. He concludes that these daycare centers "condition relations among weakly tied mothers—among complete nonintimates—in ways conducive to social support" (108). They do this by facilitating trust in other parents and by establishing a sense of obligation to those connected with the center. In his examples, the shared connection to the daycare also seems to serve as a symbolic cue that the other person is okay to trust, especially in the very initial stages of an acquaintance relationship. The mothers want and need to trust, and they rely on the shared connection to the daycare center as a reassuring sign that they can go ahead and imagine other parents as trustworthy sources of assistance.

From this perspective, the activities that form trust networks lie at the convergence of two conflicting and yet undeniable motivations: to trust and cooperate with others, and to protect oneself from trusting the wrong others. People balance these two motivations through an imaginative use of symbolic cues. When they do trust a certain other, and thereby engage in Simmel's leap of faith, it is the result of imaginatively reading those symbols as evidence of another's trustworthiness, and thereby deciding that it is okay to act on their desire to trust.

Problems of Distrust

How this imaginative and symbolic activity works at the social level is perhaps best seen within the dynamics of trust surrounding race and foreignness in America. Eduardo Bonilla-Silva (2013) describes the cultural aspects of the racial order in terms of a racial habitus. The term "habitus," based in the work of Bourdieu (1987), is defined as a mix of embodied dispositions—including tastes, preferences, and cognitive frameworks—that are formed through everyday habits and are often specific to a person's social class. Bonilla-Silva argues that the historical development of the racial order has produced a stark difference in habitus between whites and blacks, displayed in how whites and blacks tend to dress, speak, carry themselves, and have different tastes and preferences. People are usually unaware that they are "acting white" or "acting black," except in situations in which such behaviors cause conflict, and thus they are also often unaware of how their assessments of others are shaped by their own racialized dispositions.

In this way, race also frames assessments of others' trustworthiness. The set of dispositions associated with blackness, in particular, are taken as symbolic cues to be careful about trusting. Gambetta and Hamill (2005) show this in the case of taxi drivers' intuitive assessments of the trustworthiness of black versus white potential passengers. As they seek to protect themselves from the risks of robbery or assaultbased on their available knowledge and cultural frameworks, blackness becomes a symbolic cue to refrain from trusting, even if they themselves are black.

The same can also be said for indicators of foreignness. Post-1965 immigrants to America increasingly live in anti-immigrant times (Massey and Sanchez 2010). The public's concerns about the economy and the shrinking middle class fuel hostility toward immigrants, who they fear are taxing the social safety net and taking their jobs. In this context, a person who appears foreign, whether that means dressing in an unfamiliar style or speaking English with an accent, can be implicitly associated with a sense of threat.

Certainly, living at the intersection of blackness and foreignness is more complicated than it seems at first glance. In a study of West Indian immigrants, Mary Waters (1999) describes the fluidity of these categories for those who choose between racial and ethnic identities, and for whom a distinct ethnic identity provides a type of protection against the effects of the American racial order. As immigrant blacks have become more visible in American life through stories like Kwasi's, in Chapter 1, they have often been viewed as more hardworking and law-abiding than American blacks. This means, however, that "[w]hen West Indians lose their distinctiveness as immigrants or ethnics they become not just Americans, but black Americans" (5). Losing the trappings of foreignness is thus associated with downward mobility.

Adjustments to the racial order do not, therefore, ameliorate the problems of racism or xenophobia. Instead, they establish new binaries of "good" versus "bad" blacks and "good" versus "bad" immigrants within public perceptions.[17] And although Ghanaians like Kwasi and Benjamin—also introduced in Chapter 1—may initially benefit from being placed on the positive side of these binaries, their position remains tenuous. There is a perpetual threat of being miscategorized. If they find themselves working in certain jobs, living in certain neighborhoods, socializing in certain bars, wearing certain clothes, and going to certain churches, such misreadings are even more likely. They walk a tightrope stretched above two symbolic categories that trigger distrust in others—"bad" blacks and "bad" immigrants—and any misjudgment or misstep on their journey could undermine their ability to avoid such symbolic classifications. All of these issues challenge Ghanaian migrants' ability to build trust networks upon their arrival.

Choosing to Trust

In spite of the cultural categories that link blackness and foreignness to trust and/or distrust in complex ways, migrants like Kwasi and Benjamin are not passively subject to these challenges, and their trust networks are not purely a result of their social positions. As noted earlier, Tilly's writings on trust networks say little about whether people make choices to opt into certain trust networks and opt out of others; but the stories I tell in this book strongly suggest that, in fact, they do. In our conversations, Benjamin was openly aware of the importance of trusting the right people, but he also made choices about which symbolic cues to rely on and whether or not to imagine certain people as trustworthy in turn. For example, he chose to see me as a "church colleague" rather than an outsider, even though there was plenty of symbolic evidence to support either of these conclusions.

The paradox of trust—that people are often motivated to trust but also to avoid trusting the wrong people—implies two conflicting impulses that must be balanced.[18] In given situations, people may act on one or the other; and this may change when dealing with the *next* person in the next situation, depending on the relevant symbolic cues operating in each case. When and how they act on these coexisting desires introduces an element of creativity to the process, which again supports a view of personal trust as an imaginative and symbolic activity.

This also helps to explain the variations in the personal religious trajectories I describe in the following pages of this book. Two people may make very different decisions about group memberships in general, and where to go to church in particular, but share a similar motivation to develop relationships of personal trust, and a similar hope or expectation that they can establish such relationships in the context of a religious membership. What makes their patterns of trusting different, and ultimately influences the unique development of their church-based trust networks, are the variations in how specific symbols come into play within specific interactions in religious communities, and in when and how much they choose to interpret those symbols as evidence of trustworthiness.

Personal trust matters, therefore, because it shapes many migrants' decisions about their associations, as seen in the case of religious membership. It also matters because it is one of the key bases on which social divides are bridged or reinforced. Finally, it matters on a conceptual level, because by looking at personal trust, and the motivations at work when and if people trust certain others, we can recognize the power of both external constraints and the creativity of human imagination in the day-to-day lives of America's newest communities.

Immigrant Religion in America

As noted in chapter 1, sociologists have observed the importance of religion in American life generally, and for newcomers specifically, for over a century. Following in the tradition of Max Weber (1946 [1904]) and Will Herberg (1983 [1955]), numerous recent studies demonstrate the salience of religion as a vehicle of integration for those who adhere to both mainstream traditions such as Christianity and minority traditions such as Islam and Buddhism.[19] In particular, the work of Steve Warner (2007, 2000, 1998, 1997) affirms the importance of religious identity and practice for post-1965 immigrants. He shows how immigrant religious communities provide social support, cultural continuity, and a sense of belonging to newcomers, while also connecting them to broader social networks than they would otherwise enjoy and facilitating their sense of positive engagement with U.S. culture and society.

At the core of this larger argument is the distinctly American model of the congregation, a localized voluntary religious community serving multiple functions for its members and reflecting their distinct needs and interests. Early European settlers were often motivated by the desire to practice their model of Christianity free from the influence of Europe's religious hierarchy, and thus decided to avoid establishing or giving political preference to any one religious organization in the laws of their new country. Although certain religious groups have enjoyed a degree of prestige as the churches of the political elite—as illustrated by the fact that only one American president has had an affiliation other than Protestant—nonetheless American religion is characterized by legal and political disestablishment.

This disestablishment has allowed for religious membership to be a bottom-up as much as a top-down creation, largely shaped by the nature of local congregations. Although congregations are usually part of larger organizations, they are not mere reflections of those organizations, and they are highly adaptable to their immediate context. A Methodist church in rural Alabama, for example, looks very different from a Methodist church in suburban Houston, even though both are part of the same denomination. This pattern is what Warner calls "religiocultural localism" (2004, 107). Such disestablishment has also allowed for religious membership to be a space of agency for lay religious actors to create communities that are both affective—joined in emotional bonds—and effective for addressing local issues. Religious membership creates "a space available for subcultures" and "an area of empowerment for minorities" (108). Not surprisingly, the American congregation thus holds great appeal for new immigrants. They can avail themselves of its many social functions and adapt it to their unique concerns, thereby using it as a space to pursue integration if they so choose.

Of course, the picture of religion's role in immigrant integration has not always been so universally positive. A parallel perspective, exemplified in the mid-century in an article by Robert Breton (1964), argues that to the degree that religious memberships often involve large investments of time and resources, and often connect immigrants primarily to others within the same ethnic community, they in fact can reinforce a sense of separateness from the host society and limit integration. This is a particularly common fear in European discourses on migration.[20] This also seems to be more likely for the increasing numbers of new immigrants who follow traditions outside the Judeo-Christian mainstream. One study of minority religions (Wuthnow and Hackett 2003) reveals a more limited political integration among Muslims, Hindus, and Buddhists, in spite of their generally higher economic status. American Muslims have a particularly fraught relationship with American culture and its categories of identification, which leads them to resist certain aspects of cultural assimilation even as they pursue citizenship and various modes of economic incorporation.[21]

Nonetheless, there is still plenty of evidence for the appeal and the social importance of religious membership for certain post-1965 immigrants. Exploring the reasons for this, Peggy Levitt (2007) notes how the flexibility of religion as a membership category fits well with the lifestyles of transnational citizens who live simultaneously between two or more different societies. While nationality, kinship, and ethnicity are usually ascribed statuses tied to a physical place, which can make them harder for transnationals to hold onto, religion is a voluntary and portable identity. Transnational migrants can usually choose global religious memberships and find local iterations of them wherever they go.

This fits with the work of Tweed (1997, 2006) on Cuban diasporic religion, and his theory that emphasizes religion's connections to crossing and dwelling in space. Tweed defines religion as a "confluence . . . of organic-cultural flows that intensify joy and confront suffering by drawing on human and superhuman forces to make homes and cross boundaries" (2006, 54). There are many aspects to this rich definition, some of which overlap with other recent theories of religion that give a central role to superhuman or supernatural realities (Riesebrodt 2010, 72; Smith 2003, 98). Yet what is clear and distinct about Tweed's theory is how it links religion to the imminently human work of making homes and crossing boundaries. Movement in real and virtual space and religious flows are closely connected; and our modern "world on the move" (Zolberg 2006), in which there are unprecedented numbers of global migrants, is thus likely to be one of widespread religious engagement and creativity, where religious forms shaped and are shaped by transnational journeys.

This is indeed reflected in how post-1965 immigrants tend to innovate on past traditions and demonstrate a degree of fluidity in their religious identities and memberships. For example, Carolyn Chen (2008, 2006, 2005) describes how and why many new immigrants from Taiwan convert to Evangelical Protestant Christianity. Prema Kurien (2012) shows how second-generation Indian American Christians have decoupled their religion from their ethnicity and come to view religion as a personal quest, in which they are free to seek out new religious communities as they see fit, regardless of whether those communities share or reinforce their ethnic identity. And Nina Glick Schiller and her colleagues (Glick Schiller and Çaglar 2008; Glick Schiller, Çaglar, and Guldbrandsen 2006) argue that many African migrants think of religious practice as a way to *transcend* ethnic boundaries rather than reaffirm them. I found much the same mentality among the Ghanaians I interviewed. Where and with whom they practice religion is not a given; rather, it is an issue of personal choice, navigated in response to their transnational lifestyles, their distinct concerns as migrants, and the contexts of their reception in the United States.

Evangelical Charismatics and Church Choice

The voluntary approach to religion exhibited by post-1965 immigrants reflects both the congregationalism of American religion and the culture of globalizing Evangelical Christianity in Africa, Asia, and Latin America—the parts of the world from where today's transnational migrants increasingly originate.[22] The kinds of churches that have grown rapidly in these regions in the past few decades—like Evangel Ministries or the Yoido Full Gospel Church in Korea, mentioned in chapter 4—follow in the Evangelical tradition and are also usually Pentecostal and/or Charismatic. Such churches are labeled slightly differently across contexts and between observers. In Latin America, they tend to be called *evangélicos* (Brenneman 2011), while in West Africa they are often called "Born Agains" (Marshall 2009). Some scholars group them under the banner of global Pentecostalism (Miller and Yamamuri 2007; Martin 2002), Pentecostal-Charismatic Christianity (Robbins 2004; Meyer 2004), or simply global Evangelicalism (Offutt 2015; Smilde 2007; Freston 2001). In Ghana, the churches growing most rapidly as part of this historical shift are usually called "Charismatics," and are somewhat distinguished from the older Pentecostal churches (see chapter 4). I use the term "Charismatic Evangelical" to highlight both their local identity and their kinship with Evangelical groups worldwide.

The Evangelical tradition teaches that religion should be based in a personal and self-initiated relationship with God, rather than in taken-for-granted affiliations. It claims one's religion should be actively and consciously chosen, and it stresses the need to detach religion from other political or ethnic memberships. As chronicled by Robert Bellah and colleagues (1985), such religious individualism predominates in American culture. Religion is viewed as a personal project rather than a social commitment or obligation. Yet it is less well known that aspects of this religious individualism are widespread outside of the United States and Europe as well. Charismatic Evangelical Christianity is now the mainstream religion in southern Ghana, and it heavily promotes the idea of personally initiated and self-chosen religiosity.[23]

While not all who move abroad are Charismatic Evangelical in their affiliation before arriving, many of them are, and many more have attended different kinds of churches in the past but still view the Evangelical tradition as mainstream and legitimate. Indeed, from their perspective the distinctions between different Christian groups are often fluid: if one's personal religiosity is what matters most, then commitment to a tradition (i.e., Anglicanism, Presbyterianism, the Charismatic church, etc.) is less important than how a particular congregation serves one's social and spiritual well-being. Most of Evangel Ministries' members in Chicago were not raised in Charismatic Evangelical churches, but gravitated to them later on and did not tend to see this as a dramatic religious transformation. It was instead an issue of finding a good church regardless of its label. As shown in more detail in chapter 5, they wanted a church with inspiring teaching and a warm, energetic, and connected social atmosphere, whether it was Charismatic Evangelical, Anglican, Methodist, or something else.

Urban areas of the United States like Chicago provide plenty of options for such Evangelical-oriented but nonparticularist Protestants. There are Evangelical-leaning Presbyterian or Baptist churches, nondenominational congregations, and Pentecostal-Charismatic communities that share similar teachings and practices. There are also African immigrant, African American, and mainstream white American versions of each of these.

For example, Evangel Ministries is just one of dozens of small congregations in the area started by West Africans but seeking broader appeal. One particular building in the heart of Uptown (figure 2.3) had three floors of offices, many of which were filled by West African businesses, organizations, and start-up churches.

Posters on the doors of these offices advertised the many church meetings taking place there on Sunday mornings. A sampling of some of these posters is shown in figure 2.4. I photographed each of these posters on different office doors, on a single afternoon, in the building shown in figure 2.3. Some of them, like the Mount Zion Anglican Church or the Apostolic Church International, appeared to be connected to larger denominations or church organizations, while others, like Acme Vision International or Joyous Victory Ministries, were brand new. Most of them advertised Sunday morning services, as well as midweek prayer services and Bible studies. Most of them also expressed a

FIGURE 2.3 Office building in Uptown, with a large number of West African small businesses and churches.

FIGURE 2.4 Posters advertising churches founded by West Africans in Chicago.

multicultural identity, or at least an aspiration as such. The frequent use of the word *International* and imagery like a world globe and dozens of country flags expressed this.

Yet in spite of these numerous options within the ethnic community, many aspirational migrants from Ghana themselves would rather attend already established and diverse American congregations. Again, an older view of religious and ethnic identities as both fixed and closely intertwined for migrants leads to the expectation that new migrants will automatically and immediately attend the church that matches their religious and ethnic background (i.e., Ghanaian Presbyterians will go to a Ghanaian Presbyterian church). But for those I met and interacted with, such was not the case. Most of them had tried several kinds of congregations since their arrival, which varied in ethnic makeup and affiliation. They were usually comfortable in diverse settings, fluent in English, fairly educated, and looking for a style of worship very similar to the American Evangelical mainstream, which made it natural for them to choose churches outside of the Ghanaian immigrant community, at least at first. Like both native-born and other new Americans, they were looking for a congregation that reflected their distinct cultural experience. This experience was only partly defined by their ethno-national heritage; it was just as rooted in global Evangelicalism and their social class.

The Segregated Hour

When entering the religious landscape of the United States, Ghanaian migrants are constrained in their choice of church by the relationship between race and religion. The history of black Christianity in the Americas is a story of simultaneous exclusion and embrace. On the one hand, Christian moral teachings, rituals, and settings have offered many avenues to the empowerment of black colonial subjects at home and slaves taken abroad, and black Christian figures have been at times instrumental in challenging systems of oppression.[24] On the other hand, the marginalization of blacks is echoed and reinforced in the structures of American religion. Religious institutions are formally desegregated, but there remains a de facto division between black and white Christianity. Mixed-race congregations remain rare and difficult to sustain, even though many Christian leaders and laypeople consider such churches beneficial.[25] Many Evangelical churches that aspire to multiracial diversity are still firmly entrenched in white Evangelical culture, and blacks in such churches must adapt to those models rather than the other way around.[26]

Christian Ghanaian migrants in the United States tend to seek out religious diversity, as being both reflective of their experience as educated transnationals and rooted in the values of global Evangelicalism. In Ghana and Nigeria, for example, Charismatic Evangelical leaders and committed members tend to boast about their churches' broad appeal and ability to transcend social divides of social class, nationality, and ethnicity (in this case, identification with local ethnolinguistic groups). To all appearances, they have been effective in bringing those of different ethnic groups together in solidarity. So it is not surprising that many Ghanaians who migrate abroad—and who view their local Evangelical churches as close relatives of Evangelical congregations in the United States—seek out mainstream Evangelical churches as social settings where they can continue to enjoy the benefits of a multicultural religious community. It is also not surprising that most Ghanaian Charismatic Evangelical church leaders in the United States—like the pastor of Evangel Ministries—aspire to extend the unifying tradition within a multicultural church of their own.

For example, several of my interviewees had visited Willowcreek Community Church in a northwest suburb of Chicago soon after they moved to the area. The church was famous enough that even back in Ghana many had heard of it. It was a natural first choice, especially if they were keen to pursue new social ties and a multicultural religious experience. It was similar to Evangelical mega-churches they were familiar with from Ghana—it was a large congregation headed by a well-known preacher—and so they tended to assume it would also be a diverse community where their connections would not be limited to other black migrants.

Yet they often found Willowcreek and similar congregations to be very different from their experiences with Ghanaian Evangelical Christianity. Such American churches were neither multicultural nor especially inclusive relative to their Ghanaian counterparts. Existing members did not appear to be as connected to each other, or as willing to embrace and build connections with them as visitors. Even when they kept attending, the personal ties they were looking for just never seemed to materialize.

Meanwhile, aspiring Charismatic Evangelical church leaders found that in the United States, "multicultural" did not easily translate to "multiracial." Bringing Ghanaians, Nigerians, Cote D'Ivoirians, and even American blacks together in worship was much easier than bridging the racial divide. Ghanaian church leaders and laypeople tried to find and develop religious networks that bridged racial and ethnic boundaries, but in the context of American religion, they found it difficult.

These Ghanaian migrants, therefore, were presented with a particular set of religious options: attending nonmigrant congregations where they might meet more Americans, but would not necessarily be warmly received; or attending migrant congregations, which were usually very close-knit, but would be much less helpful in extending their networks into the host community. Different people made different choices, or changed their minds over time. Some opted out of churchgoing entirely. No matter what they chose, however, almost all of them were consciously balancing these conflicting concerns; and the church choices they made in turn influenced who they knew, how they lived, what they wanted, and how they saw themselves in relation to their social contexts.

Religion matters, therefore, because for many migrants the choices about where to practice religion are choices about how they want to locate themselves on the social landscape of the host country. Religion is one key domain in which they engage with—or decide to disengage from—mainstream American culture. Further, the relationships that develop in congregations directly shape the choices migrants make about their lives: when to move, when to stay, where to go, what to do, and how to raise their children. Religion is thus more than a comforting, enclave-like setting where migrants can reminisce about home and cope with the strains of migration. It is a context of reception,[27] as well as a context of connection, imagination, and agency.

3

The Sources of Risk

INEQUALITY, THE RACIAL ORDER, AND GROUP COMPETITION

IN THIS CHAPTER, I focus on the risks in the Ghanaian migrant experience that make it difficult for them to establish new trust networks. Some of these challenges are rooted in the inequalities of their home country, while others arise from the inequalities of the U.S. racial order, and being part of an ambitious and at times competitive migrant community. As the stories in this book illustrate such challenges, they also speak to larger questions of identity and what it means to experience belonging in a wider community, whether that be in Ghana, the United States, or somewhere else.

Leaving the Homeland

When I got to know him in 2010, Benjamin didn't remember much about his father. He knew only that he was a politician, killed during the December 1981 coup reinstating Flight Lieutenant J. J. Rawlings as Ghana's head of state. After Ghana's achievement of independence from Great Britain in 1957, the new government underwent many such coups and regime transitions, two of which—one in 1979 and one in 1981—were orchestrated by the military leader J. J. Rawlings. In his public rhetoric, Rawlings called his 1981 coup the "Second Coming," employing biblical themes to legitimate his second forceful takeover, and to draw a link between his leadership and the story of Jesus Christ as a liberating figure who brings justice and peace to the people.[1] For Benjamin and his mother and siblings, however, this event was far from "just" or "peaceful." They were one of many families that lost parents, grandparents, and siblings during this time of upheaval.

After this event, Benjamin's mother moved him and his siblings out of the capital city of Accra and back to where she was born and raised, in Ghana's centrally located Ashanti Region. (see figure 2.2) Although their father was gone, his mother made sure the children were well provided for. They went to the best boarding schools in southern Ghana, learned textbook English, math, and science, and spent their vacations at their mother's modest but quiet home in the country around Kumasi, Ghana's second largest city.

Although Benjamin's family lived well, the country as a whole suffered economically as he was growing up. In the late 1980s, there was a serious food crisis resulting from an economic collapse.[2] Benjamin's mother's generation struggled to purchase basic necessities, as noted by one observer:

> For those lucky enough to find any wage employment, it would take the worker more than a week to buy an American tin of rice (3 kg), more than a day to buy 3 kg of maize, ten days to buy a tuber of yam, over ten days to buy a bottle of edible oil [one pint], more than a day to buy an American tin of garri (cassava grains). . . . The plain fact is that most people count themselves lucky to have one square meal a day.[3]

This food crisis followed a troubled history of economic mismanagement. Although multiple local and global factors contributed, at least one major cause was President Rawlings's manipulations of the economy to provide gain to his political base (Herbst 1993). He distorted export and import prices such that local farmers could no longer make a living from food production. People migrated in large numbers away from the land and toward cities hoping to break into the salaried classes, but such aspirations were increasingly unattainable for the majority.

Benjamin's mother never remarried, and so as Benjamin grew up she came to rely on him more and more to support her. His ambition was to become an engineer, so he attended one of Ghana's two most prestigious universities. Life at the university was good. He had a musical sense and a charismatic personality, and was regularly asked to deejay at his classmates' parties. One day he was invited to do a guest session on the college radio station, which was a huge success. He was given a regular time slot and widely praised for reinvigorating the station's programming. Because of this, he became something of a minor celebrity in the quiet college town where he lived for four years.

When he graduated, Benjamin did what nearly all his well-connected classmates did: he took a salaried position in the capital city of Accra. He worked for the Tourism Board, which fit his charismatic personality. Every morning he would wake up, put on his suit, drive his company car to the airport, and greet foreign visitors from England, Germany, Japan, South Africa, Russia, France, the

United States, and China, among others. He would ask them what they were interested in seeing and what they were there to do, and then he would develop a tour package for them. As a supervisor, he was making a good salary paid in U.S. dollars.

While working at the Tourism Board, he also made money on the side running small-scale visa scams. He would promise people he could get them a visa for the United States for a fee, but then would take the money even if he was unable to acquire it. This type of operation was and is increasingly common in urbanizing areas of West Africa, following rapid increases in the demand for visas and the changes in U.S. immigration policy. As noted in chapter 2, a new immigration law in 1990 established a "diversity visa" lottery for countries like Ghana that had not traditionally been major migrant-sending countries to the United States. Practically speaking, this meant there were 55,000 resident visas with green cards each year made available to nationals from Ghana and similar countries. African and European nations were the main beneficiaries of this program; and among Ghanaian nationals, specifically, 1,000 to 2,000 visas were awarded yearly.[4]

Yet to be eligible for one of these visas, one must prove one had either a bachelor's degree or two years of work experience in a job requiring at least two years' worth of training. In other words, one had to show conclusively, during an in-person interview at the American Embassy, that one was unlikely to overstay the visa or become reliant on U.S. government services after migrating. The same was true if the applicant wanted to apply for a student visa after being admitted to an American college or university. Embassy officials were given a lot of authority in determining who was granted these visas, and they could reject someone based on the smallest hint of suspicion. Many in Ghana thus perceived the visa-granting process as both difficult and arbitrary, and looked for some kind of certainty, which Benjamin and his fellow scammers claimed they could provide.

So, in addition to his government pay, Benjamin started making extra cash with these scams. After only one year out of college, he was making more money than many Ghanaians saw in their lifetimes. He likely knew what people thought about his activities. But it was easy to rationalize that just about anyone would do the same in his place. He saw similar operations happening everywhere in government, where the law was treated as fluid rather than fixed. For example, it was a matter of course to pay off a police officer when pulled over when driving in the city. Police officers earned a salary, but it was not large, and their ability to ply people for bribes was understood to be part of the compensation of their position.[5] He and the police officers, and the people whose money he took, had that in common: they were all trying to make a better life for themselves in an uncertain economy.

At the time, Benjamin would not have described himself as particularly religious. He attended Presbyterian services periodically with his mother, but he did not socialize with church people or spend much personal time engaged in religious activity. That would change later on; but in the years he was flying high and dreaming big in Accra, religion had minimal importance in his life.

As he was making money from the culture of migration developing in southern Ghana, he started to turn his gaze abroad.[6] He thought if the best and the brightest were those who made it in America, he belonged there, too. Rather than taking advantage of rich relatives or applying for a diversity visa, he decided to pursue a graduate degree so he could get a student visa. He started applying to programs in business administration, and he saved up enough money to pay his first year of tuition up front. Once he was admitted to an MBA program in the United States, he received his visa. He knew the system could be brutal to navigate; and yet nothing in his experience to that point suggested he should be anything other than optimistic about his chances abroad.

Disappointment and Strained Relations

When I met Benjamin later on at Evangel Ministries and told him about my interest in Ghanaian churches in Chicago, he turned on his tour guide persona, assuring me he would get me interviews with anyone I wanted to talk to. He was also one of the first members of the congregation I interviewed in person. When we met for this interview one afternoon in downtown Chicago, he brought me a Styrofoam food clamshell full of *waakye*—a Ghanaian one-pot dish of beans, rice, noodles, and sauce. It was a dish I had mentioned I liked and missed from my time in Ghana. He bought it from a food truck, which was daily frequented by the many single male Ghanaian taxi drivers in the city.

He told me in this conversation that after five years in Chicago, his life had changed drastically. He had finished one semester of a master's program and had lived six months in the city, but by then he had tapped out his savings. He had little choice but to drop out of the degree program and look for a full-time job. He found one through an acquaintance who worked for a taxi company. Yet it was hard for him to be satisfied with working as a taxi driver. He had gone from being the "big man on campus," to working in an elite government job, to being just one of many underpaid foreign workers in the United States.

At first, he tried to work and still attend classes, enrolling at a local city college. Yet he found the education there to be little better than what he already had from the university in Ghana. He recalled, "I was asked to write an essay about my definition of success. When the teacher read it, she said it was so good and she read it out loud to the whole class. She told me that I didn't need to be at that school." So he decided it was a waste of time and money to continue at the city college. The education that would be useful to him he couldn't afford, and the education he could afford offered no additional value.

Many Ghanaian migrants to the United States come for higher education, as had Benjamin. Increasingly American colleges and universities court qualified international students. If such students are able to navigate the application process effectively, it is fairly common for them to gain admission. The college or university then provides them with an I-20 form, which verifies that they have been given admission to a program of higher education. The I-20 form is considered by many Ghanaians to be their best bet for acquiring a U.S. visa (although it is never 100 percent guaranteed).

If they do receive a visa, it is usually an F-1 student visa, which has some very specific stipulations.[7] In the first year of study, students are only allowed to seek on-campus employment, such as work-study jobs. After that first year, they are allowed to seek off-campus employment only if it meets certain criteria as "practical training" for their intended profession. They are also required to maintain full-time student status at the I-20 granting institution.[8]

This system effectively precludes the possibility of working to put oneself through school, which is why the program formally requires that prospective students prove they "have sufficient funds available for self-support during the entire proposed course of study."[9] Yet as noted earlier, whether or not that criterion is met is largely up to the visa-awarding officer of the American Embassy. People like Benjamin are often able to rally enough evidence of sufficient support without *actually* having the needed amount, cash in hand. They may also make their case on the basis of scholarships from the university promised for their first year of study, even though it is impossible to know the extent of the continuing scholarships they will receive after their initial first-year offers.

Most American students, if left in a bind like Benjamin, whereby their scholarships and savings are no longer enough to cover their schooling, will apply for federally subsidized student loans. These loans make up the bulk of student debt in the United States. Of the roughly $900 billion total owed in student loan debt, the vast majority—$864 billion—is administered by the federal government or is government-subsidized.[10] Those loans, however, are not available to most international students except in certain cases, such as refugees. Although some private agencies do offer international student loans, they almost always require the loans to be cosigned by an American citizen.[11]

Many Ghanaian students who run out of money are thus forced to drop out. If they return to Ghana, as the law requires them to do, they face the disappointment of relatives and friends back home, some of whom likely contributed significantly to send their hopeful son, daughter, niece, or nephew abroad in the first place. If they stay and work, they run the risk of being arrested as undocumented workers. Staying in the United States and *not* working only delays the inevitable.

These events in Benjamin's life put significant strain on his relationships. Apart from his mother, whom he called every day and to whom "I remit more than I even take care of myself," he did not stay in touch with his relatives in Ghana. He had an aunt and uncle who also lived in the United States, in the Washington, D.C. area, but he had not contacted them since he had been abroad. He explained why as our conversation progressed from the play-by-play details of his life to the emotional side of being a foreigner. He and I talked:

"It is hard when you are all in a foreign country, and struggle to try to make it; it is easier not to talk to people sometimes because they will worry you need something from them, or they might need something from you."

"Have you been back to Ghana since you moved here?"

He shook his head, no. "Going back to Ghana is more complicated than just getting the plane ticket, because when you go to the United States, everyone back home has a lot of expectations on you. They see what America is like on the TV, and they think that money just falls into your lap. So when you go back, you have to do a lot of work to make a lot of people happy. There are certain people that I want to make happy, like my mother and my sisters, but there are many others that would be expecting things."

"But do you miss Ghana a lot?"

He nodded. "I miss my mom the most. I talk to her every day or every other day."

He pulled an international calling card out of his pocket and showed it to me, explaining he used it to call her frequently.

"She moved to a new place [out of the capital] once I moved to the United States. I just had someone go and check on her, and the place where she is staying is okay, but not great, so I am hoping to move her somewhere else soon."

He then told me about his older sister, with whom he was very close when they were growing up in Ghana. She later married and moved to Italy.

"Did she marry an Italian man?" I asked.

"No," he said. "She married a Ghanaian man that had moved there and came back to get a wife."

Although the two siblings had been close, after she went to Italy she didn't talk to him much. Then when he moved to the United States, she started communicating with him more. He understood why after he went abroad himself. He felt the same anxiety about what people might expect from him or how he might disappoint them.

It was also difficult to establish new social ties in Chicago with other migrants like himself. When he first came to the city, he had sought out such connections, but soon felt alienated by their competitive and controlling dynamics. He explained, "Those who have been here a while can tend to look down on those who are new, and either see them as a threat or tell them they don't really know how things work over here." He got tired of being talked down to as a "beginner" who needed schooling in the American lifestyle.

He decided he "never wanted to live among my folks on the North Side," referring to the neighborhood in Chicago, Uptown, with its higher concentration of West Africans (see chapter 2). He continued, "Ghanaians are gossips. I hate that; sometimes people feel you are a threat, and I don't want to get entangled with that." He lived alone by the time we met, in an area quite some distance from Uptown. He also said he wouldn't go to African barbers, but preferred African American shops where no one knew anything about him or his background, and no one was likely to ask him uncomfortable questions. Although he enjoyed using online media such as Facebook, he was also careful to insulate himself from the Ghanaian community in such virtual spaces as well. He used a pseudonym on his profile rather than his real name, because he didn't want "certain people" to be able to find him. Later on, after I had known him a while, I found out he had deleted his Facebook account entirely.

In transitioning from a university-educated representative of the Tourism Board in Ghana to a taxi driver in the city of Chicago, Benjamin underwent what Halter and Showers Johnson (2014) refer to as an "occupational detour." According to these authors, it is common for first-generation migrants from West Africa to find themselves doing very different kinds of work in the United States than they did at home, or than they hoped to do after their migration. Those who move abroad are disproportionately better educated and better qualified relative to those who stay home; yet degrees, qualifications, and work experience in white-collar professions often fail to transfer to the new context, and the job markets in given sectors operate differently or are more competitive than in Ghana. As a result, new migrants are often disappointed by the realities of the educational system and job market in the United States. In turn, these disappointments strain their ability to maintain a strong network of relations with those back home or to build new ties within the ethnic community, for the reasons Benjamin describes.

Certainly, as migration from Ghana to the United States has become more common in recent decades, more and better information has traveled back to those at home. There is broader awareness of such occupational detours, which makes prospective new migrants better prepared for what they may face, and makes their parents, spouses, and other relatives at home more understanding when things do not go as planned. Furthermore, as the community of Ghanaians abroad has grown and become more established, the existence of global migrant networks means that new migrants are often now much better informed about opportunities abroad than in the past, and they can usually find distant relatives, old acquaintances, or former classmates in whatever foreign city they arrive in. Some of those I interviewed were on the giving or receiving end of incredible generosity between near strangers who just happened to be part of the same Ghanaian network abroad. Indeed, almost everyone was assisted at some point through such networks.

Yet as Horn-Udeze (2009) shows in a study of Nigerian migrants to Europe, there are still incentives for those who go abroad to keep their setbacks secret from those at home, so as not to appear less capable of success. Even though relatives and friends may know that occupational detours—or more specifically, major steps backward in the job market—are common, everyone hopes to be the exception rather than the rule. When such hopes result in disappointment, fear of disappointing others or being misjudged can strain existing and potential connections.

Furthermore, the existence of global migrant networks means that those who are doing well risk being called on to share excess resources with newcomers, while those who are doing less well risk being criticized or avoided. People also spread information through these networks in the form of gossip, in order to identify who is doing well and who is not, and also to exert social control over others' behavior. If a new migrant becomes too embedded in these networks, this gossip can threaten his or her ability to make new connections, because the information shared may or may not portray the individual in a favorable light.

These dynamics ultimately impact the migrants' connections to ethnic-based trust networks. As described in chapter 2, trust networks connect individuals like Benjamin to associational groups and communities, on the basis of personal trust. Such trust is an imaginative and symbolic activity that relies on meaningful cues and the willingness of others in the community to interpret those cues as evidence of trustworthiness. Yet if the cues Benjamin projects suggest he may be new to the host context, less successful, and in a tenuous position, then other Ghanaians in Chicago may be reticent to trust him on a personal level. What they can tell about him at first pass suggests trusting him may be risky; and given his situation, what he knows about gossip and the attitude of more established members of the community suggests it is risky for him to trust them, as well. Although he may indeed periodically interact with or even rely on certain other Ghanaians he knows in Chicago, these dynamics make it difficult for him to fully connect into trust networks based on co-membership in the Ghanaian migrant community. There are many like Benjamin, therefore, who keep the migrant community somewhat at arm's length, citing "gossip" and "competitiveness" as the reasons for this.

The Transatlantic Life

Elijah and his wife Catherine were the pastors of Evangel Ministries in Chicago, and when I met them they had been in the United States for many years. Before coming to Chicago, they had lived in a small town in the Midwest where Elijah worked as a family physician. There, he had the type of success story Benjamin was dreaming of: a professional career, a nice home in a peaceful neighborhood, a smart and successful wife, and a healthy young child. Yet even still, they dealt with many of the same issues that Benjamin described.

I learned much of their story over dinner at their home one evening. We scheduled it for the only day of the summer that they were both off from work and had time to spare: the Fourth of July. I arrived at their suburban condo in the mid-afternoon, after an hour's drive from the city. We spent some time chatting in the living room, and then Catherine welcomed us into the kitchen to eat. After the delicious meal, we lingered around the table as their daughter, now six years old, watched *The Jungle Book* in the next room. It was a rare chance to relax with these two very busy people.

Elijah was an intellectual, passionate about life-long learning. His pride and joy was his library, an oasis of musty book smells and the life of the mind. Both he and Catherine had been raised in rural villages, rather than in well-connected political families like Benjamin's, so their trajectories through prestigious medical schools and their achievements abroad were particularly significant.

Elijah and Catherine were also older than most when they married. Although delaying marriage was becoming less and less unusual among their friends and relatives, Catherine still received many subtle and not-so-subtle comments about impending spinsterhood as she progressed through nursing school and stayed single into her thirties. Perhaps it caused her stress at the time; but when she and I met, after her marriage to Elijah and the birth of her daughter, she expressed no regrets. She laughed at how much more worried others were about her than she was about herself.

Always a devout woman, she had for many years considered becoming a Catholic nun. As she became less inclined to take that path, she started praying for a good spouse. The pool of suitable marriage partners must have seemed small; she wanted someone who would understand and value her Ghanaian heritage, someone who would not be threatened by her education and her achievements, and someone who would share her faith and her commitment to the church. Finding the right person must have seemed even less likely once she moved to England, a strange country in which she was a temporary sojourner.

One day she had a conversation with an old classmate from Ghana who told her of another of their mutual acquaintances, a man named Elijah, who was living in the United States in a small town with a good job, and was in need of a good Ghanaian wife. Catherine vaguely remembered him from medical school. They never had more than a passing conversation then, but she agreed to allow the friend to connect them. Their transnational courtship—a fairly common occurrence in modern Ghanaian relationships—began.

Their relationship progressed quickly, even though she was living in London and he was living in the United States. They both had lively minds, warm and hospitable personalities, and a desire to be successful in more profound ways than obtaining wealth or status. Catherine had prayed for "a man after God's heart"; Elijah joked that she got more than she bargained for. As she learned later on, by joining her life to Elijah's she was signing up for much more than a quiet and stable home life.

While telling this story, they explained their view that marriage should not be seen as a necessity for the devout and mature follower of God. They saw their life decisions about love and marriage as spiritually significant and countercultural. They were rejecting the "African model" of early marriage and limited roles for women in favor of a religious ambition, and a spiritual community in which men and women were both important contributors.

Once they married, and Catherine moved across the ocean and into Elijah's house with the big library, they started trying to get pregnant. Catherine was in her late thirties. At the private medical practice where Elijah worked, in their small town of several thousand, the two of them had good friends who rallied around them in their desire to have a family. When Catherine first became pregnant, she cautiously waited to tell anyone. Yet as her pregnancy progressed, everything seemed to be going so smoothly that they finally allowed themselves to start planning. By the last month, Elijah's co-workers put up a calendar in the office on which they gleefully crossed off each day, counting down to Catherine's due date. Their "miracle baby" was born, healthy and strong.

They had been happy in their American midwestern community. The small-town environment suited them: people were friendlier there than anywhere else outside of Ghana they had lived. They knew very few other Ghanaians there, but they made friends at the physician's office where Elijah worked. They attended an American charismatic congregation that fit their conservative values and their devotion to biblically oriented preaching. As he was telling me this story over our meal, Elijah said, "We never would have given that up if it weren't for the ministry."

"The ministry" compelled them in the form of an unexpected phone call from one of Elijah's old medical-school classmates. Back in the 1980s in Ghana, when Elijah and Catherine were studying medicine and nursing, respectively, another medical student started a small Charismatic prayer group in his student apartment. Both Elijah and Catherine had been peripherally involved with that group for several years before they independently went abroad. That group mushroomed during the following decade into an Evangelical Charismatic church of thousands, called Evangel Ministries, and that medical student became one of Ghana's young and famous religious superstars. He and several of his close compatriots finished their medical degrees, and then devoted themselves full time to the growing church organization. By the time Elijah and Catherine received their life-changing phone call, Evangel Ministries had hundreds of congregations across Africa and was planting many more in Europe, North America, and Asia. They needed someone to pastor their new Chicago branch; would Elijah consider it?

Taking on the position meant major changes for their family. The pastoral role was a voluntary rather than a paid position, so Elijah had to find a new job as a physician in the Chicago area. This took him about six months. By the time both he and Catherine were employed, their places of work were on opposite sides of the Chicago metro area. In their former life, Elijah had worked regular hours in a private practice, but now he was working as a resident in a major city hospital, which involved being regularly on call and going into work by six every morning to do his rounds, including Sunday mornings. He usually came straight to church from the hospital—a 45-minute drive—to lead the congregation and give the sermon. Sometimes his ever-present pager interrupted his sermons. After stepping out to answer it, he would come back and joke with the congregation about the kind of crazy life he led, knowing that many of them shared similarly demanding schedules and balanced multiple family, work, and church commitments.

A History Lesson

During our time together, Elijah shared with me his views about Ghana's complicated past and current political situation. Like many other Ghanaians abroad with whom I talked politics, he was deeply dissatisfied with Ghana's government leaders. Although outsiders often see Ghana as a success story in postcolonial Africa, with a growing economy and multiple peaceful presidential transitions since it became a democracy in 1992, many citizens still feel there is far too much corruption, greed, and inequality. From Elijah's point of view, the multiparty system was dominated by some of the same powerful men who ruled during the dictatorship years. For this reason, he explained, he did not have a positive feeling for the National Democratic Convention (NDC), the left-leaning party that had again come into power in 2008 with the election of John Atta-Mills.

I replied that I was surprised he was not an Atta-Mills supporter, since Atta-Mills was Ghana's first president to be an open Charismatic Christian (former presidents had all been members of missionary-founded Protestant groups). While conceding this was true, Elijah noted, "The shadow of Rawlings still looms large in the NDC."

He saw Rawlings, the former military dictator now dressed up in democratic clothing, as the person truly calling the shots as long as the NDC was in power. "Rawlings was a very strong leader, and to resist being controlled by him a new leader would have to be strong as well; and Atta-Mills is not strong enough."

He then connected the continued corruption in politics to a lack of opportunity for the average Ghanaian, going so far as to say that life in Ghana for the average person was better under British rule and immediately afterwards than it is now. "Today, if you are from the rural areas, it will take a miracle for you to move forward and get ahead." He continued that even the educational system in Ghana owes much to the British. Most of Ghana's best schools, he explained, are still those that were started by foreign missionaries.

"If you look at it," Catherine chimed in, "The Ghanaians have not invented anything; all of the civilization we have comes from the Europeans."

Elijah laughed at this. "Sometimes [Evangel's head leader] jokes about how the government may soon have to go to the British, who they kicked out, and ask them to come back and run the country again."

I nodded. I had heard as much from the founder of Evangel Ministries the year before, during a Tuesday evening sermon when I was at the organization's headquarters in Ghana. The founder said it was ridiculous how each new powerful ruler comes in and blames those who came before him for all of the country's problems. He said, strikingly: "When Ghana gained its independence in 1957, they inherited so much, and yet were not able to add one inch of railway line to what was already there."

"What the missionaries had done was very impressive," Elijah continued. "I am very thankful for what the Europeans brought in terms of education and Christianity. In Aburi, you can see tombstones with German names and Swiss names, of missionaries that had come and then died in several years' time from diseases... [W]e are reaping the benefits of the sacrifices of those who have gone before us. If they had not come, I myself would probably be a Muslim named Muhammed."[12]

To Elijah, those gravestones in Aburi symbolized something valuable brought by pain and sacrifice to his parents and grandparents. He felt indebted to people of a foreign tongue and a different race, with whom he shared a religious faith. It was natural that he respected and admired them, even as he acknowledged the suffering caused by foreign rule. For these reasons, and given the country's struggles in the 1970s, 1980s, and 1990s, Elijah and Catherine could perceive British rule as better in some ways than what followed.

While Elijah and Catherine later admitted these were unpopular sentiments in many circles, I found such opinions were not so uncommon among Ghanaians in the United States, both within and outside of Evangel Ministries. These aspirational and emigrating Ghanaians had an ambivalent relationship to their home country. They reminisced about the beauty of the land, the social nature of the people, and the relaxed way of life; but they bemoaned the lack of opportunity, the bluff and bluster of the politicians, and the inefficiencies in the system: poor roads, unbearable traffic, power outages, arbitrary college admissions procedures, flooding, and rampant bribery in policing. My introduction to such complaints came through the sermons of Evangel Ministries' founder, when I attended his congregation in the summer of 2009, but I concluded over time that he reflected certain existing sentiments among his target demographic.

Inequalities and Social Ties

In their lives in the United States, Elijah and Catherine made certain choices to pursue, ignore, or avoid certain bases of social connection after migrating abroad. They had both attended good secondary schools and the same prominent medical college in Ghana, and their ties to classmates continued to be important in their lives afterwards. Indeed, for them, these ties to former classmates seemed to operate as a type of trust network they relied on at various moments of their lives. A former classmate from medical school introduced them to each other, as described earlier, and Elijah lived with a former classmate in the United States when he was still getting on his feet financially. The term "classmate" itself carries a double meaning: it is someone from the same class in school and, in the Ghanaian context where education is all-important, someone from the same social class, with similar habits, lifestyles, values, and goals.

The Evangel Ministries organization was built upon such class-based networks. The founder was a medical student who gathered several of his classmates together to form a new church organization, and as they expanded they relied upon the ties formed in medical school to identify successful professionals abroad, like Elijah, who might be interested in starting new branches. It was a winning strategy, considering that about 50 percent of medical professionals trained in Ghana were working abroad in the mid-2000s, and most of them were trained within the same central hospital system.

Apart from these networks, however, and the ties they later built within the Evangel congregation in Chicago, Elijah and Catherine did not gravitate to other Ghanaians after moving to the United States. When they lived in a small town before coming to Chicago, most of their social connections were with their American co-workers. By then they had both lived in either the United Kingdom or the United States for some time and were fairly comfortable being the only Ghanaians in social settings.

When they moved to Chicago, where there was much more opportunity for them to live near or socialize with other Ghanaians, they usually opted not to do so. They bought a home in the suburbs close to Catherine's work, and periodically traveled to the North Side of Chicago to buy Ghanaian food products, but otherwise did not pursue connections to the ethnic community. They knew few Ghanaians in the area apart from the church, but in Elijah's words, "We have not really formed a group." Thus, Elijah and Catherine seemed to be connected to a trust network based on their educational experiences—a foundation on which their church-based trust network was later built—but less so based on ethnic identity itself.

Even in his pastoral role, Elijah did not pursue cooperative relationships with other pastors of Ghanaian churches in the area. When I interviewed the pastor who started the branch before Elijah came, who later became the overseer of all U.S. branches, he said this was the typical pattern for their congregations: "If there was another Ghanaian church somewhere and I knew the pastor, of course I would stop by and say hello, but we just focus on what we are doing. . . . So, no, apart from the brotherhood of Christ, there is no special kinship."

After interviewing other Ghanaian pastors in the area, I found a range of approaches on this issue. Some of them worked closely with each other while others downplayed any links to the Ghanaian community. Churches like Evangel Ministries that ignored or avoided such links were usually the same congregations that were seen as more "Americanized." They tended to attract more educated members who spoke English fluently and lived and dressed in more Western styles. They conducted their services in English and usually met in locations outside of immigrant neighborhoods.

This was particularly apparent in how Elijah and Catherine, and Evangel Ministries' other members, interacted with the wider Ghanaian community during the yearly event of Ghanafest. As mentioned in chapter 2, Ghanafest is a festival organized by the main Ghanaian cultural organization in Chicago, the Ghana National Council (GNC). It is usually on a Saturday in August. During the late morning and early afternoon, there are a series of ceremonial activities, including prayers by local Ghanaian church leaders, formal addresses by the leadership of the Ghana National Council, and a ceremonial procession of the chiefs and queen mothers of the Chicago area. The festival also features food and craft vendors, bands, DJs, and dancing.

Yet during my first summer participating at Evangel Ministries, I did not witness most of these formal events. I decided to participate in the festival as a member of the congregation, which meant I would be picked up by the choir director,

David, and would go when the rest of the group was going. David arrived at my house around three o'clock, hours after Ghanafest started. By the time we got to the festival, it was close to four o'clock. About five of the most committed members of Evangel Ministries were handing out bottles of water wrapped with religious pamphlets. I joined in with them, to numerous jokes on both sides about a white woman inviting Ghanaians to a Ghanaian church.

The festival was large, with dozens of food and craft stalls and thousands of people coming in and out throughout the afternoon. The stalls were arranged in a semi-circle around a raised stage, on which sat a number of important-looking persons in either suits or full *kente* cloth.[13] Each of the Ghana National Council's distinct subgroups—the Ewe Association, the Brong Ahafo Association, and so on—also had its own small tent, where members would cluster, eating and talking (see figure 3.1).

Elijah was there without Catherine or their daughter. The advertisements for the festival said there would be prayers by Ghanaian pastors in the area, but it seemed Elijah was not at all involved in this way. He hung close to our group and seemed to know very few others at the festival. David, the choir director, was in a similar attitude. He was there to hand out pamphlets and didn't interact much with anyone apart from the church group.

FIGURE 3.1 People socializing at Ghanafest.

During a quick break, David and Elijah said they wanted to get some *kelliwelli*, a street snack made from fried plantains. They invited me to come along. We walked through the stalls, past the street food that was familiar to me from my time in Ghana: *waakye, red red, banku,* and various types of grilled skewered meats. Elijah was picky, stating he wanted to get *kelliwelli* right off the fire. We finally found a woman cooking some in front of us and ordered several helpings. The woman's stall was toward the inside of the ring, around the central open area in front of the stage.

While waiting for our food, we watched a traditional dance being performed by men and women in *kente* cloth. They were holding a large, ornate umbrella. I asked David if he knew what was going on.

Elijah laughed before David could answer. "He doesn't know," he said, implying that David was too Americanized to know much about the ceremonial activities of Ghana's ethnic groups. Elijah then admitted that even though he himself had grown up in the village, he now remembered little about the type of dance going on in front of us.

"I had an aunt that used to dance in the house of the fetish priest," David chimed in. He then conceded, though, that Elijah was right—he didn't know how to explain what was going on in front of us.

On the matter of *kelliwelli*, on the other hand, Elijah was an expert. As we ate it, he had plenty to say about its being good, but not "proper" and not as good as what his wife could make at home.

As we wandered back through the stalls, both David and Elijah seemed uninterested in getting more food, talking to anyone, or looking at anything else. At first I was surprised they weren't more engaged in and excited about this once-a-year celebration of all things Ghanaian. But that seemed to be the prevailing attitude among Evangel Ministries' members. With a few exceptions, others in the church were similarly lukewarm about participating in Ghanafest during the years of my research. They either complained that it was too chaotic to bring children to—one woman said she would never go again after losing track of her young son in the crowd one year—or stopped by briefly to chat with each other, advertise their church, and pick up some Ghanaian snacks they had been craving. As I got to know them better, this attitude toward the festival seemed in keeping with their general approach to social ties with the ethnic community. They certainly had such ties, but they also held the community itself at a distance.

This attitude said something about their social position. With some exceptions, they were generally of a higher socioeconomic class than many others in the wider community. At a Ghanafest event several years later, another Evangel Ministries member—a young woman in Chicago to pursue a law degree—told me that the dances at the fest are really for the older, less educated folks. She didn't get involved in such things because those weren't practices she was interested in preserving, and relationships with such people weren't ties she was interested in pursuing.

Unlike Benjamin described earlier, Elijah and Catherine never complained about competitiveness within the ethnic community as a reason to avoid it, or expressed concerns about the threat of gossip. Their attitude was more indifferent than openly avoidant, perhaps because they were slightly older, more established, and had less to worry about from risky relationships. Yet like Benjamin, they did not pursue new ties on the basis of Ghanaian identity, in and of itself. Instead, they maintained ties with some family and classmates around the globe while pursuing new ties in the context of the church. Their existing and developing relationships formed along the lines of social class and religious association. The inequalities of Ghanaian society thus also shaped the contours of their postmigration social connections, as in Benjamin's case, and made it less likely that they would establish trust networks based primarily on co-membership in the ethnic community.

Chicago's Color Line

These stories show some of the sources of risk that are inherent in existing or potential ties to others within the same community of Ghanaians living abroad. Yet these newcomers also experienced risk and ultimately distrust within another facet of social connection: potential ties to native-born Americans. Perhaps the biggest social source of this risk and distrust is the dynamic of the U.S. racial order.

Chicago is a diverse gateway city, where people from all parts of the globe live, work, and interact. Yet it is also a city with a troubled history of interactions between races. This was apparent in how Elijah, Catherine, Benjamin, and others I interviewed interacted with the environment. Their experiences reflected both the distinctness of Chicago's racial dynamics and the general challenges of being black in America.

Modern Chicago joined the list of major global cities at the turn of the twentieth century, when its population doubled between 1880 and 1890 and doubled again by 1910. Following this turn-of-the-century boom, the Great Migration brought thousands of American blacks from the South to the North between about 1910 to about 1970. This was a massive demographic change. The population of blacks in Chicago more than doubled from 1910 to 1920; and by 1920, about 83 percent of blacks in Chicago were migrants from southern parts of the country. This group dramatically transformed the African American population and the character of the city itself.[14]

The existing white residents of Chicago viewed the influx of blacks as an invasion, and they feared the black newcomers would decrease property values, take good jobs, and engage in criminal activity (Patillo 2007, 45–49). The race riots of 1919 were an expression of this intensified racial hostility. They were sparked in part by the beating and drowning of a black young man and the subsequent inaction of the police. The riots left dozens dead and hundreds injured. They were the worst of the many violent outbreaks of white hostility against African Americans that spread across the country that year, during the so-called Red Summer.

Chicago's racial feud, to use the prescient terminology of W. E. B. DuBois (1903), played out in real estate contracts as well. In the 1920s and 1930s, much of the southern side of Chicago was covered by restrictive covenants that prevented white property owners from renting or selling to blacks. Nonetheless, the number of blacks migrating to Chicago was large enough that eventually certain neighborhoods, such as Bronzeville, North Kenwood, Oakland, and much of the South Side, as well as Garfield Park, Austin, and Englewood to the west, were transformed into overwhelmingly black areas.

Many of these areas were targeted for government low-income housing projects in the 1950s and 1960s. City planners erected uniform and narrow rectangular high-rises between wide public lawns, in the style pioneered by the Swiss-French architect Le Corbusier. Initially such apartments were a sign of civic renewal and better futures for American blacks. These projects lacked the necessary continued investment in the following decades, however, and soon suffered from serious neglect. By the 1990s, most of them—including the Cabrini-Green projects and the Robert Taylor homes, for example—were slated for demolition to make way for mixed-income residences. Black residents were forced out of the city in large numbers, often to outer suburbs with even worse access to public services and transportation.

Thus, while neighborhoods have changed and populations have migrated, the pattern of extreme residential segregation remains unchanged. Blacks and whites in Chicago lead separated lives in divided spaces, and they experience dramatic differences in their access to the resources of the urban environment. Both aspects are important for how migrants from Ghana move, work, live, play, and interact in their new city.

Elijah and Catherine experienced both aspects of the racial order when they moved to Chicago from the small midwestern town where they had been living. In that town, they knew few blacks, foreign or otherwise. Nonetheless, they got along with their neighbors and were friendly with Elijah's co-workers. They attended a mostly white Evangelical church. As the one black family in most of these settings, who otherwise owned a nice house, spoke English well, usually dressed in American business casual clothing, and worked white-collar jobs, they easily fit the categories of "good" blacks and "good" immigrants.

When they moved to Chicago and took charge of the Evangel Ministries branch, however, their social networks became more segregated. As noted earlier, they moved into a townhouse in an upper-middle-class suburb and both took jobs in hospitals. Yet they found their white co-workers and neighbors to be less friendly than they had been in the small town. They spent most of their time with other members of the Evangel Ministries church and had a limited social network apart from that. Thus, they suggested to me their relationships were more racially segregated in Chicago.

They also experienced the effects of segregation through their church work. In its early years, the congregation struggled to find an affordable permanent meeting space. Their first space was a rented room in a performing arts center. Over time another congregation, which was an independent Evangelical church full of young and creative urbanites, started renting space upstairs and began to crowd out the small Ghanaian church. Evangel Ministries was soon relegated to the basement theater, where every week they had to set up and then dismantle the sound equipment, chairs, projector screen, and podium.

Eventually, the building's owners informed them they had to leave. After months of moving in and out of temporary spaces and members' homes, they found a rental space that was theirs throughout the week. I attended the first Sunday service at the new space, and it was clear everyone was relieved and excited. Yet Elijah told me it wasn't easy getting there. "People didn't want to rent to a black church, which is silly, because we have the whole of Evangel Ministries behind us!"

It was a strange thing from his perspective. One of the wealthiest and most successful organizations in Ghana, religious or otherwise, wanted to rent a space in Chicago, and yet potential landlords were resistant to their application. Even though Elijah was a doctor, dressed well, and knew well how to navigate such business transactions, landlords still saw him as a representative of a black church, which they viewed as a riskier tenant.

The space they eventually found was several miles from the center of downtown, in a neighborhood of working-class homes and crumbling warehouses. It was a narrow, sterile room with commercial-grade carpet, fluorescent lights, and white walls. It was on the second floor of an old industrial building on a nondescript back street, across from another Pentecostal congregation of Latinos, and totally undetectable from the outside. Only the larger Latino church hung a banner over the front doors each Sunday morning.

Elijah's search for a meeting space in the urban landscape echoed that of black migrants in earlier decades. Those coming in large numbers from the American South transformed abandoned storefronts and other corners of the city into places of worship. Facing a crowded built-up environment and prejudiced real estate practices, they actively carved out new areas for meeting, praying, singing, and organizing. Such "storefront churches" ushered in a new style of African American worship—more experiential, outreach focused, and feminized—that is now a cornerstone of the black experience throughout the city.[15]

Yet Elijah and his fellow church members were working with very different frameworks as they approached the task of making space in urban Chicago. They were like and also unlike other black storefront churches. As Elijah explained, they had "the whole of Evangel Ministries" behind them; and where they came from in Ghana, that name spoke of wealth and legitimacy. The organization had extensive resources and would always come to the rescue if one of its branches had financial trouble. Nevertheless, one of its branches had difficulty getting a lease because of the perceptions that landlords symbolically associated with black churches.

It was thus not only alienating but also disorienting to be excluded and refused. Like other aspects of the American racial order, it struck Elijah as a strange and even ignorant miscategorization. It was a disjuncture between their own perceptions of their social status, rooted in their experiences as middle- and upper-class members of a mainstream religious movement, and the cursory perceptions of strangers working with different symbolic indicators of trustworthiness.

Such miscategorizations showed up in other stories I heard, and they were particularly grating for those who were most different from predominant images of the urban African American. One example came from another Evangel Ministries member, Anna, who like Elijah and Catherine had lived in the United States for many years. She and her husband Timothy were both successful professionals who lived in a commuter suburb. Anna was a medical doctor, working as a resident physician in a city hospital.

On one particular afternoon, Anna picked me up after work so I could come back with her to their home, where I had promised to give Timothy a piano lesson. It was a long drive and we made multiple stops on the way, so it gave us plenty of time to talk about Anna's feelings about her life in America, and in Chicago in particular. It also took us on a scenic tour of diverse Chicago neighborhoods.

We started in the heavily white and wealthy North Avenue shopping district. We went to Crate & Barrel, where she was looking for big, wide bowls to serve *fufu* in. *Fufu* is a traditional Ghanaian dish usually made from some combination of cassava or corn flour, cooked slowly to form a stiff porridge, and then served with some type of soup or stew. As she perused the white porcelain dishware of different shapes and sizes—some wide and shallow, some square, some round and deep—she said that really, she only ever made *fufu* when she had relatives in town.

"I don't prefer it myself. It's too filling, and all the starch is bad for you. It's probably been like five or six years since I actually sat down and had a bowl of *fufu* to myself." Her mother was visiting, however, and was making *fufu* on a semi-daily basis; but she was complaining that Anna and her husband Timothy didn't have the "right" bowls to serve it in. Finally she found what she was looking for, and we went up to the cash register, commenting on various items of home decor we liked. She joked about how in her younger days she used to have no money and plenty of time to spend it, while now she has more money but none of the time.

As we left the store, she started talking about her experiences in school and working in the medical field in Chicago. I asked her if the experience had been good, and she responded that it was about 50 percent positive, 50 percent negative. "Here," she said at one point, "Everything is about race. It's the first thing anyone asks: Are they white or black?"

This played out in particularly aggravating ways at work: "If you are a black woman, they always assume you are a nurse." She gave an example of when she was treating a patient along with another doctor who was not American, but who "looked very white—he was Columbian, I think." The patient had seen this doctor, and so when Anna came in to check up on him, the patient said, "We already talked to the doctor, we don't want to talk to you." She responded, "I'm sorry, but I'm his boss. If anything is going to happen with your treatment, it has to go through me first."

This kind of interaction was common for her at both the elite private university where she went to medical school and the city hospital where she currently worked. It was frustrating to her, because she and her husband had always been privileged by Ghanaian standards. Although they met after moving to the United States, their families knew each other and came from a similar well-connected and wealthy class in Ghana. Most of their family members had lived or studied abroad at one point or another, and many of them worked in high-ranking government or business professions in Ghana. Also, much about their life in the United States seemed typically middle-class American: balancing the demands of home and work, paying off school loans for their higher degrees, hiring a cleaning service to help with the housework, and outfitting their condo in a commuter suburb with brand-name dishware, furniture, and appliances. It was thus both unfamiliar and aggravating to be talked down to in such a way as a black woman.

Later on, she talked about her reactions to Chicago's existing racial segregation, as we drove through Englewood, a predominantly black neighborhood and a notoriously high-crime area. "When I was doing my residency here," she said, "We came down into some of the schools in these areas to do service projects, and I was so sad to see how many students there were for each teacher. There was no way they could really go forward in that environment. As an immigrant, I am here to take advantage of what is here, but there are so many people who can't, or they just don't have the mentality."

"Did you know that such neighborhoods existed in the United States before you came here?"

"No, I really didn't," she shook her head, "Though in movies and music there was some indication of it."

One afternoon, she remembered, she had given a ride to one of Evangel Ministries' church members. This was the only member of the group who was African American, born and raised in Chicago, as opposed to being a first- or second-generation immigrant. This young woman, Candice, lived in a housing project that Anna had found extremely frightening to drive through: "The neighborhood was so scary, and it was just me in the car. . . . I didn't want anyone to feel bad, but I told her, 'I'm sorry, can I just drop you off outside?' Taxis don't even go in there, and so if you go in they all know you're not from there and they just look at you."

In those neighborhoods, she felt many of the same emotions that I would have: sadness, trepidation, and the weight of the huge divide between herself and those who lived there. Her experience was complicated, however, by something else—the fact that in America, as someone who is black, she can be symbolically associated with those communities. She can be seen as black in its negative connotations within America's racial order and distrusted on that basis, even as she enjoys a far more comfortable life than many American-born blacks in Chicago, and feels a similar mixture of compassion and distrust in regard to the urban underclass.

Not surprisingly, I also heard stories of negative interactions with law enforcement. Several stories came out on one occasion when David, an Evangel Ministries member who often gave rides to church events, was chauffeuring me and several other members to a meeting. We were in a suburban part of the city when he realized he was headed in the wrong direction. Although he saw a place for a ready U-turn, it was posted as illegal, so he went out of his way to find a legal way to get back on track. He commented that as a black man he was sure he would get pulled over and ticketed if he made the illegal U-turn, which sparked a series of stories from others in the car about how often they, too, had been targeted by police for small violations.

On a more serious level, as violence against blacks at the hands of police escalated in the years during and after my research, I paid close attention to the Facebook posts of my Ghanaian friends and acquaintances, both in Chicago and elsewhere. They posted about how they had to talk to their children about interacting with potentially prejudiced police officers, having the conversations that African American parents have had with their children for decades. Learning the rules of racial distrust in America—the same "simmering distrust" that President Obama lamented in 2014 after racially charged shootings in Ferguson, Missouri—was increasingly a matter of survival.

Admittedly, in specific instances it was difficult to know for sure whether and how much racialized distrust was operating. There may have been many reasons why, in Anna's story, the patient assumed the light-skinned Colombian male was the doctor and she was the nurse; and why Elijah and Catherine's social networks were more racially segregated when they moved to Chicago. Some of the congregation's rental applications may have been rejected for very different reasons than that they were a black church. Each of these incidents was weak evidence alone.

Yet cumulatively they sent a clear message. That is how racialized distrust operates: through small denials, subconscious inclinations, and slight discriminations, which result in an overall experience of alienation. Anna could only chronicle one small recent example in detail, but what mattered was the weight of the many similar exchanges she dealt with in her years of medical training and service. Through such mundane interactions she learned that here, "Everything is about race." She learned she can be viewed with skepticism far beyond what is deserved—that she and other black immigrants can be seen as guilty until proven innocent in the imaginative reckoning of social trust.

A Beginner's Guide to Trust in America

The sources of risk involved in moving from Ghana to Chicago with high aspirations—in the context of inequality, the racial order, and group competition for resources—were perhaps most starkly illustrated in the story of Sandra. I met her on a Sunday morning at Evangel Ministries a few weeks after she had arrived in Chicago from Ghana. Although I didn't usually ask to meet people for one-on-one interviews until I got to know them better, I was interested to talk to her while her experience was still fresh, so I asked her for an interview that very week. She tentatively agreed.

The next Saturday afternoon—a sunny day in June—I pulled up to the tall brick apartment building where she was staying. The building was in Uptown, Chicago's bustling, immigrant-dense neighborhood on the North Side. Sandra ran down quickly and hopped in the car. As we drove several blocks to the coffee shop, she told me that she was currently staying with her cousin in that building, but was looking for a new apartment of her own.

"Are there a lot of Ghanaians who live in that building?" I asked.

"Yes, a lot. Actually, my cousin is in Ghana right now so it is just me staying with his two daughters."

She explained her cousin had told her before he left the country that she really needed to find her own place before he got back. She had just looked at a place that morning, but got some initial resistance from the landlord. "Since I am just a beginner I have no credit, so I need to find someone to cosign for me." The term "beginner" was one she used frequently in reference to herself.

We drove past the building where she was applying for an apartment and she pointed it out to me.

"Is it a nice place?" I asked.

"It's okay, for a beginner."

I looked up at the building. It was one of the many mid-century high-rises of the Uptown neighborhood (see figure 3.2). Many of these buildings were originally built as "apartment hotels" during the early 1900s, when Uptown was a thriving commercial area intended by developers to rival Chicago's downtown. The building Sandra pointed out still had the mark of the architectural fads of the 1920s, yet it now carried a distinct air of neglect.

The neighborhood overall had changed dramatically since its heyday, becoming first a center of working-class migration from rural areas of the United States and Eastern Europe, and then a hub for international newcomers.[16] By the 1990 Census, the foreign-born population of Uptown had grown to constitute about 33 percent.[17] Uptown became a neighborhood of cheap housing and poor schools, but also one of the few areas in Chicago where African migrants could find grocery stores selling products imported from their homelands, barbers familiar with their preferred styles of hair-braiding, accounting and legal services tailored to their special needs, and restaurants serving their traditional cuisine (see figure 3.3).

Uptown was where Sandra was "beginning," like many newcomers before her. Yet although it did seem to ease her transition to be surrounded by some people from her homeland, the language of "beginning" implied that she saw Uptown as a temporary jumping-off point rather than a permanent home. Most of those whom she had just started going to church with at Evangel Ministries—including Elijah and Catherine, Benjamin, and Anna and Timothy—lived in suburban areas of Chicago and only visited Uptown when they needed a special item from the Ghanaian Market. For them, the measure of success was to be able to move *away* from the ethnic community.

When Sandra and I arrived at the coffee shop that afternoon, I offered to buy her a coffee or tea, but she declined. I sensed she felt a bit nervous about my interest in her story. When I got my coffee and sat back down with her, I pulled out the standard consent form I used for interviews. She took it, looked it over, placed it in front of her, and folded her hands on top of it.

FIGURE 3.2 A typical residential high-rise in Uptown.

"You can go ahead and ask what you want to know," she said. Her body language conveyed she wanted to wait and see how the conversation progressed before she committed to anything with her signature.

She started to warm a bit when talking about her upbringing, and when she learned I had been to the area of Ghana where she grew up. She told me how she studied business management at the polytechnic university and then worked

FIGURE 3.3 A Ghanaian restaurant in Uptown, located in a strip mall between a Chinese restaurant and a Mexican grocery.

for a year at the Ghanaian equivalent of the social security administration in her hometown. While working there she met her husband. He was another recent university graduate who decided to pursue the pastoral profession. He was training for the ministry in an organization Sandra was only vaguely familiar with, Evangel Ministries. She soon got to know the group quite well, as this young man started to pursue a more serious relationship with her. Since he was becoming a pastor there, it was important to him that she also become a member, and that they go through premarital counseling using the Evangel Ministries model.

One of the early challenges to their relationship was Sandra's plan to move abroad. This plan developed after traveling to the United States to attend a conference representing the company she worked for. While there, she stayed with her cousin, who had a new daughter. Her cousin was proud his daughter was an American—it was a symbol of how far he'd come, and how comfortable his child's life would be compared to the one he'd had in his village. He urged Sandra to consider coming abroad for a stint as well. She should do it, he told her, for her children.

His words stuck in her memory, and she decided to at least start the process of applying for a residency permit in the United States. She heard nothing about the application for about a year. Just as she assumed it was a lost cause, she was granted the visa. In light of this, she and her soon-to-be husband had to adjust their plans. They decided to go ahead and marry, but she would still move abroad to see what kind of success was possible. She came with the idea of getting a degree in cosmetology and making some money for their new family.

As she talked I tried to imagine what that conversation at the airport must have been like. Did they reassure each other that he would follow in her footsteps soon thereafter? Did they avoid that question entirely? Did they mostly sit in silence as they waited for her plane to start boarding? Although the living apart was intended to be temporary, they didn't know exactly when it would end.

With these questions on my mind, I asked, "Do you think your husband would eventually come to the States to join you?"

She responded with a shrug and a sigh, "That's my hope, but he's so much involved with the church there ... and I am not yet due to file for him." She was referring to the mandatory timeline of waiting before she could serve as his sponsor for a family reunification visa.

She told me she left her child from an earlier relationship there in Ghana with her husband, and found out she was pregnant again soon after she arrived in Chicago. This news brought even more intense internal conflict surrounding her decision to move. If she gave birth to their child in the United States, she would be raising the child alone, at least for a while; yet the child could also become a U.S. citizen, and that would dramatically improve his or her future opportunities.

While she was telling her story, her phone rang—it was her husband. She answered and spent about five minutes chatting with him in *Twi*. When she hung up, she apologized for the interruption, and explained that he is not really comfortable with her being here. Just recently they had a conversation during which he tried to convince her to return.

This made sense, given her early experiences. Although her cousin had been the most convincing voice encouraging her to move abroad, when she finally did, he was much less supportive of her than she expected. He provided a place to stay but quickly decided she needed to move out. To him, she was a burden he could not afford to carry indefinitely. She started looking for an apartment, but every landlord she met required her to have a cosigner on the lease. She also started braiding hair for money, and was meeting Ghanaians and Nigerians in the city as clients. Yet she often heard them gossiping about others in the community and worried they would gossip about her as well. Her experiences of competitiveness in the community echoed Benjamin's, and again made it difficult for her to establish trusting ties to other migrants.

Gradually as we talked, Sandra's account shifted in tone. At first she gave me matter-of-fact and simple answers about the details of her background and her move to Chicago. Her hands continued to rest on the consent form, which she still was not certain she wanted to sign. As we kept talking, though, she started to talk more readily and with more feeling. Her hands started gesturing to give emphasis to her frustrations.

"It is so difficult being here and not knowing what people's motives are, and not being familiar with the way that things work. If you could hear some of the stories, you would be so sad. . . . Even when we succeed in our education, we have to compete with you guys . . . and you don't trust us."

This frank statement about trust and distrust spoke to her discoveries about what America is really like, as well as to the very interaction we were engaged in. My first thought was that this was likely the first time she was able to express this sentiment to a member of the host community, and she was bravely taking the opportunity to do so. My second thought was on the nature of this particular disappointment: to do everything "right" as a migrant, succeeding in education and trying to transition into the workforce, but still being met with distrust. It was not what she hoped America and Americans would be.

As we left the coffee shop, she got another call. This time it was a distant acquaintance in the city that had agreed to cosign her loan. I heard her schedule a time to meet him, and then she hung up and reported the good news. I congratulated her. She reflected again on how hard it was to make things work here, since she had no idea that not having "credit" would keep her from being able to rent an apartment.

"I had also been told to stay away from the credit card office," she explained. Many of her informal conversations with other West Africans in her building had given her the impression that "credit card offices," i.e., various credit and loan providers, could easily take advantage of her by charging high fees and interest.

I nodded, "Yes . . . but, well, the best way to get credit is to have a credit card, and make sure you pay it off regularly and consistently." As I spoke, though, I was half-hearted. I wasn't sure how ready she was to get a crash course in the U.S. credit and banking system, especially as she already seemed a bit tired now from our lengthy discussion.

She shook her head again to signal her confusion. "Most Ghanaians will just use cash," she told me. "Since it is easier to trust it when you have it in your hand and can see it."

The word *trust* had come up again, this time in relation to an unfamiliar monetary system. Yet both times her usage of the term spoke to distinct challenges to trusting as an imaginative and symbolic activity. On the one hand, it was hard for her to imagine the people at banks and credit card companies as trustworthy, especially given what she had been told by other migrants. Based on her unfamiliarity with the U.S. system and her experience in Ghana, where the average person relied on cash rather than credit, it seemed too risky to try to build credit with such companies, even if she was told it would benefit her in the long run.

On the other hand, she was frustrated that people like her weren't trusted in spite of their accomplishments. The landlords she interacted with, for example, may have seen her black skin and simple clothes, and heard her tentative English, and read these symbols to mean she was a risky tenant—a "bad" (i.e., poor, desperate, isolated) migrant to rent to. This contradicted how she thought of herself: a dedicated mother, a religious person with strong values, and part of the Ghanaian educated class.

Sandra's frustrations, like Benjamin's described earlier, were thus part of the tightrope walk of being an aspirational Ghanaian migrant in the United States. In her interactions with her cousin, who withdrew some of his support after her arrival, there was the threat of being seen as a bad case, someone who would drain his resources rather than contribute to them. Similarly, in her interactions with clients, there was the threat of being looked down upon as a "beginner," someone who knew nothing about Chicago and had nothing to offer, who would perpetually work a dead-end lower-class job as a hairdresser. Finally, in her interactions with landlords, there was the threat of being seen as a "bad" immigrant—someone who was broke and desperate, and likely unable to consistently pay rent—or being seen as a "bad" black, someone with a poor upbringing and no work ethic. It was certainly not inevitable that in every interaction she would be viewed as untrustworthy; but given the symbolic categories operating in each of these settings, it was an ever-present possibility.

Intersections

The concept of intersectionality has become essential to the sociological study of race in America, as a more nuanced way of looking at the effects of the racial order.[18] Scholars such as Patricia Hill Collins (2009) contend that there is no single experience of blackness; rather, there are distinct experiences at the intersections of social identities, which reflect overlapping systems of domination. This approach has predominantly focused on the intersections of racial and gender discrimination, but more recently has been applied to other overlapping systems that establish unequal relations between social categories.

As discussed in the introduction and chapter 2, living at the intersection of blackness and foreignness in America is complicated. The experiences of black migrants and American blacks are not the same. Many Ghanaians—such as Elijah, Catherine, and Anna—do not adopt the *habitus* of African American culture; they do not "act black" in their speech, dress, eating habits, or mannerisms. Rather, they tend to embody a higher-class *habitus*, particularly in relation to the

Ghanaian social order. This means that when black immigrants of their social class come to the U.S., they are in some ways well suited to move comfortably in mixed professional and social settings. For this reason, as Waters (1999) argued in the case of black Caribbean immigrants, they are sometimes distinguished in the public consciousness as more desirable tenants, employees, students, or friends, and by implication, are seen as more trustworthy than African Americans.

Yet even though new black migrants are often viewed more positively, at the intersection of blackness and foreignness, miscategorization by others is a frequent occurrence, and any miscategorization in a negative direction challenges the possibility of trusting and being trusted in a given situation. For someone like Sandra in particular, who does not have the education, status, or cosmopolitan family experience that someone like Anna has, the threat is even more real. How she talks, dresses, carries herself, and does her hair are all markedly different from Anna, and reflect her restricted resources and limited experience abroad. Her ability to distinguish herself from the African American underclass, and signal that she is a trustworthy person within the symbolic categories of the U.S. racial order, is tenuous, and highly dependent on how things play out in her first few years in Chicago.

Other situations not contained within these particular stories, but that I heard about in the course of my study, included university students who found it difficult to work with American classmates; nurses whose co-workers told them they only got their job because they were black; taxi drivers who were belittled by their passengers; and even romantic relationships that were suddenly severed by a partner who felt the other one was dragging them down. Each of these situations was different in its particulars; but in their totality they expressed a general trend of people being categorized by others as untrustworthy, based on how those others read the cues and perceived the risks of exchange.

Aspirational migrants from Ghana thus face challenges in the establishment of personal trust networks in multiple settings, whether they are dealing with Ghanaian relatives, friends, or acquaintances, or with native-born Americans at work, in school, or in basic economic transactions. These challenges arise in part from three major social structural factors: (1) the unequal relations between classes in both Ghanaian and American society; (2) the racial order in the United States, which both vilifies aspects of black American culture and draws a sharp line between upstanding and degenerate forms of blackness; and (3) the competitive character of ties among aspirational migrants who are seeking a better life under these constraints. These factors inhibit the imaginative and symbolic activity of trusting others in a variety of situations, and as a result, they challenge these migrants' ability to establish networks of personal trust in the host community.

4

The Draw of Religion

ACCESSIBILITY, PORTABILITY, AND PROMISE

THE RELIGIOUS LANDSCAPE of Ghana is vibrant and dynamic. On a given Sunday morning in Accra, lines of people in their Sunday clothes wait for their turn at the taxi stop; or pack into *tro-tros,* the local form of public transportation; or if they have the means, drive their cars to one of hundreds of different places of worship. In the southern parts of Ghana, the largest number of people are Christians; but just what type of Christianity—and which congregation—they prefer varies from person to person. It is common to switch throughout one's life, or to participate at some level in more than one group. Since the 1980s, locally originated Ghanaian Evangelical churches have been the major beneficiaries of these trends, attracting tens of thousands to their meeting places each Sunday morning.

In this chapter, I highlight some of the reasons why such churches have been particularly appealing to young, aspirational, urban-dwelling Ghanaians, the population from which emigration disproportionately draws. I also show how the appeal of these types of churches—which are actively planting numerous branches around the country and the globe—is related to rapid changes occurring in Ghanaian society. I argue that such churches provide an accessible, promise-filled, and portable basis of new social connection for young people living in the midst of such changes, whether or not they ever go abroad.

A Church of One's Own

Stephen had always lived in Ghana. Yet his life was still transatlantic in many ways. When he was young he lived with an uncle, aunt, and two cousins, while his mother temporarily lived and worked in the United States. His uncle had similarly spent time abroad and had married an American wife, so the family with which Stephen spent his formative years exemplified a mixed Ghanaian American heritage.

When he was about eleven years old, he visited another relative in central Ghana for several weeks. When he came back to his aunt and uncle's house, he was surprised to find that the family, which had never been very serious about going to church, was now attending a new congregation—Evangel Ministries.

"What I heard was that someone invited them," he recalled, as he and I sat in a rooftop restaurant on the University of Ghana campus. "So, because I lived in their house, I mean, I didn't have a choice—I had to go. So the first time I attended the church, I liked it."

"And did you ask them why they started to go to church when they hadn't before?"

He scratched his head, thinking. "Um, I remember, I think that I spoke to my other uncle, there were two . . . so I asked him why [they started going], and he said that they were in the house one day and the one in charge of the church—he wasn't the pastor by then, he was in charge of the church—came to evangelize to them and invited them to church on Sunday, and they decided to go."

I nodded. I had been attending the Evangel Ministries main branch in a suburb of Accra for several weeks, and had become familiar with their habit of going door-to-door to invite people into the congregation.

I encouraged him to continue: "And when you first went with your uncle, what about it at first was appealing to you?"

"Let me say that, when I went the first time I was surprised that church would have so much life, really, because even though it was a young church, our number was less than thirty, I think, at that time. . . . I was surprised that they were so nice, I had never seen that before.

"The first day I attended I spoke to the pastor of the church; he spoke to me, asked my name, asked where I live. And then offered to come and visit me, which he did. And then, he asked me to join a ministry in the church . . . and I was surprised that at that young age I was being offered the opportunity to do something in church, because I was thinking that before you can do something actively in church you have to be of a certain age, you just cannot, you know . . . "

I probed: "But you were eleven."

He nodded. "Yah, I was eleven, saying, join this ministry, I was surprised, okay, so it is a good opportunity to work."

"So did you join a ministry shortly after?"

"Yah, I joined the welcome ministry. I mean, the next time I went back to the church, it was the next week, so, I joined the welcome ministry."

His uncle, aunt, and cousins grew less interested in the church and their attendance trailed off. Stephen, however, decided to keep going on his own.

At the age of twelve he would get up on a Sunday morning, before the rest of the family, so he could be at Evangel Ministries in time for the meeting of the welcome team.

The pastor was young and felt approachable to Stephen, and they became friends. The pastor soon found other ways for Stephen to get involved. "He thought that I could do more than just being in the welcome ministry, so he offered me the opportunity to learn how to play an instrument. He asked me to find somewhere I can learn, he was willing to pay for it."

"What instrument did you learn?"

"The piano."

"So he paid for the fee?"

He nodded and smiled. "Yah, for some time. And then afterward, we had someone from the main branch to come down to our place to teach, so that one wouldn't have to pay. Yah, so I learned the piano, and alongside I learned the drums also. I also learned the guitar as well, so I was involved in the music ministry, then also the choir, so I was playing for the choir . . . at times I could sing; I was just doing all those things."

About a year later, when he was thirteen, his mother moved back to Ghana and his uncle and aunt moved to the United States. He returned to living with his mother. She was raising him in a Presbyterian church before she left, but wasn't surprised that he stopped going when he moved in with his uncle. What did surprise her was that her preteen son had found a new church of his own. Stephen asked her if it was okay if he continued to go to Evangel Ministries instead of her Presbyterian church.

"When I was young I used to say that I wanted to play the piano, and the drums, so seeing that someone is offering me the opportunity to learn how to play the piano, become who I really wanted to be, and the pastor was so nice—came over to my house to meet my parents, talk to them—she was impressed."

Stephen's mother was in the end pleased he found his own place to worship, meet people, and pursue opportunities. Like many other parents of the young Ghanaians flocking to churches like Evangel Ministries, she recognized that this church provided something for Stephen her traditional Presbyterian congregation could not.

The process through which Ghanaian young people like Stephen have found a new degree of ownership of their religious lives through the rise of the Charismatic movement echoes insights into North America's bottom-up congregationalism. Ghana has followed the model of formal religious disestablishment, and congregations there are increasingly multifunctional communities that reflect the local culture and concerns of their members. The Evangelical Charismatic movement in particular is Ghana's first mainstream religious movement formally disconnected from global—and primarily Anglo-European—denominational structures. Its congregations are fully free to develop a localized style and provide a space of religious agency for less powerful groups, such as youth and women. Just as in North America, therefore, where people of diverse ethnicities, classes, and ideologies talk about finding "a church of our own" (Warner 2004), in Ghana young people like Stephen often find a church of their own within the Charismatic Evangelical movement.

"I Just Wanted to Be Like Him"

Evangel Ministries continued to play an important role in Stephen's life as he grew older. He and his mother moved across town, so he could no longer go to his original Evangel Ministries branch, but he found another within a five-minute walk of their new home. He was nearing the end of his high school years by this time, and was struggling with his education. He applied to several of his first-choice university programs, but was rejected because his grades had been consistently poor. It was a difficult time for him, in which he grappled with the question of how to move forward.

"I had intended to go to medical school, but my grades didn't serve me that much to go there. So, I was confused, I didn't know where to go, I didn't know what to do really. And then I applied to a university—that was, like, two years ago. I wanted to do engineering, and I didn't get the admission. So, I was very sad, I was down. Then I applied to the polytechnic also; I didn't get admission. I was very, very . . . I felt disappointed. I thought probably I couldn't do it anymore. Maybe I'll just have to end it, and find a way to build a future from that point."

There was a turning point in this story, however, that once again involved Evangel Ministries. "I spoke to some people in church. They kind of gave me encouragement like, no, you can do it. You can do it, and nobody is born a failure, everybody has a future. I remember that one person I spoke to in church told me that, 'you can go to the university, and I know when you go to the university you will do very well.' . . . That person attended this school and did business administration. She said, 'you can go to the university and you can do well, I think you should go to the university.' [She] bought the forms for me, forced me to apply. And she endorsed them for me, actually. I got the admission, and now I'm here."

"Wow," I said, "and did she encourage you to do business administration?"

"No, she didn't," he laughed. "I think I was just trying to imitate her life."

"Because she was being so helpful?"

"Yes, and she's also married to a man who also did business administration; he's a banker. So I think my whole idea of banking shifted because of that."

He laughed again, remembering how he would copy this man down to even small details. "I mean, I always wanted to have the same kind of life that he had. I used to dress just like him. If I wore a new tie, I would knot my tie the way he knots his tie. The kind of tie he would wear with his shirt, I would go and look for that same tie, I would wear that same shirt. I just wanted to be like him, I wanted to have that, the way he came off the university, how he got married, and all that. I just wanted to have exactly the same kind of life."

This couple showed Stephen what a better future could look like. They modeled how to be optimistic in the face of failure, how to identify a worthwhile ambition, and even how to dress the part of an upwardly mobile professional. To know that he wanted an upper-class lifestyle was one thing; to really *see* it, and to receive encouragement from two people who were living it, was something else entirely. His involvement at Evangel Ministries supplied this opportunity.

Over time, however, his commitment to the church organization started to eclipse his ambition to work in banking and business. He got a job in the Evangel Ministries office, managing the accounting and attendance data for the growing international organization. Through this position he learned more about Evangel Ministries' global scope, and developed a lot of respect for the founder's intentionality in its design. He also started to imagine himself contributing to the organization in more significant ways.

He explained, "If I were to start a company right now, which I thought of at a point in time in my life, I don't want to have a company just here; I want to open a global company that is going everywhere. I would want to go to the U.K., to the U.S., everywhere, I mean try to make things work. Do you get it? So, I think that if our founder was to start a company instead of a church, he would also want to grow it as much as he wants to grow the church."

Stephen decided to finish his business administration degree, but use it within the organization rather than in business. He told me his current ambition was to be a full-time leader of one of Evangel Ministries' international branches.

"I kind of caught the interest in being in the full-time ministry. I wanted to go as a missionary, and save other people who do not know about Christ. Yeah, preach the gospel in towns. And then I think one day also I was given the light about these Western missionaries that came to Africa, and how they gave their lives right here, in a town or in a country where nobody knew them. Just because they wanted to bring Christianity to Africa. I thought I could also do the same. If I could go to a country where Christ is not known, and then by just preaching to one person, I am alright, I am okay to do that."[1]

It was a vision he would probably not have considered when he was a shy boy of eleven. Now, though, much seemed possible that hadn't before. His was no longer going to be a story of obscurity, scraping by, or what-might-have-been. His was going to be a story of respect, service, and personal fulfillment. Although he would not likely get rich as an Evangel missionary, he would never have to worry about whether or not he would be able to take care of his basic needs, for he had seen how the organization takes care of its own.[2]

As noted, Stephen never lived abroad, at least not by the time I met him. But the way in which his religious membership shifted his aspirations for the future, in large part owing to the close social ties he found there that modeled a different set of accomplishments, foreshadowed what I later observed among those who lived in Chicago, and indicated from the start the power of religious-based trust networks to shape personal histories. Stephen's story thus shows how Charismatic religious membership can both help Ghanaian young people achieve their goals and later transform their goals. It meets them where they are and changes who they are in turn.

Sunday Morning in Accra

While visiting Accra, Ghana's capital, I spent weekdays at the university working alongside graduate students at the Regional Institute of Population Studies (RIPS) at the University of Ghana.[3] On weekends, however, much of my time was spent with Ama. Her cousin, Sylvia, had married an undergraduate classmate of mine, and when Sylvia heard I was traveling to Ghana, she gave me Ama's contact information. Ama had recently finished her degree at the University of Ghana, where she studied theatre and dance. She was currently working at her national service, which is a government-mandated year of service employment required of all graduates of accredited tertiary schools. Ama and I quickly connected, spending our Saturdays at birthday parties, shopping in the Osu district, or going to the beach. Coincidentally, she was also a member of Evangel Ministries, and so we also saw each other most Sunday mornings.

She first brought me to Evangel Ministries' main branch on a drizzly Sunday morning in late June. I woke up early in my room in a hostel of the University of Ghana. The hostels are like dormitories, usually built of cement blocks. Since it was summer, the hostels were quiet, populated by studious and mature graduate students. I had a long way to travel that morning, from one side to the other of the Accra metro area, so I left before most in the hostel awoke.

Outside the main campus gate I looked for a *tro-tro* to take me into town. A typical *tro-tro* is a white Toyota conversion van—a reliable vehicle serving as the backbone of communal transportation across sub-Saharan Africa—with a young man, known as the conductor, hanging out the sliding door yelling the name of the van's destination. *Tro-tros* are owned and driven by private entrepreneurs, but they are the public's way of getting around, so they are best understood as a kind of "public-private" transportation. I hopped into one whose conductor had been yelling, "Circle! Circle!," which is shorthand for Kwame Nkrumah circle, Accra's central traffic interchange.

After reaching the circle and taking a taxi from there, I arrived at Evangel Ministries' headquarters. It was an impressive campus of buildings, crowded with people in their best clothes. As I waited for Ama to arrive, I noticed a sign on one building indicating it was a health clinic. Other buildings looked to be full of classrooms and offices. I also noticed a series of vans painted with the Evangel Ministries logo. One by one, they came through the gate and more people in blouses, flounced skirts, and heels—or suits and heavily polished black dress shoes—piled out of the vans. Ama found me there about twenty minutes later, and we walked into the main sanctuary together.

I was, first of all, impressed by the enormity of the space. It was constructed in a simple style, reminiscent of an enormous government or university meeting hall. I then noticed a crowd of people in formal dress—even a step up from what most others were wearing—enter at the front and sit in the front rows. Ama explained to me that there had been a wedding at the church yesterday, and this was the wedding party. Indeed, I could spot the happy bride and groom. The bride was in her wedding gown. As the service began, the announcer called everyone's attention to the young couple and they received a hearty round of applause.

A large group of musicians and singers—about 100 or so people—stepped onto the stage and started leading the group in song, as more and more people took their seats around us. The songs started off slow and were contemplative. Our neighbors to either side stood and swayed to the music, with their hands lifted and their eyes closed, and sang heartily along with the melody. All the words were in English, and I recognized a few of the songs from American Evangelical churches I had visited in the past.

Two men in suits led the worship, switching a handheld microphone between them. Once, when one man gave his partner the microphone, Ama leaned over and whispered to me, "That's George; he's my favorite pastor."

"Why is that?" I asked, matching her whisper.

"Because he is like a father figure to me."

I took note and looked back at the pastor, who was energetically directing the musicians to pick up their tempo. Suddenly they broke into a fast and heavy drum beat. Many of the musicians were jumping up and down to the beat as they sang, and a few took off their suit jackets to free their arms to clap overhead as well. Congregants were dancing in the aisles, and many more were jumping in their seats. As the song concluded, the room erupted in loud applause and shouting.

The energy reminded me of a rock concert. I remembered something another young woman, Mary, had said about Evangel Ministries: "other young people go to discos, but I go to church!" This was the place she went to dance and be happy, she said.

Another emotional high point was during the sermon. The founder of Evangel Ministries was traveling, so another one of the many pastors preached that morning. Just that week, legendary pop star Michael Jackson had died unexpectedly, and his songs were playing on heavy rotation on Ghanaian radio. As the preacher warmed up his audience, he had a special surprise: he called up a young man from the front of the crowd who did a picture-perfect moonwalk—Jackson's signature dance move—and then danced to the base line of Jackson's song "Thriller." The whole crowd either jumped or fell out of their seats with laughter and cheering.

The service concluded with an alter call to the familiar tune of "I Surrender All," a favorite in the American Southern Baptist and Pentecostal traditions. Dozens of people came forward, and after being prayed for by the pastor, were ushered out the side door to a room where, Ama told me, they would be served cake and given information about how to get more involved in the church. The pastor then asked anyone visiting for the first time to stand. A young man in the row in front of me turned around in his chair and urged me to get up. I politely waved him off since I didn't want to leave Ama, who told me the newcomers would also be taken to a special room and given cake, soda, and one of the founder's books.

The service concluded and the rain started coming down in torrents. People scurried to their cars or the Evangel Ministries vans to head home. Ama and I crossed the parking lot to another building, dodging puddles. Ama was a member of the welcome ministry and it was time for their meeting.

The young men and women in the room where we entered were almost all dressed in black and white professional clothes, with a brightly colored scarf or tie. They all looked to be teenagers, or even younger—I thought again about Stephen being asked to be part of the welcome team at age eleven. The female pastor leading the meeting came up and greeted us, catching up with Ama on how she was doing. Everyone was served some of the cake left from the welcome reception provided to newcomers.

The meeting itself then started. It was short, and most of the time was spent listening to the instructions of the pastor, Tonya, on a range of topics. She was a tall, fashionable woman with a strong presence. She spent the beginning of the meeting telling young ladies how they should—and should not—dress, with exhortations to avoid "skinny" jeans and T-shirts. At first I was confused by this focus on dress; but it started to make sense when I thought about how young the people around me were, and how they served as the first face of Evangel Ministries to visitors. Personal appearance and decorum were as important as knowing how to show people to their chairs.

She also lectured them on how behaving well at home is important for the church: "I know many of you, your parents do not come with you to church," she said. "If you are naughty at home, your parents will think, 'I don't want to go to that church where my naughty child goes.'"

She reiterated what had been said in announcements that morning: that each person in the church should bring three new people to visit in the next month. Next week was family Sunday, she reminded them. They should behave well at home so their parents will want to come to church with them.

Another point of business she covered was the website for Evangel Ministries, which she reminded them had recently changed its web address. "Make sure you visit it!," She said. "I was talking with my brother, who lives in Virginia, and he told me that sometimes he goes to the website just to see my picture and see what is going on in the church. So please, be high-tech!" She told them that if they don't know how to get online, they should go to an Internet café and have someone explain it to them. The group of young women and men giggled at this thought. She responded by reiterating, "Sometimes we are too 'blackish' in our way of thinking; we don't like technology. So be high-tech!"

Finally, she talked about the marriage school, reminding the group it is mandatory for people who want to get married in the church to do six months of counseling beforehand. The group was getting rowdier, and several teens inserted jokes about marriage and dating. Ama leaned over to me, saying that the church tells young people they will find a good marriage partner as long as they marry within the church.

Tonya adjourned us after this. Ama and I spent time meeting some of her friends. We then left to have lunch at a small food stand on the other side of the wide parking lot, as the rain had stopped and the sun had come out bright on the drippy city.[4] The whole experience had lasted many hours, and was dynamic, engaging, and social. Evangel Ministries, it seemed, was the place to be on a Sunday morning if you were a young, single, educated person in Ghana like Ama, and the church went out of its way to make such people feel welcome.

History and Legitimacy

Evangel Ministries is one of about a half-dozen large Charismatic organizations in Ghana, and there are dozens more that aspire to the same kind of growth. The rise of such churches follows several other phases of Christian growth in West Africa. The first was the period of European missionaries, which peaked in the late-1800s. The most active groups were the Anglicans from England and North

America, the Presbyterians from Germany, the Methodists, and the Catholics. Although these groups now have a strong presence in Ghana, in this early mission phase the conversion of the local ethno-linguistic groups was slow. What success the missionaries achieved was largely due to their investments in schools that offered an increasingly valuable skill—literacy—while teaching Christianity to their students.[5]

A second phase began in the early 1900s, which involved both the advance of Pentecostalism in Africa and the spread of locally originated movements that merged Christian teachings with West African culture. Ghana's Church of Pentecost, founded in the 1930s by Apostolic Church missionaries from the United Kingdom, exemplifies the former trend. The Apostolic Church was part of the global movement of Pentecostalism that started in 1906 in Los Angeles, California, during the Asuza Street Revival. The Pentecostal movement began as a small church group under the leadership of the African American preacher William Seymour that started to experience a wave of supernatural healings, visions, and *glossolalia* (i.e., "speaking in tongues").[6] This religious revival movement was international in its orientation from its first stages, and many of its initial participants—including those that founded the Apostolic Church of the United Kingdom—traveled around the globe to spread their particular Spirit-filled and experience-focused version of Christianity.[7]

When the movement spread to Ghana—which was the British colony of Gold Coast at the time—it drew in many converts.[8] The Pentecostal churches, including the Church of Pentecost, distinguished themselves from the missionary churches by being much more passionate in their expressions, such as dancing and speaking in tongues, and by focusing on the miraculous power of God to heal people, drive out demons, and answer prayers. They advertised religion as the solution to the everyday problems and concerns of the Gold Coast residents: sickness, poverty, and oppression.

This phase of Christian growth was also driven by a second trend, the rise of independent African movements and churches, as exemplified by the conversion movement of William Wade Harris. Harris was converted to Christianity within the Anglican Church, but later started his own traveling prophetic ministry across West Africa. He was known for preaching Christian doctrine and working to abolish the traditional use of fetishes, while upholding the traditional practice of polygamy, which put him at odds with the European missionaries. Like the Pentecostals, he applied Christianity to the direct concerns of colonial West Africans, making something familiar and appealing out of something foreign.

In the 1910s and 1920s, Harris attracted large numbers of followers. Some of these followers later formed the Harrist Church, still present in Cote D'Ivoire, while many more joined the mission churches following their conversions.

Between the work of people like Harris and the Pentecostal churches, the spread of Christianity accelerated, and the result was a remarkable historical moment of religious change.[9] While in the late 1800s, Christianity was the religion of the few and the foreign, by the mid-20th century the majority of Ghanaians were Christian.[10]

The third phase of Christian history aligns with the post-independence period beginning in the 1960s. During this phase, the mission-founded churches shifted toward a more indigenous leadership, while new church organizations founded by Ghanaians started to proliferate. It was clear by this time that Christianity was here to stay in Ghana, even if many of its European founders had left. It was also clear that Ghanaian Christianity was now taking its own course, sparking its own innovations, and choosing its own leaders. By the 1980s, when Evangel Ministries began, this atmosphere of innovation and localization was pervasive; and although some scholars, like Paul Gifford (2004), characterize such Charismatic Evangelical churches as Ghana's "new" Christianity, they are also the inheritors of a long tradition of African Christianity's merging of local and global influences.

As noted in the introduction, these new churches fit within a global shift toward Evangelical Christianity across Africa, Asia, and Latin America. Although there are many local variations on this pattern, there is also remarkable similarity across these regions in the types of churches that have attracted the most adherents in recent decades. They tend to be locally originating, while also borrowing heavily from an emerging global Evangelical culture; they tend to exhibit affective rituals characteristic of Pentecostal and/or Charismatic groups; and they tend to be outreach focused, as often exhibited through an agenda of global church planting. While many reasons have been suggested for the unprecedented growth of such churches, most scholars agree they thrive among the young, urban, aspirational, and globally oriented classes. In part, their growth has also been a response to uncertain postcolonial political and economic contexts, as well as a rejection of the hierarchical and traditional religious structures left by European colonizers.[11] This recent phase of Christian growth in Ghana is thus part of a larger pattern of Christian growth across the Global South (Offutt 2015).

Any religious landscape as vibrant as Ghana's also involves competition and conflict. Innovation and vibrancy are the norm, but so are debates about legitimacy—that is, whose version of the Christian faith is valid and beneficial for followers. When new congregations are founded, there is often an ambitious, entrepreneurial figure at the head, someone who believes he or she has a special call from God or a message that people need to hear. Yet these claims take time to be vetted, and are often initially met with skepticism from the increasingly jaded religious public.

Specifically, such congregations are described as "one-man churches": congregations that are about the founder and not the faith. They are criticized for stealing gullible believers from the more established churches, and many ultimately succumb to corruption and in-fighting. It is impossible to know how many such churches have existed in Ghana during the past few decades—the stories we hear are those who are successful in their claim to legitimacy—but almost everyone in Ghana claims to know someone taken in by one of these churches, and many people express strong feelings about how they take advantage of the poor and uneducated.

These issues came up one Sunday afternoon when Ama and I went together for lunch at her aunt's home. This aunt, Theresa, was the mother of Sylvia, the woman living in the United States who had connected me with Ama in the first place. Her house was hidden behind a high cement wall and had a beautiful garden. When we arrived at the front door, Theresa greeted us warmly and asked for news about Sylvia and her new husband.

Before lunch we sat in the living room, drank fruit juice, and chatted. Theresa showed us a picture album of her children abroad, whom she visited on a fairly regular basis. She was often going back and forth between Ghana and the United States, both when her husband still lived and his work took them abroad and now that he had passed and all her children were in America or in England. Even though her place of residence was Ghana, her life was also transnational.

Eventually the conversation turned to Evangel Ministries. Theresa, a long-time devout Anglican, was curious to hear what we had to say about it, since she was becoming more aware of its influence. Her own children all lived in the United States, but she had three wards living with her and two of them went to a school run by Evangel Ministries. One of these kids, a pre-teen at the time, attended on Sunday mornings. The founder of the church also lived in her neighborhood.

"I am being swallowed up by Evangel," she joked.

I let Ama field most of Theresa's questions. Ama focused on the good that Evangel Ministries was doing for young people who don't have work.

"They give a lot of people jobs, because all of the schoolteachers, the security guards at the church, and other various employees of the church are all Evangel members and are all paid very well. Their security guards are paid the minimum wage, and most places guards do not even make that.

"They also have a very grueling process of becoming pastors in the church, where people have to take classes, then spend two years of field work in some branch of the Chapel, followed by writing exams. This is so not just anyone can go around calling themselves a pastor."

Theresa responded positively to this, reflecting the common sentiment that would-be pastors are a dime a dozen. "This is a good thing, so you don't have people going around, calling themselves pastors, using watered down pieces of scripture and exploiting people."[12]

In this exchange, the underlying issue was the legitimacy of Evangel Ministries as more than a one-man church. In her comments to Theresa, Ama was describing the good that Evangel Ministries was doing for people by providing jobs, and their efforts to vet and properly train their own pastors, as evidence that they were a responsible, legitimate Christian organization rather than an upstart predatory movement. Ama herself was very critical of the one-man churches. She explained they attract people looking for a quick fix to their problems, and they are entirely focused on the pastor: "You will see, people won't even go to church when the pastor is not there."[13] Yet she believed Evangel Ministries was different: it was an upstanding Charismatic church, not a one-man get-rich-quick scheme.

The Churches of the Moment

The thousands of people who attended to Evangel Ministries each Sunday seemed to agree with Ama's assessment that this group was more than a "one-man church" or a flash in the pan. In less than three decades, Evangel Ministries had become a major social phenomenon and a household name. Like many of his peers leading similarly popular Charismatic organizations, the founder's name was often near the top of the "100 Most Influential Ghanaians" list compiled by the eTV television network. When he made provocative statements on political and social issues—which happened often—they were reported and analyzed in the mainstream media. His many books and audio recordings on diverse topics sold thousands of copies. Although he was not universally loved, he certainly had established legitimacy as a religious figure.

To understand why this *particular* one-man church became a legitimate religious institution rather than fading into obscurity would likely require a detailed organizational history, with attention to its available resources, the leader's charisma, and prescient decisions made along the way. In general, however, such organizations tend to do well for four related reasons: (1) they give off a youthful vibe and make religious participation fun; (2) they offer pragmatic instructions on topics of relevance to the aspirational Ghanaian; (3) they capitalize on the available time and energy of young people; and (4) they facilitate new social connections between members.

Annie, a young woman who recently graduated from college in Ghana and moved back in with her parents, described Evangel Ministries and similar churches as the places where "the heat is on." In a highly religious country, they were the "it" churches of the moment. Annie's parents lived around the corner from Evangel Ministries' headquarters, and she attended there fairly often for their midweek evening service. Unlike Stephen and Ama, she was not a member of Evangel Ministries. Annie's family had been Anglican for several generations, and that was still her primary religious identity. Yet she found certain things about the church quite appealing and thought of it as a fun and worthwhile thing to do on a Tuesday night. She participated in both churches simultaneously, for different reasons.

I first met Annie on a Sunday afternoon at her home after a morning service at the Evangel Ministries headquarters. It was a warm, humid day, and I was with Daniel, a graduate student at the University of Ghana who was a Charismatic himself and was helping me get acclimated to the city. Annie was a family friend of his, and he assured me she would not mind our visiting her unannounced after church.

We arrived and sat on the porch, and were greeted by a housemaid. She told us that Annie was napping and no one else was home. Daniel told the young girl to go wake Annie up. I tried to object, since I had no desire to gain a reputation as the foreign researcher who liked to rouse people from their beds, but Daniel waved off my objection. "She is like a sister to me," he said.

When she finally arrived, rubbing her eyes, she corroborated with a smile, "I wouldn't be coming out here for anyone else but Daniel."

Annie clearly liked telling stories, however, and after several minutes she started to become livelier as she talked about her church involvement. She first got involved at Evangel Ministries when she was a student at the University of Ghana. "When I was on campus," she remembered, "they [Evangel Ministries] used to have a student's fellowship [in my dorm], and by then, I used to go to church alright, but I didn't have anything during, like, from Monday to Friday, I didn't have any activities. So, I just took a stroll there, and it was exciting, and then . . . when I came out [i.e., graduated] I knew they had branches, there wasn't just one. So then I felt there was another opportunity to get involved in that."

"So now you attend both churches, really?"

"Kind of."

"And do you feel a desire to switch to Evangel and have it be your only church, or do you like having both of them?"

"Not really, you know, it's for different reasons. When I go to the Anglican Church, I am going to teach the kids. And, I mean, if you are going to feed somebody, then you need to be fed. So, I go [to Evangel] to be fed, so I can go and feed. That's basically it. It's not like switching completely or anything, but trying to balance it so that you don't give what you don't really have."

I pressed her on this more, asking her about what it means to be "fed" at Evangel Ministries.

"I believe that the pastor there . . . he's much more focused on the people and their interpersonal relationships. Like, they talk about loyalty, I mean they go into detail as to how you manage to behave, and in what we do, what you should look out for. You know, we read the Bible alright, like they talk about specific people, but this [pastor] teaches you exactly how to find that person in the Bible in front of you . . . so you grow up, knowing exactly how to know this kind of person and what you should do."

This certainly reflected what Daniel and I had heard at Evangel Ministries on our visits. On one occasion, for example, the pastor talked about certain kinds of successful people who fail to acknowledge those who came before them and who paved the way. He very practically described how his listeners could identify these people and avoid them, since such kinds of people are fundamentally takers rather than givers. Although the lesson was rooted in stories from the Bible, many of the points were reminiscent of what one might hear at a conference entitled "How to Succeed in Business."[14]

Annie also joked about the church's heavy attention to dating and marriage, and how the leaders "guarantee" that committed members will find a mate—who they refer to as "beloveds" to distance themselves from the wider culture of casual dating—if they look only within the church. She thought this focus on marriage was at times a bit obsessive: "I believe it's good, depending on the individual, but sometimes you realize that people go to the wrong places for the wrong reasons. . . . And people also, and some people have the good intent, and they go there, and now it's like it becomes pressure for them. Because, if you are going and always thinking about, 'Oh, grab a beloved, get somebody,' you know those things, it's like finally you get to the point where it's like, okay, you want to do it, but the brain behind it may be wrong."

In spite of this potential pitfall, however, the emphasis on facilitating good romantic partnerships seemed a natural outgrowth of their focus on the needs of youth and on providing accessible social connections. If the church was intentionally designed to support the development of relationships between members, why shouldn't it also be a setting for finding romantic ones?

About midway through our talk I asked Annie to explicitly compare and contrast the Anglican Church with the Charismatic churches.

"Oh, it's like one of them likes to be silent, another likes to be loud, singing pretty. As in, God likes it quiet, that's in the Anglican churches, and all these other churches. But when it comes to the Charismatic churches, it's like we sing more, and that thing is there, the desire is there, you know, it's like you are aggressive or something, so it comes to you."

This energy surrounding the spiritual life was something she viewed as encouraging and inspiring. While in the Anglican Church, "whether or not you read your Bible is nobody's business"; in the Charismatic church, she could always find someone willing to chat about inspiring material or engage on spiritual matters. Annie's Tuesday nights spent at Evangel Ministries were great fun—both because of the music and preaching and because of the opportunity to socialize with her peers—and they were also, she felt sure, going to help her become a better person.[15] Like Stephen and Ama, at Evangel Ministries she found an accessible community, adapted to her distinct concerns as a young adult, which gave her a sense of confidence in her personal growth.

Although Annie attended the main branch of Evangel Ministries, it was a campus branch that first drew her in. This was true for many others I talked to. New branches were being started all over the country—not to mention the wider region and the world—which added an additional element to Evangel Ministries' appeal: portability.

Many of Ghana's middle- and upper-class young people lived multi-local lives. They grew up in one town or village; attended boarding school somewhere else in their teen years; went to university in yet another location if they were fortunate enough to continue their schooling; did their required national service year in some other neighborhood, town, or region; and finally moved to larger cities to look for work. Many also moved between relatives' homes in their childhood years, as Stephen had, or traveled abroad later on. Yet just about anywhere they went, at any phase of this growing-up trajectory, they could find a branch of Evangel Ministries. This, made their connection to the organization imminently portable. It moved with them, across geography and through life phases.

As is common in African countries today, Ghana has a disproportionately young demographic makeup. In 2013, youth between the ages of ten and twenty-four made up 31 percent of the total population.[16] These youth are growing up in a very different context from their parents and grandparents. They are more educated and more aware of the world outside of Ghana, owing to the rapid advancement in public primary schooling and information technologies. The primary school completion rate for both sexes is now just under 100 percent, as compared to 67 percent in 1981; and the rate of students entering the last year of secondary school grew from 46 percent to 69 percent in roughly the same period. Concurrently, the number of Internet users per 100 people grew from less than 1 in the early 2000s to about 20 by 2015, and the urban population grew by an annual rate of 4 percent.[17]

As a result of these trends toward widespread basic education, greater Internet connectivity, urbanization, and globalization—along with the widening gap between those who make it into the middle class and those who don't—Ghana's young people are mobile and adaptable by necessity. The increasing population of matriculating students have set their sights on higher education, whether at home or abroad, or on professional salaried jobs found in major cities. They need a portable and forward-thinking religious community to keep up with their changing lives, and the new Charismatic churches provide that.

Christian organizations have long been global in their mindset and motivated to expand their reach transnationally. The Charismatic movement in Ghana owes much to streams of Christianity coming from elsewhere, and its biggest congregations tend to be extremely focused on global proselytizing, as Stephen, the young man working for the Evangel Ministries headquarters, explained. Similarly, Bongmba (2007) argues that the global outreach of African-initiated churches into North America is firmly rooted in the teachings of the Christian tradition. Yet for young Ghanaians in the Charismatic movement, this impulse is arguably even more central to their faith expressions, given the increasing likelihood that many of them may end up living abroad. Having a "portable faith," as Bongmba describes it, is personally valuable, as well as solidly in keeping with Christian traditions.

The Charismatic Transformation

A central aspect of global Charismatic Evangelical culture is the personal transformation involved in becoming "born again." People who identify as born again or claim to have had a born-again conversion experience are found across Christian traditions. The term itself refers to John 3:3, a biblical passage in which Jesus says, "unless one is born again he cannot see the kingdom of God." Yet Charismatic Evangelicals put particular emphasis on becoming born again as a specific moment or process of spiritual transformation. This emphasis is so strong that in some settings, such as Nigeria (Marshall 2009), the movement itself is often called the "Born Again Movement" and members prefer to identify as "Born Agains," above anything else.

In my prior research (2010) into born-again conversion narratives in Malawi, I was struck by the emphasis placed on certain aspects of lifestyle change. Being born again was about taking on certain behaviors: sexual self-control, staying in school, dressing well, delaying marriage, and not cheating others in business. It was associated with moral restraint and discipline, and with the adoption of certain habits that signified a "modern" rather than a traditional orientation.

Likewise in Ghana, becoming fully part of the Charismatic movement involved few changes in belief but many elements of lifestyle change. The lecture given by the pastor of the welcome ministry, on the morning that I attended the meeting with Ama, revolved around how the young people should change their habits—that is, dressing more modestly, being "high-tech," inviting friends and relatives to church, and living peacefully with their parents. Further, during the time I spent in Ghana, not one of my interviewees identified a distinct doctrinal difference between the Charismatic churches and their counterparts; the differences all revolved around the adoption of new habits.

The habits promoted by the movement were particularly applicable to the demands of succeeding in Ghana's changing social and economic environment. They tended to be seen as modern habits: dressing professionally, in Western-style clothes; using the Internet and other communications technologies; actively pursuing education and formal knowledge; and following Western models of partner selection on the basis of personal choice and compatibility rather than extended family interests. As noted by Birgit Meyer (1998), such movements in Ghana see conversion as a "complete break with the past." For Ghanaian young people, such a conversion brings a sense of promise as they seek to move into a brighter future. It implies that the transformed individual can gain a new ability to shed the fetters of the past, including the burden of African "backwardness," and succeed in a modern Ghana where the old rules no longer apply.

This transition was particularly dramatic for Daniel, the man who introduced me to Annie and accompanied me to her house that day. Daniel was at the university pursuing a master's degree in population studies. He had come far from his childhood in a small village in western Togo; and his progress, as well as his developing aspirations for the future, was closely intertwined with his Charismatic transformation.

Daniel's conversion to Charismatic Evangelical Christianity was more dramatic than many others I talked to because his family was "animist," in his words: they followed the traditional religion of the Ewe, his people group, who live in Togo and the eastern part of Ghana. His childhood was spent in Togo with his mother, and he never knew his father. At the age of fifteen, he decided to move to a city in Ghana to live with his uncle, where he expected to find more opportunity and better schools.

"When I came," he recalled, "My uncle asked whether I wanted to go to school or learn a trade. So, I said, no, I want to go to school. So when I came to Ghana, I was sent to Primary 6."

While attending primary school in Ghana he had his first brush with Charismatic Christianity. "I was invited one day to a Bible study, a family Bible study. It was a man who was teaching his own children the Bible, so I was invited by a friend to go."

"One of your schoolmates?"

"Yes, one of my schoolmates. So, I joined him . . . and I was so touched by what I was told from the Bible. So my mind, my view about the world, about what I believed in, everything was changed.... And that was the end of it. I felt so good, I felt great, relieved and set free, and so I started going to church."

Yet this choice didn't sit well with his uncle. Unlike Stephen's and Annie's parents, who were Christians themselves and thus had little objection to their teenager's interest in Evangel Ministries, Daniel's uncle was adamantly against the "born again" movement.

"It infuriated my uncle," Daniel continued. "He got angry. He said, 'Why do you have to become a born-again Christian? No!' Because as a born-again Christian you don't have to worship idols. We don't pour libations to the gods, we don't call on any spirit apart from the spirit of God."

"And in your church they teach you not to do those things anymore?"

"Exactly. They are dead works. And my uncle was angry. And he was like, 'Okay, you came to me in Ghana, you came to stay with me; and if you think that you will no more worship what I worship, then you have to leave my home.' So it was a struggle, and then finally in November 1988, I was driven out of the house."

Daniel's rejection of his family's traditional practices, and reference to them as "dead works," was both a theological point and a personal one: they had no life in his eyes, no relevance to the world he was now living in.

His story continued: "So, I was driven out of the house, and I didn't know where to go. I didn't know anybody, and I couldn't speak English at the time. I couldn't speak Ga, I couldn't speak Twi, I could only speak Ewe.... So, I was, like, so what am I going to do? So you know this popular market, called Malata Market... so we have street children, they push truck there, they carry busload for them and charge them for money. So I was going to stay in Malata Market, with those boys because some of them were my mates, they were coming to school. So I could just stay with them, and work and look after myself and go to church, because church became so important to me."

"Did you leave school?"

"No, I didn't leave school. I was determined to go to school. So I was praying to God to help me go to school.... So I went to the pastor [of the church I was attending], and I told him, 'This is the issue. I have been sacked from my house because of Christianity, I don't know what to do, where to sleep.' So he took me to a deacon, a leader in the church, to put up with him for the night. The next day, we would go to my uncle, which we did." He then added, "And that deacon became my adopted father, who adopted me and looked after me for about twenty years before he died last year."

I nodded. Daniel had mentioned this man before.

"I stayed that night. The next day we went to my uncle to talk to him. He rejected all of us. He drove us out of his house. He said if I am not willing to denounce my faith and come back to idol worship, the old faith, then he wasn't going to receive me. So, I received letters from my grandmother, my grandfather, my mom . . . all telling me to come back to the idol worship. Or at least, I should go to Catholic church and not born again church, not charismatic."

"So they said Catholic was okay? Why is that?"

"Because Catholic, you are permitted to still worship idols, you can still pour libations, you can still go to the fetish priest, and they don't mind. But I realized no, that's not the right way. Once you say no to something, turn your back on it, and face what you are now seeing, what you are now facing, which is the new faith I'd found in Christ."

"And you were still seventeen?"

"Yes, seventeen, thereabouts. So, I don't know, I just felt that God will take control, God will care for me. Because I've read in the scripture that, from the Bible, that if your father rejects you, God will not reject you. He is your father. He will give you sisters and brothers, and mothers and fathers."

"Did you have a Bible that you were reading . . did you own one?"

"Oh, yes. In fact, I bought the Bible about three times and my uncle saw all of them, because I was reading the Bible a lot . . . even though my English was bad, my reading wasn't good, but I was just forcing. In fact, the Bible taught me how to read, and how to speak English. Because I was going out, speaking to people, doing outreach, preaching to people using English."

He continued: "I told the pastors, 'I am not going to stay with my uncle. You don't be afraid. Maybe you don't have a way, any place for me to stay. But I have somewhere to stay. God is in control.' And I had in mind going to stay in Malata Market and push truck, get money, feed myself, have my freedom of worship, and then go to school. That was my mind.

"The pastors they were startled . . . they were like, 'No, no let's think of this boy.' So they picked me, we went back home, and that was the end of it. And I stayed with the pastors. So my life has actually been in the church and with the pastors since I became a born again in 1988. I've always stayed with pastors. And so I was there, and I finished my JSS, Junior Secondary School, through the help of the church, because I served a lot. I washed for the pastors, I cleaned their cars, I helped with the house chores . . . you know, help people, and they also help you. So through that, I went through JSS, Junior Secondary School. And then I applied for Senior High School, and I attended one of the best schools in Ghana."

At several points in Daniel's schooling he ran into financial trouble, and it looked like he would have to withdraw. Yet each time, a friend or a surrogate parent from his Charismatic church networks helped out and made it possible to continue. In high school he was close friends with another born-again schoolmate, whose parents were wealthy and owned a hospital. Throughout his school years this friend would periodically give him things he needed: a new school shirt, a new pair of shoes, a bag of groceries. This friend also spoke highly of Daniel to his parents. "So they—the doctor and his wife—said, 'Daniel, if you need anything, come. We will help you.'"

On one particular occasion he had accrued a large amount of school debt, and he couldn't receive his diploma until it was paid off. He finally turned to his friend's parents. "With difficulty, I went there [to their home]. I said, 'Mom, this is the situation. I finished, but I've not paid my school fees for three years and it's piled up, and they want the school fees before they release my certificate.' So she said, 'Okay, Daniel, don't worry. You go, and come back.' She said that when dad comes back from work, she will discuss it with him, and then get back to me. So I went, and the next day, I went back and the money was given to me. And so I went to pay my fees. And then got my certificate."

After this time he developed the desire to become a pastor himself.

"Before then, I had a lot of visions and dreams. I saw Jesus Christ in my dreams several times, calling me, speaking to me, telling me what to do. . . . That was actually the reason I desired to become a pastor, because I met Jesus in a dream several times, calling me to do his work. So after secondary school, I straightforward went into ministry. And at the time, my desire was to go back home to my roots, Togo, and speak to my people to leave idol worship and become Christians. So I went to Togo, and I was in Togo for six years doing the work of God there. . . . You know, it was challenging. My family did not understand me, they threatened to kill me. Maybe you can understand, but there are occultic practices, and these things, they can harm you. They can have a harmful effect on you."

"So were you frightened?"

"Oh, yeah, yes, but I had to pray a lot, fast and pray, so that I will have the courage and the boldness to be able to stand before them and speak. Yah, I fell sick several times . . . but today as I speak to you I have a lot of my family members who are born again Christians in the charismatic church. My mom just got baptized last month. She listened to me, and finally she decided to give her life to Christ. She now goes to church all the time. I have sisters, brothers who now go to church, and that's it."

Making it financially in the country of Togo was difficult for Daniel, however. "I wasn't getting a job because the certificate wasn't enough, maybe. So, I said, oh, I think I should come back to Ghana, go to university, and after university I can secure some job while working at the work of God as a pastor."

That was how he ended up at the university in Ghana, earning his four-year degree and then pursuing a master's degree. He was going to graduate soon when the two of us met, and his hope was to find a well-paying teaching job so that he could be free to start his new Charismatic church on the side.[18]

Daniel's story was one that stayed with me for many months thereafter. His movement from the rural areas of Togo to urban Ghana, his struggle to go to school, his entry into the Charismatic movement through a classmate, his fervent rejection of "occultic" traditions, and the assistance he received from his new born-again networks all demonstrated the significance of the Charismatic transformation. For Daniel, the Charismatic movement carried him into the "modern" world. It enabled him to succeed in work and education, it gave him the necessary connections his family could not provide, and it instilled in him a sense of promise and possibility. Although his conversion from the Ewe religion to Christianity did involve a shift in belief, which was less true for young people raised within Christianity like Stephen and Ama, the changes in his habits and his lifestyle were equally if not more important. These changes were made possible by new relationships of personal trust: close ties to his pastors, his classmate, and his classmate's parents, who trusted him with their support simply as members of the same religious community.

The Structure of Support

Within Evangel Ministries, the emphasis on changing one's lifestyle runs parallel to its emphasis on developing close ties to others in the church. Although it has a membership in the tens of thousands, the organization encourages participants to get to know each other and to rely on each other. One of the pastors, George, explained to me that the founder did extensive research on successful Evangelical churches elsewhere and pragmatically followed their models.[19] One of his exemplars was the Korean pastor David Yonggi Cho, of the Yoido Full Gospel Church, which is widely touted as the world's largest single congregation.[20] Yoido has large services on Sundays but also a network of small groups that meet in homes, dorms, places of work, cafés, and restaurants throughout the week. Evangel Ministries uses the same model, labeling these small groups as "fellowships." The leadership understands that good music, engaging teaching, and entertaining events will attract young people initially, but close friends and personal support will make them stay.

One young woman, Mary, whom I met as she worked in the coffee shop selling pastries and sodas, told me her fellowship was where she really gets close to other members. She also said her fellowship was made up of people from all classes and ethnic groups. She attended the birthday parties of other fellowship members, which ranged from white-tablecloth, multiple-utensil affairs to backyard picnics where guests ate with their hands and sat on upturned buckets.

According to Mary, those in your fellowship should be your go-to group for social support. They would pool resources to pay for your school fees if necessary and visit you when you were sick. "If you are not in a fellowship, you cannot complain," she noted. This was how the church provided the structure of support that many Ghanaian young people were seeking.[21]

I also saw this structure of support play out vividly for Ama, in an incident a few weeks before I left Ghana. It was a Saturday afternoon, and we went to see a film at the Accra Mall, a newly built upscale shopping center near the university. Our taxi dropped us on the other side of a busy intersection from the mall. As we made our way across, Ama stepped into a busy but seemingly clear street, and with little warning a *tro-tro* came around the corner and struck her across the side.

Fortunately, it was not traveling fast. Ama had the wind knocked out of her, and the event gathered a big crowd of onlookers, but she could stand and communicate easily. In a series of exchanges almost too quick to keep track of, several people in the crowd took charge of the situation; they flagged a taxi; pushed Ama, myself, and the driver of the *tro-tro* inside; and sent us off to the hospital so Ama could get a chest x-ray and be seen by a doctor. The now miserable driver was told he must cover the cost of her treatment—which amounted to the equivalent of U.S. $40—and he did so with a pitiable demeanor but little argument.

Ama lived with her mother, had several half-siblings, and had sporadic communications with her father. Yet when we arrived at the hospital and sat in the waiting area, her first call was not to a family member; it was to George, the pastor at Evangel Ministries. Ama explained that her mother would worry too much, so she wouldn't call her till she had been seen by the doctor and knew that everything was okay. George, on the other hand, was a calm and reassuring voice on the phone, and offered both his presence and financial assistance if it turned out we needed it.[22]

Ama didn't hold any important positions in the church, and she didn't spend much time at Evangel Ministries apart from Sunday services. Although she was nominally part of the welcome ministry, she didn't even attend on a weekly basis. Yet one of the church's key leaders had made himself readily available to her. I heard such things could happen in the church, but now I was witnessing how such a big church managed to still be so relationally accessible for this young woman.

As I flew home the week after my eventful afternoon with Ama at the hospital, where fortunately we were reassured she was going to be fine, I realized the special genius of the movement for making itself accessible to Ghanaian young people. They talked directly and at length about young people's most significant concerns, and they met some of young people's most important needs: to meet new people and have fun. By scaling this model up to the level of a transnational network, they also made membership imminently portable for a generation whose reality is marked by movement both within and between countries.

In grade school, in high school, in college, in the city, in the country, in Europe, in America, and anywhere else Ama and her contemporaries find themselves, Evangel Ministries is likely to be there.

In each of the stories from Stephen, Ama, Mary, Daniel, and Annie, the movement toward the Charismatic Evangelical church was a response to their distinct concerns as a young person in Ghana, and it also revealed a shift in the bases of trust networks in their lives. As Stephen struggled to decide how to plan his future, as Daniel pursued his education away from the village, and as Ama coped with a mild accident, each of them relied on others in the Charismatic church. In the more extreme cases like Daniel's, these church-based trust networks replaced his family as the people he relied on most. Other cases like Annie's revealed more subtle changes—she still lived with her family and stayed connected to the Anglican church, while coming to rely on the Evangel Ministries community for a few specific needs. Nonetheless, together these stories show how in the context of becoming an adult in Ghana, the accessible, portable, and promising style of religion promoted by Evangel Ministries and its contemporaries offers more than appealing messages. It provides new social connections that enable young people to meet the demands of a changing world.

5

The Culture of Connection

PRACTICES AND PRINCIPLES

WHAT MAKES A good church? The question is one many Christians in North America, whether or not they are transnational migrants, actively seek to answer. Common terms like "church hopping" and "the religious marketplace" reveal how people increasingly see religion as personal and voluntary. It is something they approach almost as consumers, adapting doctrines and rituals in relation to their preferences. Robert Wuthnow (1998) calls this a move from religious dwelling to religious seeking. He rejects the idea that Americans are becoming dramatically less religious but acknowledges the predominant approach to religiosity has changed. Religiosity is now seen as a personal process of seeking—often in perpetuity—the religious practices and principles that best fit one's lifestyle and concerns.

Christians in Ghana, particularly younger people, tend to approach their religiosity in a similar way. As noted earlier, they often switch between congregations that reflect different streams of Christianity, or even attend several simultaneously. The question of what makes a good church is a relevant one to them as well. If they do move abroad, that question must then be answered in practical terms. They must choose a church to go to.

Yet relative to other religious seekers, as aspirational migrants they face some distinct challenges that shape how they answer this question, particularly the challenges chronicled in chapter 3. In this chapter, I argue that these challenges make them particularly motivated to seek out congregations where the practices and principles make up a culture of connection. I show how new migrants from Ghana choose churches to attend; how perceptions of what makes a "good church" are often about sociability within a congregation, and whether it demonstrates a culture of connection; and how congregational cultures of connection both rely on and reinforce the activity of personal trust. Through this mechanism, religious memberships can provide a basis for new trust networks. I also discuss important limitations and counterexamples. Such stories ultimately support the claim that finding connection and social trust is central to the project of finding a good church, and also explain situations in which this process is inhibited or breaks down.

Bringing Faith Abroad

Sandra, the recent arrival in Chicago whose story began in chapter 3, talked with me at length about why she attended Evangel Ministries. She joined the organization in Ghana before coming to the United States; but the more transitions she went through and the more difficult decisions she faced, the more important it became to her. As she lived apart from her husband, and at times doubted the wisdom of her move to Chicago, the presence of the Evangel Ministries branch was a major reason why she continued to stay on, and why her husband continued to accept their situation as well.

Coming from the eastern region of Ghana, Sandra was raised Presbyterian, but was not particularly devoted to the church. After graduating from college, and while working an office job in her home region, she met an energetic young man involved with Evangel Ministries. He convinced her to come to Evangel Ministries with him, first, and to marry him, second.

"What stood out to you when you first went to Evangel Ministries in Ghana?" I asked, in our conversation that Saturday at the café.

She thought for a moment. "I think they are very principled, and they focus on each individual, especially the youth. I think they are also stronger than the Presbyterians on the Bible."

"Were your parents bothered when you switched?"

"No, since it's all the same God, the same Bible." As in Stephen's case, then, her church switch was normal, and acceptable to her Presbyterian family.

She admitted that at first she found the "aggressiveness" of the church disorienting. She was not only brand new to the Charismatic environment, she was also engaged to become the wife of a pastor, and Evangel Ministries takes this role very seriously. She was scrutinized in a way she was unused to leading up to the wedding.

"We were married in Evangel Ministries, and it was wonderful, but it's so . . . they are so much involved, so critical about everything, your background, your spiritual walk, and it was really hard because I wasn't a member from the beginning." Suddenly seeming concerned that she might be sounding too negative, she added, "But after counseling, it was okay."

"Do you think this would have been different if you were married in a Presbyterian church?"

She shrugged. "I can't tell, since I never had an experience, but everything they do in Evangel is so based on the scripture. They will counsel you for a long time."

I nodded. Yet it also seemed Sandra's experience would have been distinct because of her less religious background, her unfamiliarity with Charismatic Christianity, and her plans to move abroad after the wedding, rather than stay and help run her husband's church. I imagined she had to work extra hard to prove her commitment.

After the challenges of her initial transition, however, the church became something essential to her life. When she moved abroad, her husband activated his church networks to make sure she would be taken care of in Chicago. He knew the head of the North American branches, Reverend Mark. He reached out to him on the phone, and then Reverend Mark called Elijah—who was pastor of the Chicago branch by that time—to let him know he should contact Sandra. Not only did Elijah then call her, but he also sent someone to pick her up for church the very next Sunday.

"That's one very wonderful thing about Evangel pastors," she said. "The moment this one calls this one, you see this one respond immediately.... When I came here, Reverend Mark responded so quickly to my husband, and that same night Pastor Elijah called me."

Before her marriage and her move to Chicago, she had been in the United States for an extended period visiting her cousin, who recently had a child. During that time she attended a different Ghanaian Charismatic church along with her relatives. When she came back in her own right, however, she found a congregation of her own she was personally connected to through her husband. From the perspective of those in the Evangel Chicago branch, she wasn't just another newcomer; she was an expected and honored member of the organization.

She remembered her first Sunday: "When I entered, I was happy because there is peace, those there, they don't have time for gossip... and I felt welcomed, the church is very good at that, even today a church member called, just to check on me."

She still received weekly rides to church every Sunday from Gift, a young taxi driver: "He calls me, I don't even have to call him." She also appreciated the inspirational, forward-moving messages from the leaders.

"When I first came, I heard the pastor's wife teaching Sunday School, and I thought, 'Wow, you can't be here and be growing backward' ... then I heard the pastor teach, and I had never experienced teaching like that.... When you find yourself in a lazy environment, even if you are a hard worker, you will just get more lazy; but when you find yourself in a hard-working environment, then you will start working harder. At Evangel, they know how to work with you, they approach you, they bring you in."

Not all of her Ghanaian neighbors in Uptown saw Evangel Ministries in such a positive light, nor did all of them go to church. Her cousin no longer attended anywhere regularly, and his daughters went periodically to another Ghanaian Charismatic church in town. When she chatted with people in the hallways of her building and told them where she had been attending, she got the impression many of them saw Evangel Ministries as a "Western Church," because of its focus on reaching out beyond the African community. This was apparent in their reliance on English: for those who were still "struggling to speak English," in Sandra's terms, Evangel Ministries' English-only policies were off-putting. She explained: "When it comes to worship, you flow better in your own language . . . they can't really flow in English."

Yet for herself, Sandra preferred Evangel Ministries to the alternatives, whether those alternatives were less "Western" Ghanaian churches or American Evangelical congregations. Indeed, even though there were American congregations in the area that would have been very similar in terms of teaching and worship styles, she had been warned by her neighbors about them. A Nigerian woman who had tried out an American church told Sandra they "were not welcomed," and so she didn't go back. I imagined that if Sandra felt unwelcomed in much of her day-to-day life, she had no desire to feel unwelcome on Sunday mornings, too.

"Did she tell you why she wanted to go to an American church?" I asked.

Sandra nodded. "It's because African churches are a lot of trouble . . . not all are very educated, so they involve themselves in a lot of unnecessary talk."

This, then, seemed to be why her sense that Evangel Ministries' members "don't have time for gossip" was so important. From her perspective, Evangel in Chicago avoided the "gossip" problem of most Ghanaian churches, as well as the "unwelcoming" problem of American churches. Sandra said she was confident that if she could just convince some of her neighbors to make the longer trek to where Evangel Ministries met and push through the unfamiliarity of the language, they would see why it is a good congregation.

The fact that Sandra was personally unknown to the Chicago Evangel Ministries group, and they were unknown to her, and yet from the first she was willing to see them in a positive light, said a lot about personal trust and its foundations. There was an element of imagination at work, bridging the gaps in past experience, when Sandra said "Those there, they don't have time for gossip," even though she did not know from personal experience or testing that this was the case.

Her ability to imagine them in such a way also had a symbolic basis. Something about the group at Evangel Ministries cued her to see them as more educated and hard-working, and thus less prone to the type of gossip found in some African churches that she equated with being uneducated. The group's tendency to wear professional Western clothes, talk in English, carry the tools of their professions—like Elijah with his pager on his belt and his iPad at the podium—likely served as such cues. Yet just as important was their shared connection to the organization itself where her husband was a pastor. Combined, cues based in social class and in shared religious membership allowed her to make the initial leaps of trust with these former strangers.

Sandra also relied on her church-based relationships to take care of her mother, who was very old, quite alone, and living back in her village in Ghana. Recently, Sandra convinced her mother to let Sandra's husband travel to her house and baptize her. After Sandra's husband did so, he called the pastor of an Evangel Ministries branch in the old woman's neighborhood to ask him to keep an eye on his mother-in-law. That other Evangel pastor then periodically visited her to pray with her and make sure she was doing okay. As a younger Ghanaian abroad, having someone to physically check in on her aging parent in the village was a great gift to Sandra. It was yet one more way in which she trusted her church-based ties, and in which those ties helped her address the challenges of her transnational life.

A Good Church

Anna and her husband Timothy were two of the core members at Evangel Ministries in Chicago when I started attending. Unlike Sandra, who was only starting to get involved, they were deeply embedded in the life of the small congregation. They came every week, took on a number of responsibilities for making the church run, and often spent their whole Sunday morning and afternoon worshiping, working, and socializing with the congregation.

Timothy hoped to help improve the quality of the worship music by learning how to play the keyboard. At that time, there were few musicians attending Evangel Ministries, so during most services the choir sang along to recorded music. When Timothy learned that I had studied the piano for many years as a child, he eagerly asked if I would be willing to give him a lesson.

We had our first lesson on a weekday evening. We spent about 45 minutes going over the basics of reading music, and I taught him how to play a song we often sang on Sunday mornings. The phone rang and he went to answer it. It was Benjamin, calling about playing golf that following Saturday. He told Benjamin that he was "with my piano teacher, Nicolette!" and then told me, "Benjamin says hi!" I noted it was the second time Anna and Timothy received a friendly call from a church member while I was with them that day.

After he hung up, we sat down and talked more about his life and his history with Evangel Ministries. Like his wife, Timothy came from a globally oriented and well-off family. His parents had lived abroad in the past, though they settled in Ghana afterward; and many of Timothy's siblings also lived in the United States. A couple of them even lived in the Chicago area. Timothy was raised in Ghana and came abroad when he entered college. He went to a highly ranked liberal arts college, and began a professional career. He met Anna through friends after moving to Chicago, when the two of them were both fairly established. They married and moved to a commuter suburb of the city, where they had two small children. As described in chapter 3, their life was similar to other metro-area professional couples, foreign born or not.

Their lives looked quite different from Sandra's: they were not new to the area, they had no need to find new jobs or an apartment, they lived together rather than apart, they had more stable connections in the area among their family members, and they were financially much more comfortable. Yet like Sandra, they found Evangel Ministries in Chicago to be a good church.

As Timothy explained the appeal, he noted it was not something that drew him in before he went abroad. He knew about Evangel Ministries while living in Ghana, because a couple of his brothers were attenders there. Yet he was less interested. "I never really got into the mega-church thing; though it is an attraction for some, I've always been the opposite. You know, I don't really see the guys in Switzerland, for example . . . for me, it's really what I have with the church here."

By talking about the "guys in Switzerland," he was referencing the organization's drive to be a global church and to excite potential new members with that vision. For him, at least at first, this was not an inherent draw; it didn't matter much to him whether there were other Evangel Ministries members in foreign countries around the globe. However, his following sentence also suggested that now, on the other side of his migration, there was something in the Chicago Evangel Ministries branch he found important—"what I have with the church here."

I was curious to know more about what that was. I first asked about the church's ethnic composition: "Is it an advantage to you that Evangel is mostly Ghanaian?"

"No, that's probably why it took me so long to go back when I first visited. I didn't want to do all Ghanaian. I had been going to International House,[1] which had a really good mix."

International House was a large, predominantly African American congregation on Chicago's South Side, which also had a fair number of white, Hispanic, and South Asian congregants. This was the first church he and Anna attended after they married. Given their backgrounds and the kind of settings they were used to in other areas of their lives, such a congregation seemed to make sense for them. They looked for a church with "a good mix" of people. In this, they were far from alone: many others I talked to also preferred a multicultural congregation to a homogenous one, all things being equal.

Yet Timothy and Anna found that all things are not equal when comparing large multicultural congregations to small homogenous ones. Although they liked International House, some controversies with the leadership came up—Timothy did not explain this to me in detail—and at the same time Anna and Timothy moved to the other side of the city. This meant they were once again looking for a church to go to. Although they tried to find a diverse congregation they felt good about, it was difficult.

"I really wanted to find something with a good blend [of different people]," Timothy reiterated; "but you know, it's tough to find a good church."

Neither he nor Anna told me exactly how many different congregations they tried during this time, but I got the impression it was quite a few. There was one Charismatic Evangelical congregation in their neighborhood they really hoped would work. It was mostly white, but the preaching and the practices—including the nice praise music—fit what they were looking for.

Yet there was a problem at this church that became clear after some months. They were not able to connect with the members the way they wanted to. Anna, who told me her version of the story on a different occasion, described it in this way: "I got tired of just going and not really feeling like people were reaching out to us and making friends. I like to be more active in church. I don't want to just go in, hear the message, and then leave every Sunday. I wanted a place where I really felt at home."

Her sentiments echoed those of others in a similar position. It was very common for Ghanaians of their class and situation to attend mainstream Evangelical churches that were mostly white or African American rather than Ghanaian. They were comfortable in diverse settings at school and work, fluent in English, and preferred a Charismatic Evangelical style of worship that was easy to find in the United States in nonethnic congregations. In a narrow logistical sense, therefore, they had no need of an ethnic church. Along with the preference for diversity Timothy described, this combination of factors made nonethnic churches desirable.

Yet it was also common for them to find such congregations ultimately unsatisfying. Another woman with a similar experience, Helen, explained this similarly as a lack of personal connection in the community. She was frustrated that the American Evangelical church she and her husband attended for several years failed to support them during a time of illness. To her, it was unheard of that church members would fail to visit and assist a fellow member who was sick. This incident inspired them to switch to a Ghanaian Charismatic Church like Evangel Ministries.

Given that several of Timothy's relatives were Evangel Ministries members in Ghana, when the branch came to Chicago he heard about it through the grapevine. Because it was a Ghanaian church he was reticent to join, and it took him a while to go back after his first visit. Over time, however, he and Anna did start to attend more regularly, and as they did they were more and more drawn in. In Anna's words, during a service on New Year's Eve she thought to herself, "Hmm, maybe this is it."

By the time I met them they were firmly rooted in the community.

"Any church I went to before, I didn't enjoy as much," explained Timothy. "Now it's become more of a family, we get along, we do things together. In Ghana. . . . Well, here you get closer because you don't have much going on beyond that. . . . I have friends at work, and my relatives, but we see each other only once in a while, you get closer to the people you got to church with. . . . In Ghana, I know my neighbors, anyone I went to school with is right there and I can see them, so my closest friends are not necessarily in the church."

Before he moved to the United States and settled into his new life in Chicago, churchgoing and church-based ties were thus not particularly central to Timothy's life. Unlike the young people talked about in chapter 4—John, Ama, Annie, and Daniel—and even several of his siblings, he never underwent a Charismatic transformation while in Ghana. He never felt the need to, although he certainly would have considered himself a Christian during that time. It wasn't until later, when the semi-permanence of his life in America set in and he and his wife were actively looking for social connections, that the kind of church life exemplified by Evangel Ministries' small foreign branches became desirable. Other bases of social connection—neighbors, classmates, work friends, and the like—were weaker or harder to maintain in his current situation, so the church and its members became primary.

His statement also suggested that getting closer to the people they went to church with fit better with the rhythms of their life. Sunday was the one time of the week they were both usually free from work; and to get both of their small children ready, dressed, fed, and in the car to travel across the city to visit with others was a once-a-week sort of task. As a result, Sunday mornings and afternoons were their primary time for socializing throughout the week. It mattered a lot, therefore, whether they actually liked spending time with the people they committed that time to, and whether those people were equally committed to the social aspect of church.

This being the case, it made sense for him and Anna to leave the American Evangelical congregation, where they were not able to find such close connections; and ultimately to choose a small homogenous Ghanaian church, where their desires and expectations for what church ties could and should be fit those of the other members. In one sense they attended the church *despite* its homogeneity, although in another sense its homogeneity made it better able to provide something else—a culture of connection—they considered essential to a good church at this point in their lives.

Just as when Elijah and Catherine were talking about their educational and religious trust networks in chapter 3, Timothy made it a point to say that membership in the church wasn't about its ethnic identity per se. This came out when I asked what he thought might be different about Evangel Ministries in comparison to other Ghanaian churches in Chicago.

"Evangel definitely has a different feel.... I think what we might be struggling with, in pulling Ghanaians in, is that in other churches people want to go there and sing Ghanaian songs.... I understand the reasoning; they say that that's the only place we can get together to feel Ghanaian.... Some people have even asked me why we don't sing Ghanaian songs at Evangel."

"Is it important for you to 'feel Ghanaian' at church?"

"I don't really have a need for it, I guess. It is fine to have the desire to be around other Ghanaians, but it shouldn't be your number one priority in going to church.... The first priority should be getting close to God."

He then mentioned another aspect of what he saw as Evangel's distinctiveness. "In Evangel, you have people who are well-accomplished, have been successful in other areas . . . and you see there has been a lot of sacrifice for them to do what they are doing, so for starters you know this guy isn't here to take my money, because he could make a lot more money doing what he was doing before. . . . Rev. Mark's [the pastor before Elijah] wife was a doctor, and she was in my school in Ghana, so you know these are good people who don't need to do this for the money—it says a lot."

His statements revealed how ethnicity and class did and did not matter in his search for a good church. He talked about the "accomplished" status of most of Evangel Ministries' leaders, and how this contributed to their legitimacy in his eyes. They were not doing this for the money, but rather as an act of calling. Given the debates described in chapter 4 about "one-man churches," it was important for Timothy to find symbolic cues for trusting Evangel's leaders, for him to imagine them as trustworthy religious men and women rather than self-serving entrepreneurs. The cues he saw were their accomplishments, and the indicators of their upper- or upper-middle-class position: the way they dressed, talked, and carried themselves, while also being friendly and welcoming. These indicators connected to social class made a difference in his ability to imagine Evangel as a group of trustworthy people he wanted to invest in, just as they did for Sandra on her first visit to Evangel as described earlier.

He also said celebrating one's heritage at church was fine, but it shouldn't be the first priority, thus downplaying the role of ethnicity itself in the kind of church he looked for. He knew other Ghanaians in Chicago for whom the ethnic identity was more central to their religious practice: they liked to sing Ghanaian songs and pray in *Twi,* for example. Yet he saw himself as having different priorities and preferences. According to him, Evangel Ministries stayed small in part because it wasn't designed to celebrate Ghanaian heritage so much as establish a multicultural Evangelical church, and this put some less Americanized Ghanaians off.

However, as I did more research into the various Ghanaian congregations in Chicago I found Timothy's perspective to be more common than he implied. Many people—not just those who were as well off or well connected as Timothy—looked for churches with upwardly mobile leadership and less emphasis on Ghanaian ethnicity.

The perspectives of many Ghanaian pastors reflected this. While there were some congregations, particularly those with an older demographic, who did seem more rooted in Ghanaian traditions—these were the churches who would help run the Ghanafest and whose members were more involved in the Ghanaian National Committee cultural association, for example—there were many others who espoused the same multicultural vision and deliberately deemphasized Ghanaian culture in order to bring more non-Ghanaians into the church.

For example, one research study done in Chicago the early 2000s (Stevens 2004) chronicled a major split in an established congregation over this issue. One faction believed the church should be more Americanized, and thus more accessible to people outside the Ghanaian community. When they were not able to sway the leadership they started a new church. By the time I was conducting my research, both congregations were active; but notably, even the more traditional church had established an English-speaking, Americanized service in order to extend its reach beyond the Ghanaian community. When I interviewed the pastor of this church, he espoused the same multicultural vision as Evangel Ministries' leadership: that their church was about religious kinship first, and ethno-national kinship second. The same was true for a half-dozen other Ghanaian Charismatic Evangelical pastors I interviewed, who were either presiding over older congregations or starting new churches of their own. Each of them described his congregation as "multicultural" rather than Ghanaian.

In part, then, new Ghanaian migrants tended to see a good church as one with trustworthy leadership, and one with a more multicultural emphasis that deemphasized Ghanaian ethnic distinctiveness. A good church could easily be one composed of non-Ghanaians. Most important, though, a good church had a certain kind of congregational culture that supported the type of social connection they wanted and expected from church life. Thus, although Timothy and Anna suggested the *best* kind of church would be one that was diverse but also as socially connected as Evangel Ministries, they came "back" to an ethnic congregation because they failed to find that connection in more diverse settings.

Sunday Morning in Chicago

By the time I had this conversation with Timothy, I had been attending Evangel Ministries in Chicago for several months. When he mentioned, "What I have with the people there," I knew from observation what he was talking about: it was Evangel Ministries' congregational culture of close connection between members. It was the many hours spent together each Sunday, the relaxed way of socializing before and after services, the jokes told, the songs sung, and the updates shared about each other's lives. It was the energy he got from those thirty or so people each week—the people he was "closer to" because "you don't have much else going on beyond that."

Although I had been to Evangel Ministries in Accra the summer beforehand, when I first came to Evangel in Chicago I had very little idea what to expect. I imagined it was smaller and thus had a slightly different feel, but no one I knew had ever been there or could tell me much about it. All I had was a phone number and an address listed on the Evangel Ministries' branch directory web page.

When I called the number, a quiet male voice said only, "Hello?" It seemed I had reached someone's cell phone. I launched into my prepared introduction. He listened and said he was no longer the pastor at the Evangel Ministries branch in Chicago. He was the overseer of all the U.S. Evangel branches now—his name was Reverend Mark, whom I would later meet during one of his visits to the Chicago branch. There was a new pastor now in Chicago, Pastor Elijah. Rather than giving me Elijah's phone number, though, he said I should probably just visit there on a Sunday morning and talk to him personally.

The first Sunday I went was in early June, and the weather was unusually cold and gray. The address I had for the congregation was a community arts center in a commercial area. I found it easily in walking from the public train. On the main floor of the building, another Evangelical church was meeting. It was advertised with large banners over the building's main entrance, and I saw as I walked in that this congregation was made up of young, mostly white urban professionals. When I entered, their greeters assumed I was visiting their congregation; they were surprised when I asked for the "African church," but directed me down a back hallway to a set of double doors with no windows. I could hear music coming from the room as I walked toward it.

I opened one of the doors and peeked in. I saw a banner across one wall—"Evangel Ministries International." I was in the right place. The room was a small theater, with a stage at the front and about seven rows of chairs spread across the room. On the left next to the stage was a medium-sized book rack filled with books by Evangel Ministries' founder. On the stage was a podium, centered on a round red carpet, and a portable projector screen on the left.

Although I arrived right at the scheduled starting time, it felt as if I had arrived very early. The service hadn't started yet, and there were just a few people standing around chatting, setting up the projector screen, and testing the sound system. I was greeted by two men, one in his forties and wearing a suit and glasses, the other a bit younger, a bit taller, and wearing a dress shirt and slacks. They were very friendly. The older man introduced himself as the pastor, Elijah, and the younger man said his name was David. They were both excited to hear I was in Ghana the previous summer, and were eager to know whom I had met when I was there and what I had thought of Evangel Ministries' headquarters. They invited me to sit down, and said they would talk to me again after the service was over.

From my chair I watched the slowly building buzz of activity around me. There was a low hum of conversation and laughter in the room. Children ran around, hopping between different adults' laps. About fifteen minutes later, a woman in a dark blue suit with a wide smile and glasses came onto the stage. She announced it was time to pray. The dozen or so folks present started making their way to the rows of chairs. They stood in front of their seats with their heads bowed or upturned and their eyes closed. They started praying out loud in low voices, and above this murmur the woman on the stage—I later learned she was Catherine, Elijah's wife—encouraged them with statements like, "The Lord is good!" and "We give you all the glory, father!"

After ten minutes of such prayer, the people settled into their seats and Catherine started teaching a lesson based on several short passages from the Bible. The topic was, "What we use the Word of God for." Her points included: "We use the word of God to help with our standard of conduct," "We use it as a light for guidance," "As a word of assurance," and "As a solution to problems." When she made this final point, the problems she related it to were anxiety, fear, and depression. She then talked about how to pray in the right way so that our prayers will be answered. She said sometimes we "ask amiss," and we need to pray according to the word of God. She talked about the book *90 Minutes in Heaven*, which tells of a Baptist minister who died and went to heaven, and then was raised back to life because of the prayers of another minister. The one thing he learned through the experience, she concluded, was that God answers prayer.

The group was still small at this time. There were four children under the age of ten and a girl who looked about fifteen sitting in the front left rows. This girl had a table in front of her, with a computer that controlled the projector screen. During Catherine's teaching, she would scroll through slides with the Bible verses written on them. There were also two older women sitting in the front right side, the pastor sitting in the very front row on the right, and four younger men clustered around the sound stage at the back. Yet through the lesson, more people started filtering in. By 11 o'clock, the room held about twenty adults. Everyone present appeared to be of West African heritage. People wore nice suits or dresses, though there were a few women wearing head-to-toe traditional Ghanaian fabrics.

After the lesson was over, the pastor invited the choir to the stage for the music portion of the service. Two older women and two young men came up, and one of the women stood in front with a handheld microphone. There were no instruments, so we sang along to a recording; but people sang no less fervently than if a live band had been performing. They stood and swayed or clapped to the music, and during one energetic song a few people went into the aisles and danced. All the songs were in English, like the songs that were sung at the headquarters in Ghana. The singing lasted thirty minutes or so, and was followed by about five minutes in which people walked around greeting each other. Many people—in fact, just about everyone in the room—came up to me to say hello and welcome.

Next was the pastor's sermon. It was based on a book about prayer written by the Evangel Ministries' founder. He held up the book to show it to us as he began, and reminded the group they should be reading it during the week and bringing it to church on Sunday. Everyone in the congregation should have one, he said, since he had given them out several weeks ago.

In his sermon he talked about how much influence the spiritual world has in the physical world. In fact, he said, what happens in the political and financial worlds is directed by the spiritual world that we can't see. He noted: "Prayer is how we tap into the spiritual."

Giving personal examples of answered prayer, he told us he had fervently prayed for God's will to be done when he decided to move to the United Kingdom and then to the United States for the medical profession. He told us how, when he lived in Ghana, a friend from medical school went overseas and then came back needing a place to stay. He told this friend to stay with him even though his place was small, and "we lived like brothers." Then, when he himself had decided to come to America, he didn't know anyone there. So this friend, because of the generosity he'd shown him before, invited him to come and even sponsored his visa. This friend then hosted him for the next year and a half as he was getting on his feet. He concluded that, "If you submit your will to God, he will close some doors and open others, so that amazing things can happen."

I was struck while listening to his story by his experience of uncertainty and change, by the way he and his classmate relied on each other during such changes, and by his framing of this in terms of faith in God. He portrayed the guidance of God—working through the friendship of trustworthy others—as the hook on which he could hang his confidence in the midst of the itinerant transnational life.

After the sermon concluded and the leaders collected offerings from the congregation, Elijah asked anyone who was attending for the first time to stand up and introduce him or herself. I and two other Ghanaian women did so. One of these women said she was in Chicago visiting relatives, and the other said she just recently moved from Ghana. The congregation clapped to welcome us, and Elijah said he would meet with us afterwards. He then asked if it was anyone's birthday, and a young man (whom I later came to know as Benjamin) went up to the stage. The pastor then prayed for him and the whole congregation sang "Happy Birthday" to him.

After the service, Elijah met with the three of us who were new in the back left corner of the room. We all chatted a bit, and he took my number and said he would call me later in the week (which he did). I then had several conversations with other people in the room, including two women who were both nurses and had lived in London and New York before coming to Chicago. After a few short conversations of this kind I assumed it was time everyone would be leaving, so I headed out the door and walked to the train.[2]

While I didn't know it at the time, on that first visit I actually missed much of what the church does together. I left far too early, assuming that since the formal service was over, the group would be dispersing soon. I did what Anna described to me later as the typical habit of churchgoing at most American congregations: filing in, sitting through the formal service, and then quickly leaving.

Evangel Ministries' gatherings, on the other hand, lasted much longer—sometimes by a matter of hours—after the formal service. About a month later, on a Wednesday evening, after a midweek service, the extent of this practice finally sunk in. It was early July and the sun was just setting at nearly ten o'clock, casting a warm glow on the old warehouses surrounding the performing arts center. On this particular night, I was offered a ride to the train station from Benjamin, which I accepted. I thought it would be about fifteen minutes before we left, but it turned into an hour, and for the first time I started to experience what for many Ghanaians is missing at the typical American Evangelical congregation: lots of real socializing after services. The pleasant weather and the big turnout for the meeting had everyone in a good mood. Mary, a consistent long-time member, turned to me and said, "This is how Evangel always is . . . nobody wants to leave. It's like that at every branch."[3]

The truth of this was increasingly clear to me the longer I attended. For those who were most embedded in the church, the community offered consistent times for hanging out with others in a laid-back atmosphere and provided some of their closest ties. The formal routines of the church included two services a week—one on Sunday and one on Wednesday nights—but members also often got together on Friday evenings at the pastor's house for a prayer service, and those who were in the choir saw each other for rehearsal on Saturday afternoons. Then there were birthday and Christmas parties throughout the year, which members usually celebrated together. Weddings and funerals within the congregation were also important. Once, for example, a few members drove together to Virginia to attend the funeral of the mother of another member.

For a few members, too, some specific church-based relationships became even closer. Benjamin, for example, found a friend in the congregation, Gift, who was also in the choir and also drove a taxi. On weekends, the two of them were inseparable: they drove their taxis for fares on Friday night, then Gift often crashed at Benjamin's apartment, and in the morning they went to the gym to work out. Later on Saturday they had the choir rehearsal together, also at Benjamin's apartment; and then again bright and early Sunday morning, they were together giving people rides to church, running through the songs one more time, and setting up the sound equipment. The Sunday morning service was just the last in a long series of activities they did together each week and weekend. *This* is what it meant to be "active in church," in Anna's terminology, used earlier. It was quite different from the culture of the American Evangelical congregation she and Timothy had tried beforehand, where everyone went to church right at the starting time, sat through a short service, left immediately afterward, and rarely interacted through the week.

The Culture of Connection

Scholars of religion have increasingly focused on how the nature of specific congregations shapes people's religious experience. Nancy Ammerman's (2005) study of congregational life in the United States both reflects and reinforces this focus. She argues that although congregations can be grouped within larger traditions—that is, Catholicism, Evangelicalism, Black Protestantism, and so on—what they actually do together also develops locally in response to the interactions of leaders and participants. In particular, U.S. congregations often provide a basis for relationships: they facilitate people having fun together, they give people a sense of solidarity, and they enable people to establish new social networks, both with each other and with other voluntary organizations devoted to charity work and community service.

Yet while congregations of many different traditions share these same goals, they vary in the degree to which this vision is realized. In some congregations, members find some of their closest friendships; in others, co-participants remain little more than acquaintances. And collectively, whether the former or the latter experience is more typical matters for how the church *feels* to both members and new visitors. A particular congregation can feel warm and friendly, or more distant and cold. Given this, and recognizing the loosening of people's commitments to given traditions and their desire to find churches that best fit their needs, it makes sense that the social feel of a congregation can matter a lot for whether new visitors consider it a good church.

We would also expect people to place even more priority on the social feel of a congregation if they have a particular need for new connections. Thus, while Ammerman finds communal rituals and the emphasis on relationships to be trends in American congregational life generally, Steve Warner (2000) finds them to be particularly important within migrant congregations, since migrants both tend to need more support and have fewer ready avenues through which to find it. The sociability of migrant congregations is not qualitatively different from what is found in nonmigrant congregations, but it is rather intensified.

Thus, for example, a particularly connected American congregation might make it a habit to throw each other birthday parties, and many members might spend time together outside of church services; while in a particularly connected migrant congregation like Evangel Ministries, members will socialize for hours every Sunday and Wednesday night, will give each other rides to and from church, will visit each other in the hospital if sick, will help each other move, will watch each other's children for free, and will give each other a couch to sleep on for months at a time, if needed. The risky conditions of their lives, and the challenges to finding relations of trust in other areas, make such an intensified sociability both desirable and expected.

These practices of intensified sociability within certain congregations define a culture of connection. Within such congregations, people value and even expect close social ties; many if not most of the ritual practices of the group have a component of relationship building; and the moral principles most often emphasized by the leadership and lay members alike reinforce mutual obligation and support between members. In such congregations there is also the implicit assumption that the social aspect of the congregation can and does eclipse other objectives. Social connection is not only important to members of such congregations; in their regular habits, it is prioritized above other things. In such moments of individual and collective prioritization, the true significance of sociability for members comes through.

Timothy and Anna's story exhibits how they personally prioritized the social feel or culture of a congregation above other concerns. On one level, they considered a good church to be one that was diverse rather than exclusive to a particular ethnic group. Yet in the end, they were willing to leave a diverse church that lacked a good social feel for one that was homogenous but had a strong culture of connection. They were among about a dozen members at Evangel Ministries who in theory wanted to avoid a church with a strong ethnic identity but sacrificed this desire for the sake of something more important—in their words, "love," being "more active in church," "friendliness," "being accepted."

Likewise, the routines I observed at Evangel Ministries in Chicago showed where their priorities were ultimately grounded. As a branch of a large, globally oriented Evangelical organization, they were constantly being encouraged by their upper leadership to grow bigger, to reach out and bring more people—particularly non-Ghanaians—into the congregation. Yet as a congregation with an intense culture of connection, they also developed routines that at times were at odds with the evangelistic objective.

This came out most tellingly in a conversation I had one day with Elijah, the pastor. One day after church he approached me and said, "I have a very sincere question for you, and I would like a sincere answer."

Curious, I encouraged him to ask his question.

"You've been around for a while now, and I'm wondering if there are things you've noticed about how to make the church more accessible to other Americans like you. I know you are doing a lot of writing and thinking about things, and I know I'm putting you on the spot, but I really want to know. I know that the issue of time is one, but I want to know if there are others."

By "the issue of time," he was referring to how the church service rarely if ever started when scheduled. From the pulpit, he often encouraged the group to be more punctual, because he knew this lack of timeliness was going to discourage Americans from joining. Yet because it was an established practice for those with cars to pick others up for church in the morning, and because members lived scattered across the city and traffic could at times be unpredictable, it was difficult for everyone to arrive by the start time. The congregation's habit was to wait until at least most of the core members had arrived before beginning the service. Elijah could either fight that habit by starting on time anyway, and thus spend the first part of the service talking to himself, or wait until everyone arrived. Almost always, he did the latter.

This was why at my first visit I felt I had arrived early, even though I was "right on time." I soon learned there was the official starting time and then there was the real starting time, and the real starting time depended upon completing the necessary preparations and having a critical mass of members present. After some months, once I had gotten used to this way of navigating time, I witnessed two other new visitors struggle with it. It was a married couple, a Ghanaian man and an American woman. They arrived at ten o'clock, Evangel's advertised starting time, while people were still setting up the chairs and the choir was still rehearsing. A bit disoriented, the man had approached me. "What time does the service start?"

"Sunday school should start soon," I replied, "probably in the next few minutes. Then the service will start around 10:45."

"Ah, well, maybe we'll go wander around and come back at 10:45," he said. He then introduced himself and the woman, his fiancée. He had been once to the Evangel Ministries in Ghana, but that this was his first time visiting in Chicago. His accent suggested he went to school in the United States rather than in Ghana. He also seemed slightly irritated about the time delay. From behind me, Elijah hurried up and greeted the two of them, and they ended up staying through the service. Yet they didn't come back again after that day.

This loose way of navigating time was even more pronounced for choir rehearsals on weekends. I joined the choir about six weeks after starting my participation in the church. On one particular Saturday afternoon, I was told rehearsal would be at two o'clock and Gift would pick me up. Just after two I got a text from Benjamin saying that the rehearsal had been changed to four o'clock and Gift was still going to pick me up. Another two hours passed, and then Benjamin called again and said he was near my neighborhood and could come get me. He had been taking someone to the airport, and he had just called Gift, who wasn't ready to leave and get me yet, so Benjamin decided he would just do it.

He pulled up about ten minutes later and I walked down and got in the passenger side. He explained he had been helping a friend move all day, and then had taken him to the airport because he was moving to Houston. "He is also a church member—Kwame, do you know him?" Yes, I said, I had met him.

He apologized for the rehearsal being delayed. He had been up driving his cab until two in the morning the night before, and unfortunately business had been very, very slow. He then took another friend to the airport. This was time in his cab when he wasn't making money, but he couldn't charge his friend for the ride. He noted it was something very different between Ghanaians and Americans. "Ghanaians will never take payment from a friend for something! Here, even if your *mother* watches the kids, you will pay her."

I agreed it was true, laughing a bit.

"Even in this rigid environment," he said, "in the church we still have to help each other, and keep things free and relaxed."

While I was working hard not to feel aggravated about the delays and the schedule changes, Benjamin saw them differently: they were all part of being "free and relaxed" enough to respond to people's needs as they came up. He saw the wider American cultural environment as "rigid," but saw the church as a place to resist this, and to put cooperation, sociability, and connection first.

It made me think again about my conversation with Elijah about the issue of "time" and his desire to bring more Americans into the church. On the one hand, pursuing the aim of bringing in more Americans motivated him to push the congregation to start at the schedule time; but on the other hand, doing so too forcefully would be seen as a concession to the rigidity of the American environment, and would be counterproductive to the free and relaxed patterns that allowed them to prioritize connection. Keeping it free and relaxed meant they could give and receive support, and enjoy the social side of their congregational life more fully. It was not surprising Elijah was ambivalent about this issue and that he ultimately went along with the free and relaxed routine.

Continuing our conversation on the way to rehearsal, I asked Benjamin, "Have you been to other churches in Chicago?"

"I've visited two other churches, though I don't really remember their names. They were African, mostly Nigerian and Ghanaian. But I couldn't really see myself fitting in with the people there. At Evangel, I feel like the difference is the love that people have for each other."

"Were those other churches a lot bigger?"

"Yes," he replied. "I guess that being a smaller church, it is easier to give everyone good attention. You know, at those other churches I knew even more people there than I first knew at Evangel, but I chose Evangel because of the love of the people. I didn't know anyone there at first, I got to know them afterwards. I like that it is smaller."

He then thought for a moment, realizing how this might sound, since over and over again we were being encouraged by Elijah and by visiting higher-ups in the organization to bring more people into the church. "But that doesn't mean I don't want the church to grow," he added. "I definitely want to see it grow and see new people come into it."

These comments of Benjamin's further illustrated the tension between two different objectives—growing the church while still "giving everyone good attention"—and how the latter was most often prioritized. In general, Elijah, Catherine, and the rest of the members talked *a lot* about how important it was to invite people in and help the church expand. Yet their use of time and space defaulted to a much more relaxed, less regimented model, even if it undermined the goal of growth.

This tension is once again not unique to migrant congregations. The question of whether close-knit congregations find it more difficult to expand, given that being small is often what helps to facilitate closeness, has been asked in a number of congregational studies. One study argued that, "For newcomers, it may be hardest to make friends in 'friendly' congregations" (Olson 1989, 432), because core members are satisfied with the closeness of their relationships with each other and so are less motivated to reach out to new members.

Given what I was told about the structure of Evangel Ministries in Ghana, the organization's leaders were conscious of this possibility and worked to avoid it in the main branch. They intentionally sought to combine resources and programs that would only be possible in a congregation of thousands with small-group intimacy through the small-cell or fellowship model.

For Evangel Ministries' overseas branches like the one in Chicago, however, their reliance on Ghanaians abroad in the founding stages, and the tendency for those Ghanaians to prioritize a culture of connection over church growth in practice, meant it was common for such branches to stay small. Evangel Ministries in Chicago grew very slowly during the time I was there, in fits and starts, and I learned by attending the regional Evangel Ministries camp meetings—described later—that few branches in the United States were much bigger.

Being small, however, enhanced the culture of connection among those who did become core members of the group. Because the church was small, attendees would interact with the same people week after week, getting to know a few people very well rather than many people peripherally. Being small also meant that each participant was valuable, and each person's efforts were necessary in the operation of the church. Arranging the chairs, setting up the stage, testing the microphones, singing in the choir, and organizing events were things we all did together, because with only two dozen consistent members, everyone had to pitch in.

The relaxed, collaborative style of the church was again apparent within the choir. As mentioned, the choir was a subset of the church's core members, usually the younger adults and teenagers, who would rehearse every Saturday afternoon (although as suggested, just *when* on Saturday afternoon varied from week to week). Rehearsals did involve singing practice, of course, but they also involved lots of laughter, conversation, and snacking on Ghanaian food in between songs. The particular Saturday described earlier, when Benjamin picked me up late because he was helping a fellow church member move, was no different. We rehearsed at Benjamin's apartment, and when we arrived I found Gift and Benjamin had conspired to bring me a big helping of *waakye* from a Ghanaian food truck. I shared it with the other five people who were present. This included the former choir director David, who had moved out of state by that time but surprised us with an unannounced visit during our regular choir rehearsal.

Even the more formal rituals taking place on Sunday mornings and Wednesday nights enhanced a closeness between members. Something as simple as the regular monetary offering fed into the overall culture of connection. Every Sunday members would be called to the front to give whatever contributions they may have brought that day. They would file to the front and stand in a line to give their gifts. Elijah would then thank each by name and say a blessing for them and their lives. This practice was quite different from what I had observed in American Evangelical churches, where giving is typically more discreet, and I mentioned this to Elijah when he asked me what I thought they could do to make Americans feel more comfortable in the church. I said that in most American churches, offerings were either taken during the "passing of the plate," or dropped into a box in the back of the room at the end of the service, and many Americans might not feel comfortable being made to give so publicly.

Elijah responded with surprise, saying it never occurred to him this would be a problem. "In Ghana, it is so common in any church for people to just bring up their offerings," he said.

Yet once again, the more time I spent at Evangel Ministries, the more I came to view this as more than just a small difference between cultures that could easily be changed to make the congregation more appealing to Americans. Going up front to give money was another important component of the congregation's culture of connection. On the side of the givers, it was a ritual of commitment and investment: it symbolized both how they valued what the community provided and how they felt safe being public with their contributions. On the side of Elijah and the responding congregation, the reception and the prayer were rituals of recognition. To the giver, they conveyed the message: "We see you; we thank you; we accept you as one of us."[4]

Finally, the act of worshiping together supported this experience of connection. Pentecostal-Charismatic ritual is affective and expressive, often including singing, jumping, and dancing; loud, public, and spontaneous prayer; dynamic preaching styles; and the characteristic practice of *glossolalia*—that is, speaking in tongues. Each of these elements was regularly part of Evangel Ministries' Sunday morning service. Singing together, in particular, was an emotional high point connecting members to each other. We would all participate with our bodies and voices. We would stand up and let go of physical inhibitions. For myself, the singing time was when acute feelings of being different were lessened. The music had an emotional power that partially assuaged my sense of being an outsider; and from the relish with which others were singing and dancing, I imagined they felt some of the same things. My experience with singing thus echoed Gerardo Marti's (2012) study of how music can be a tool within interracial congregations to transcend social divisions.

Such visible expressions of emotion within Pentecostal and Charismatic rituals have led some scholars to argue that people convert to such congregations because of the emotional experience they provide. In a study of Charismatic Evangelicals in Guatemala, Robert Brenneman (2011) uses the theory of emotional energy developed by Randall Collins (2005) to explain conversion to these groups. Collins's theory argues that humans are motivated by emotional dynamics rooted in the social world. People seek out positive emotional energy; and such energy is primarily the product of successful rituals of interaction, particularly when they occur in chained sequences in the context of relationships. Building on this theory, Brenneman argues that such emotion enhancing interaction rituals within Charismatic Evangelical churches can help explain why participants find them.

I similarly observed that the vigor of formal rituals and the enjoyment of informal socializing felt good to participants, and kept them coming back. Yet I saw this as only one aspect of sociability—albeit, an important one—rather than the primary explanation for their involvement. Intensified sociability at Evangel Ministries involved a complex of positive emotions along with practical benefits and symbolic affirmations. Members gave each other rides to the airport and helped on moving day, which were practical and material benefits; while they also enjoyed the emotional highs of making music together and the symbolic affirmations of being prayed over when they came forward with their monetary gifts. All these aspects were enjoyed within the same church ties, and all were part of the experience of close connection with those others.

In Evangel Ministries', therefore, people oriented themselves toward building close connections. They valued sociability, and they expected that value to be reciprocated by others. This was evident in Sandra's initial delight at being received so warmly by the congregation; in Anna and Timothy's decision to prioritize the social feel of the close-knit congregation over their desire for a multicultural worship experience; and in Benjamin's preference for Evangel Ministries over other options because of "the love of the people." The practices members engaged in also almost always had a relationship-building component. This was true when members picked each other up for church or relied on each other for support in difficult times; in how they prioritized such practices, even to the potential detriment of other aims such as expanding the church; and in their emotion-enhancing rituals, like chatting, laughing, singing, praying, and publicly giving gifts.

"More than Just Church"

Along with these practices of sociability, Evangel Ministries' leaders and members emphasized moral principles that supported building close connections, particularly the virtues of mutual obligation and religious-based solidarity. Participants talked about church as family in formal and informal settings. This was apparent in the regular dialogue within the small Chicago branch itself and in the larger organizational setting of Evangel's "church camps."

Every summer, Evangel Ministries' regional leaders organized camp meetings for their congregations across the United States. These were weekend-long sessions of singing, preaching, and socializing. They were spaces where Ghanaians and other Africans connected to each other and experienced solidarity beyond their local community. They were also settings where the ethos of the larger organization interacted with and shaped the culture of its many local branches. Since the meeting schedules were very intensive—services throughout the weekend were three or four hours long, lasting late into the night and starting early the next day—and much of the time was devoted to preaching by Evangel Ministries' leaders, the two camp meetings I attended taught me much about the values being promoted within the organization.

The first night of the camp meeting in June 2010, I arrived in the evening with several of Evangel Ministries' Chicago members. The camp took place at a hotel in the Chicago suburbs. I shared a room with three other young women from different branches, but none of them had yet arrived when I checked in. I dropped off my bags and then went downstairs to the meeting room just before the opening session was scheduled to begin.

The meeting room was a typical hotel conference hall that had been transformed into a church sanctuary. There was a stage set up at the end of the room, with a drum set, a keyboard, and several microphones arranged on either side of the podium. Over the stage was the same banner we used each week in Chicago: "Evangel Ministries International." There were about ten rows of chairs set up on either side of the center aisle. At the back of the room, tables displayed the many books and sermon tapes produced by Evangel Ministries' founder, available for attendees to purchase.

Although I was told the first evening service was going to start at ten o'clock in the evening, when I arrived at that time the room was nearly empty. There were a few people in the room conversing in small clusters, and a few others praying softly or wandering around. Someone told me a group from another city was quite late, so the leaders were waiting on them to begin. Soon a few musicians set up and starting playing praise songs, and more people came in and joined the singing. This relaxed mixture of praying and singing continued for another hour. By nearly eleven I was falling asleep on my feet, so I went upstairs to the room to rest. I intended to go back down after a quick nap, but promptly fell asleep until six o'clock the next morning. When I suddenly awoke, I noticed a text message on my phone from David, Evangel Chicago's choir director, timed at one o'clock in the morning. It said, "We are starting the meeting now."

While washing my face and getting dressed, I got a call—it was David again. He told me the morning meeting was about to begin. Although I had slept a luxurious seven hours, it was a rookie mistake. Everyone else had been at the meeting until three in the morning and was gearing up to meet again at seven.[5]

This pattern continued throughout the weekend. Meetings would start early in the morning and go for several hours. We would break for an hour to eat breakfast, and then meet again for four or five hours. Lunch was just a few snacks or coffee during the meeting. After another two-hour break in the late afternoon and then dinner, the meeting would start again and go late into the night. Usually we had about three or four hours between the end of the late-night meeting and the beginning of the meeting the next morning.

Roughly three-quarters of the weekend was spent doing one of two things: socializing and listening to sermons. The socializing was similar to what happened each week at Evangel Ministries in Chicago. Conversations were relaxed and lengthy. People lingered together over meals when the leaders allowed them longer breaks. Loud laughter often rang out in the breakfast room. Calling it a "camp" was certainly appropriate: at times it felt like a boot camp, especially when the preachers would push us to keep going after hours of instruction; and yet other times it felt like a summer camp, with little sleep, lots of talking, and lots of fun.

The sermons, too, combined instruction with entertainment. The guest preacher, a Reverend John visiting from Ghana, was dynamic, engaging, and often hilarious. He had the crowd alternately roaring with laughter and cheering multiple times over. He made references to mainstream culture, sex, male/female relationships, movie stars, and the gap between Ghanaian and American habits, all the while conveying the values and the vision of the organization.

The overwhelming theme of Rev. John's sermons was the importance of committing fully to the life of the religious community. He admonished his listeners to "get serious" about their church activity, and to devote lots of time to church life throughout the week. He told women to wear "shoes for working" on Sunday, rather than high heels: "on Sunday you should come prepared to work!" He exclaimed. A principle he often repeated was to "maximize Sunday usage," by using one's Sunday to not only hold services but also visit sick members, have choir rehearsal, and discuss important church business, such as finances and outreach programs.

He also talked frequently about how Evangel Ministries functioned like a family for both himself and its other devoted members. He taught that God not only creates people and things in the world, but that another one of his works on the earth is to "put the isolated into families." "Evangel is not a church, it's a family!," he said during one message. "If you stay and become grounded here, you will see that these relationships are more than just church."

He proceeded to tell a supporting narrative from the Bible.

"Jesus was preaching once and was interrupted by a man who said, 'Your mother and brothers are outside.' Jesus was surprised, but then Jesus used the moment as an opportunity to say, 'Who are my mother and brothers? Are these not my brethren? Anyone who does the will of God is my mother, brothers, and sisters.'"

He looked down at the microphone and paced toward the other side of the stage. "On my fortieth birthday, which was some years ago,"—he looked up at the crowd and winked, and everyone laughed—"we were having a party, and eating and dancing, and fellowshiping, and suddenly I realized that not one of my siblings had called me that day." He repeated, "not one!" and lifted his pointer finger high into the air. It was his church family he celebrated with, not his biological one. To this, the congregation again responded loudly. Some stood up and clapped and cheered. This was one of many occasions over the weekend when they were encouraged to think of their relationships in Evangel Ministries as "more than just church."

Later that same day, he made a similar comment: "A time will come when you will stand alone, and only a church member will be with you!" He made this statement while once again encouraging listeners to commit more time on Sundays to the work of the church.[6] The dual themes of relationship building and church work were inseparable. Relationship building *was* church work, and vice versa.

Evangel Ministries' leaders were thus aware of and eager to promote shifts in members' networks toward church-based connections. The organization relied on existing networks, usually those built on family or on the shared educational experiences of certain social classes, to identify leaders for its global branches and to collect an initial core group of participants for each new congregation. Yet the organization also promoted the idea that the church itself could form a new basis of connection: it could be a new kind of family. The large branch in Ghana followed the fellowship model in order to provide participants a sense of intimacy even in a congregation of thousands, and the small branches abroad were made up of people who spent lots of time together on Sundays and throughout the week. Its leaders preached the principles of mutual obligation and commitment to the group as much as any other topic. The tone of their preaching alternated between exhortation and promise: exhortation to commit and to give, and promise that if they did so they would find true community.

One final incident toward the end of the camp meeting reinforced the connection between exhortation and promise, and specifically how being receptive to the exhortations depended on trusting the promises. It showed me in a deeply emotional way how I myself, as someone in a unique position both in and outside of the church community, responded differently from others to the more forceful exhortations of the leaders.

As noted earlier, at the camp there were many books or sermon tapes by the organization's founder for members to purchase. The founder had recently released a comprehensive collection of sermon tapes, in a glossy and professional package, that cost about one hundred dollars. After multiple encouragements throughout the weekend to buy this compilation, Reverend Mark—then the overseer of all North American branches—stood to give us one final push.

"You need to have this," he said, as he held the package up for us to see. He asked everyone in the congregation who didn't yet own the compilation to stand up. I stood, along with about twenty others, in a crowd of roughly sixty people. Rev. Mark then spoke to us directly.

"I want all of you to buy one. . . . I am your pastor; will you obey me?" He repeated this question twice, and the "Yes!" from the crowd was more resounding on the second response.

"Okay, clap for yourself, but only if you mean it," he said, and everyone clapped.

Feeling conspicuous, I hoped he would then allow us to sit; but he continued on. "Okay, how many of you honestly cannot afford it?" Four women across the room raised their hands. One by one, Rev. Mark addressed them publicly.

To the first one, he said: "You can't afford it right now? Who is your pastor?" Another pastor in the front raised his hand, and said it was true, that the woman had not been working for one year. The pastor said he would like to take care of it for her. "Alright, he will take care of it for you," Reverend Mark replied, and everyone clapped again.

He then asked the second woman a similar question. He seemed skeptical because of her nice clothes and her Americanized accent. "Really, you cannot afford it?" he said. She looked embarrassed and said she couldn't at the moment. Rev. Mark then heard someone say something from the back.

"Your pastor in the back, she has it for you back there, so just go back," he told the woman. Rev. Mark did the same for each of the other women, agreeing to pay the cost of one of their compilations himself. Each time the crowd responded with a round of applause.

I bristled at this experience. My initial reaction was to distrust the motives of Evangel Ministries' leadership: the force with which they pushed the sermon tapes seemed to reflect an excessive devotion to the founder of the organization, and even a desire to exploit for profit. My field notes from that day recorded my emotions right alongside the details of what I had seen:

> *I was burning with frustration at this point, both from having been put on the spot and forced to buy the tapes, and from having spent such a long time listening to these sorts of encouragements. I felt angry, that they were elevating*

everything that the [founder] says to such a high level, and it felt somewhat dangerous to me. So I went and got my food from the buffet and took it out to the patio by the pool [of the hotel], alone. As I was thinking for a bit afterward, I started to cool down, and the thought came to me: Is it so bad? What if that sort of thing actually makes people feel cared for?[7]

It wasn't an easy question for me to answer, yet I did reach at least one conclusion. I decided that when you trust someone, you are more likely to see what they do in a positive light, and be receptive when they exhort you to do something. This is true even if it means the person exercises power over you, as Reverend Mark did when he pressured the group members to purchase the sermon compilation. As my emotions showed, I did not trust Reverend Mark enough to interpret his directions as being in my own best interest. I stood up when he asked, but only out of a dedication to fully enter into the experience—and after the exchanges that followed, I mostly wished I hadn't.

Yet the willingness of the other women to raise their hands and be honest about their financial situation, and their visible appreciation at being gifted the compilation by their pastors, seemed to indicate they *did* trust him—at least more than I did. Their responses suggested they were more fully invested in the idea of Evangel Ministries as a family—even to the extent of seeing its leadership as parent-like figures and accepting their exhortations. Indeed, many members referred to the founder or another leader as a "spiritual papa," like when Ama told me the pastor George was like a father to her.

Thus, my intuition that Reverend Mark's forcefulness might actually make the members feel cared for touched on the nature of the church-as-family trope. In a family, parents exhort their children to behave in certain ways and promise them love and support in return. Living and talking by analogy to such relationships, Evangel Ministries' leaders took on a parental tone of exhortation, while also promising that their congregations could provide the support members needed. Members who adopted this perspective responded receptively to those exhortations, and trusted both leaders and fellow members with their time, their emotions, and their resources. Imagining Reverend Mark as a father figure, they interpreted his strong words in a positive light, suspended any doubts they might have about his motives, and expected good things from his leadership and from the community.

Such exhortations and promises in the discourse of the organization, in combination with the practices just described, created a culture of connection, while also relying on and supporting the ongoing imaginative and symbolic activity of personal trust. They were possible because people used meaningful cues to imagine the others in the group as trustworthy in their initial interactions, and they encouraged and enabled people to take further leaps of faith with each other over time. As with the daycare mothers studied by Small (2009), shared membership in the group conditioned these relations toward trust and obligation; and this process was furthered through the practices and principles of the congregational culture.

The relationship between congregational culture and personal trust as an imaginative and symbolic activity was thus circular. In the first place, newcomers relied on meaningful symbols as cues that they could imagine the group and its leaders as trustworthy people. This trust was enacted in their gradually increasing investments of time and energy. As those investments increased, and they spent more time with the group, they identified even more cues to trust at an even deeper level. By the time they were committed to the group, and had been involved in this mutually reinforcing process for months or years, their level of trust dramatically shaped how they read and interpreted the acts of the group and its leaders. They saw the command to spend money on the founder's sermon tapes as an act of care, for example, rather than how I initially interpreted it as an act of manipulation.

This circular process was also visible in the personal narratives recounted earlier. In Sandra's story, her positive reception into Evangel Ministries was in part based on her husband's role as an Evangel pastor in Ghana—a good indicator of her trustworthiness—and on her own positive experience with Evangel Ministries leaders. Her phone call to Elijah, and his offer of a ride to church that same week, were the initial leaps of faith they engaged in because of how they read the symbolic cues about each other. Similarly, her account of entering for the first time and knowing that here was "peace," and that the members could be trusted "not to gossip," was based not on experience but on what she saw—friendly, well-dressed, accomplished, and fairly Americanized people—and what that symbolically indicated about their likelihood of helping and not harming her.

Likewise, before spending much time with the people at Evangel Ministries, Timothy and Anna could see cues right away of how accomplished their leaders were. It was hard to miss the fact that Elijah was a working physician, for example, with his pager on his belt and his iPhone at the ready. They could also see that Evangel Ministries put less emphasis on ethnic identity than did other Ghanaian congregations, which fit their own orientation. The songs were in English and most people came to church in business casual American dress more often than in traditional Ghanaian clothes. On the basis of these cues, they imagined that this congregation, in spite of its homogeneity by race and nationality, could be trusted to meet their need for a good church. This is what is meant by the idea of trust as an imaginative and symbolic activity; and it shows how it can enable and be enabled in turn by congregational cultures of connection.

I make a similar argument elsewhere, when my co-author and I analyze prayer and liturgy within two black immigrant communities as *constitutive-ends practices*, oriented toward the development of relationships with others and with the divine (Mooney and Manglos-Weber 2014). In constitutive-ends practices, the means and ends of the activity are inseparable; while in means-ends practices, the end goals are distinct from the means of achieving them, and different means can be selected depending on their availability and efficacy. For example, working at a job can be a means to gain wealth or social status; but there are other means to the same goals, and the means itself can be discarded or exchanged if it is no longer viewed as the best way of reaching those goals. On the other hand, activities in the realm of art, play, and relationships often have internal or inherent rewards, and in this sense they are constitutive-ends practices. The activities themselves are both the end goals and the means for achieving those goals. Indeed, the very distinction between means and ends becomes meaningless in such examples.

Likewise, practices of sociability, which take place in greater frequency and with a greater intensity within congregational cultures of connection, are constitutive of the imaginative and symbolic activity of personal trust. The practices themselves thus have two levels of meaning. On one level, driving across the city to give a fellow participant a ride to church is a routine of sociability, characteristic of a culture of connection. On another level, it is an imaginative and symbolic act of personal trust. It implies the trustworthiness of both parties, and it is possible because they both choose to imaginatively interpret available symbolic cues as positive evidence of each other's trustworthiness.

Other Good Churches

All these examples come from Evangel Ministries, a congregation many found to be a good church, which was also almost entirely ethnically homogenous. Many members said they had attended non-Ghanaian churches in the past, or would ideally like to find one; but without real counterexamples it was hard to know whether what I observed about the culture of connection was merely a function of shared ethnicity or something that could stand apart from the ethnic connection.

During one conversation with a man named Jeremiah—whose story is told in chapter 6—he told me that based on his experience, about one-third of Ghanaians in Chicago attend Ghanaian churches; another third attend non-Ghanaian churches; and another third don't attend anywhere at all. This was a rough, off-the-cuff estimate, but it conveyed a sense of the diversity of church choices made by Ghanaians in the area. In my second summer of research, then, I sought out others who seemed to find what they were looking for in nonmigrant congregations, to see if it matched the emphasis on connection and trust I was finding at Evangel Ministries.

Sylvia was a young woman who had almost exclusively attended non-Ghanaian congregations; and her aunt in Chicago, with whom she spent her teen years, also attended a non-Ghanaian church. Sylvia's parents had lived in the United States while her father was in dental school, and during that time Sylvia was born. Shortly afterwards they moved back to Ghana, so Sylvia spent her early childhood there. When she was fourteen, her parents decided she should be sent to Chicago to live with her aunt Dotty, who also had two daughters just under Sylvia's age.

Sylvia came to Chicago around the time Dotty and her husband divorced, so for most of Sylvia's high school years it was herself, her aunt, and her two cousins in the household. Dotty worked two jobs to support the girls and later on started her own catering business.

When we sat down for an interview, Sylvia recalled how Dotty was not always inclined to socialize with other Ghanaians. "She had a push-and-pull relationship with the culture, She would gravitate towards them at times and then pull away from them at other times."

I asked her to elaborate on the possible push factors.

"The Ghanaian community is very . . . not competitive, but I think . . . competitive," she laughed. "People can be kind of showy. There is some jealousy and envy and some embarrassment when you don't have things that others have. It can put strain on marriages, if you can't do certain things your friends can do, and you look at each other and wonder who's to blame."

Sylvia didn't say so directly, but I wondered if this had been part of the reason for Dotty's divorce. I heard similar stories of how the tensions of transnational life and the gossip within the ethnic community could contribute to the end of people's marriages. From her very first years in the United States, then, Sylvia was socialized to stand somewhat apart from the ethnic community—or at least to avoid getting too intimately involved.

Reflecting this, Dotty brought the girls to an African American Episcopalian congregation. Dotty was deeply involved with this church, and Sylvia remembers one woman from the church in particular, a close friend of her aunt's, who was a fixture in their household. They called her "Gramma"; and Sylvia told me laughingly how as a child she never knew exactly whether this woman was black or white because of her light skin. The church itself had about 200 members, and was about 70 percent African American, 15 percent white, and 15 percent a collection of other ethnicities and nationalities. Sylvia remembered a few other Ghanaians attended there, but most of them came because her aunt invited them. There was also a large youth group Sylvia was involved in. Although Sylvia remembered sensing she was different from the other teens, she also remembered being excited to get out and "try something new."

After graduating from high school, Sylvia went to college in the Chicago area. During this time she sometimes went to her aunt's church, and sometimes went to chapel services and prayer meetings with her classmates, but never looked actively for a church of her own to attend. She had little awareness of or interest in Ghanaian churches in the area in particular.

This changed, though, after she finished her master's degree and found her first job. A co-worker invited her to visit a small Evangelical congregation with him. This church met in a storefront in a predominantly Latino/Latina neighborhood. She went and she liked it—the people were friendly and the preaching appealed to her. She became a regular and active participant, and it was in this church congregation that she later met her American husband.

I knew of the church. It was populated with twenty-something professionals who were politically progressive and interested in urban revitalization. It also had a strong ethos of racial integration. Because of this, it had become more diverse. Sylvia described it as, "more Caucasian, but a growing African American group, maybe some Latino."

Ultimately, though, it was the social feel that was most important to Sylvia. "There was an intentionality about building community," she said. "It was actually more like in my Ghanaian culture . . . people there will often just show up at your doorstep to hang out."

Sylvia had never regularly attended a Ghanaian congregation, but she had a sense that "intentionality about building community" was more common in Ghanaian circles than in American ones. Nevertheless, she was able to find a non-migrant congregation that allowed her to experience the closeness characteristic of "Ghanaian culture" within a more diverse community.

After she married, her husband's graduate-school plans took them to a new city, and they said goodbye to the church where they had met and developed many close friendships. They settled into their new place and started looking for a new church. It was a challenge, in some ways—as a biracial and binational couple, they needed to find a group that felt like home to both of them rather than just one or the other. They ended up in a racially mixed Episcopal church much like the one Sylvia had attended with her aunt Dotty as a teenager.

She laughed in acknowledgment when I pointed out the similarity between Dotty's church and the one she attended now. She noted, though, that she hadn't been deliberately looking for an Episcopalian church. "The community seemed embracing," she said, explaining her choice.

For her and her husband, therefore, choosing a church wasn't about specifics of denomination, ethnicity, or nationality. It was about finding an "embracing" community. As for Timothy and Anna, Sandra, Benjamin, and Dotty her aunt, the social feel was crucial. Although each of them ended up in congregations within different denominational traditions and with very different ethnic and racial compositions, they all shared a similar perspective on what made a good church. They valued multicultural diversity, while also ultimately prioritizing congregations with cultures of connection whether or not they were diverse.[8]

The Non-Attenders

In addition to those who attended mostly Ghanaian congregations and those who attended mostly non-Ghanaian congregations, there was a third and final group that didn't attend any church at all. It was rare for Ghanaians to be completely non-religious or atheist, and most considered themselves either Christian or Muslim. Among self-identified Christians, however, there were some who kept organized religion at arm's length. Although this seemed counterintuitive, given the many social benefits other migrants found within congregations, such counterexamples actually revealed a lot about the significance of religious association and ultimately supported my overall argument about how new migrants choose a church.

Franklin was an example of a congregation-avoider. When I met him, he was a fairly new arrival from Ghana, in his early twenties. He was in Chicago to study film. He identified as a Christian, and he had visited several congregations of different sizes, ethnic makeups, and denominations since moving there. Yet after nine months he did not find a congregation he could commit to, and he became convinced that organized religion in the United States wasn't for him. One of the congregations he visited, in fact, was Evangel Ministries; and yet while others like Sandra, in chapter 4, described being drawn to the place right away, his reaction was quite different. He acknowledged they were friendly and welcoming. But for reasons he later elaborated on, it was not the specific kind of "friendly" he was looking for.

As we talked on a cold, rainy afternoon in a Starbucks café near his university, I could tell he was an intense young man. He gestured expressively with his hands and had a lot to say about identity, art, and being African. He was also frank about his frustrations with the Ghanaian community, on the one hand, and with the white mainstream culture of cinema, on the other. Already his experience in the United States had not gone as he expected, and he was particularly disappointed with the lack of diverse voices and perspectives in his classes on film. The education he was getting was not what he had hoped for.

"I came here for one thing, but am finding some other thing. So there's an area of film called 'third cinema,' like West Africa, South America, India, and some other places. It's what is known as the 'poetics of refusal'—it's a rejection of the Western hegemonic forms of representation."

He was introduced to the third-cinema movement in a class, and his main focus for his career shifted as a result. He decided he would finish his program, but would then move forward with a major transnational and transcultural project from the third-cinema perspective.

"I call the project Sembène, after the guy who is the father of African cinema, and I am networking with some other Africans and South Americans and finding a way to tell our stories in a way that is us, because that genre is dying out, because of all the commercialization.... So I am looking towards raising funds and starting a new movement that will mean something for us. So that means that I also realize that I want to teach.... I've always taught back home, so I'm trying to learn all I can so that I can teach.... So I will go home, but I need to get my feet wet here and then go."[9]

I asked if he had planned for a long time to come to the United States.

He nodded. "I knew that I would come to States, knew long ago, even though given the chance, I would not do it again. What I'm looking for is not here. But it's good because it's making me see."

"Where do you think you will find what you're looking for?"

"That's in South America, Brazil and Cuba," he replied, citing the hubs of third cinema, "Next summer I'm going to go to Brazil."

Being in Chicago was also hard in other ways, specifically in how different it was from his life in Ghana. "I miss [Ghana] like crazy every day. First of all, my boys are not here; when I get off work at home, we check in with the boys, we share our struggles and victories together, and that's the nice thing where we are not jealous of each other's achievement . . . and the freedom of just knowing that you are home.... Here, I can only work twenty hours a week, and I can only work on campus . . . the thing is I don't even have the time to take on other jobs."

This problem of loneliness and idleness got worse in the summers. "It's just depressing, like this summer, these long four months of a break, it's just a killer, it makes me understand that, wow, I'm by myself. See, I've closed from work, where am I going? I'm not much of a loner, my status is not usually being alone."

He then talked about his family. "I miss my mom every day, and my sister calls me every day . . . and you are missing it if somebody dies, somebody is getting married, and I never thought I would never be around for these things!"

These comments reiterated the general shock of isolation affecting Ghanaian newcomers to the United States, regardless of their economic situation. Franklin enjoyed a privileged position compared to other migrants. His parents paid completely for his schooling, supported him in doing whatever he wanted for a career, and would likely support him in his pursuit of his ambitious film project. He mentioned that when he lived in Ghana, he drove his own BMW. Yet the social strain of living abroad by himself was still intense. Like Timothy, he described Ghana as a place with a rich social life, filled with neighbors, family, and classmates; and described Chicago as a place with little going on socially, where he found himself "a loner" much of the time.

By the time we had this conversation, I had heard many similar stories that ended with finding a good church to meet those needs. I changed topics to see if this was something Franklin had considered.

"Have you been to a lot of churches here in Chicago?"

"MANY churches," he said, laughing, "it's like some kind of prostitution going on here, just church trotting!"

He said he had a pattern of trying out and tagging along to various churches around the city. "When I first came to Chicago, I was living with a friend, a random stranger from my program. I went looking for something in my neighborhood, and went to a church where they were all Ukrainian, and I think I was the only English-speaking one, but I walked out before it was over, I was done." He laughed again, remembering the experience.

"The next time I went to church I went to visit friends in Maryland, and I went to a Ghanaian church, but that was just a visit. But the next time I went to church for myself here, it was a Lutheran church. And I liked it a lot, it was fun, you know truth is truth and so I knew that this is the stuff, and I liked the fact that it was different."

It was an ethnically Norwegian church, so he knew it was a bit out of the norm for him to go there, but something about it drew him in. "They were very warm nice people, so afterwards it's like a tea where everyone gets together and chats after church . . . but there was not a lot of young people, as usual with these orthodox churches"—he was using "orthodox" in the Ghanaian sense to mean non-Charismatic, older Protestant and Catholic churches—"I went there for a while, as long as I stayed in that area, though I went only four or five times or less."

It seemed as if the Norwegian Lutheran congregation had intrigued him at first because of their initial friendliness; but it never turned into a basis for real social connection. When he moved again and the Lutheran church was no longer close by, he tried a youth-oriented American Evangelical church. In its makeup, it was much like the urban church of young professionals where Sylvia attended and met her husband: modern worship music modeled after pop radio, a twenty-something crowd, and a progressive ethos. Yet unlike Sylvia's experience with her church, Franklin found the social feel of this congregation to be lacking.

"The 'MTV church' I call it," he said. "It's a Western church, a place where you come and it's like, you don't know me, I don't know you." There was a cool vibe, but little of the warmth he was looking for. His "MTV church" analogy implied attendees were more spectators than engaged and socially connected participants.

Coincidentally, this congregation met in the same building as Evangel Ministries at the time. The American Evangelical church was on the ground floor and Evangel Ministries met in the basement. Because of this, there was one Sunday when he visited Evangel Ministries, but by accident—he had initially gone to attend the American Evangelical church. "So I went with this girl, and we got there and got in late, and there was this other church meeting there, so we thought, let's just visit there."

He then gave some backstory about why he hadn't ever visited there—or any Ghanaian church—before that day. "I had avoided them, on frivolous grounds. First of all, anything that is too grounded in home I don't deal with. . . . I don't think that we have come this far to recreate another Ghana. I feel that I achieve best when I don't try to hold onto my former life, and Ghanaians have this sense that they will make you feel like you are still at home."

Like others, particularly those of his social class, he found many reasons to avoid getting too involved with the ethnic community. "But so I did go there [to Evangel Ministries] on accident," he continued, "I showed up, and it was nice, nice people, but I'm not trying to sign up. . . . And they are a bit aggressive, too, so that's why I decided, I'm not doing this."

He then put his position even more strongly: "I wouldn't go [to church] with Ghanaians. I am always trying to avoid a gathering of Africans. I think we talk too much, we gossip too much and we are in everyone's business."

I asked him why this is.

"Because the West is somewhere we come to seek greener pastures, and there is like this foolish competition. There is the same culture even in the church. I am always aware of that. Even back home, if you try to be too nosy and too into church business, you won't find me in that church . . . there is a limit that I think we should go as far as that. And I don't like any church that polices behavior too much."

He continued, growing more animated. "Look, most people that end up here are high achievers anyway, I don't need anyone to tell me you need to do well in school, I would rather just talk after church. . . . Can we not always try to make it look like we are this unique group? And I seem to be a bit of a maverick in how we should present ourselves. . . . Doing film is a bit off from the Ghanaian community. . . even at home, people ask, 'Oh, there's a degree for film?' People were asking me, like, 'What, you serious?' but they also want to avoid you because they worry that you won't be successful."[10]

In these statements he echoed the frustrations of others about the competiveness of the ethnic community, and how it is caused by high aspirations and the desire to distinguish themselves from "bad" immigrants or "bad" blacks—to be a "unique group." Like Benjamin, he talked about how fellow Ghanaians made assessments of others' likelihood of being successful—and by extension, their likelihood of being a helpful versus unhelpful connection—and decided to either pursue or avoid them as a result.

These issues made Franklin adamant about not attending a Ghanaian church. Ironically, then, he saw Evangel Ministries as too "ethnic" in character—too aggressive, too "grounded in home"—even though I knew many of the members chose it in part because it emphasized Ghanaian identity *less* than other congregations in Chicago.

In all of this, his attitude toward churchgoing didn't seem to be fundamentally different from that of others I talked to; he just felt even more strongly about avoiding the ethnic congregation. This was true even though he also had been unable to find an American church with the right social feel. It meant that, for now, he had no church. He held Christian beliefs, and enjoyed talking at length about theology and philosophy with friends and classmates, but he had not found a religious congregation worth committing to and investing in.

Importantly, Franklin had been in the United States for a short time, was busy with school, and did have some friendships with classmates; and it still looked likely that his stint in Chicago would be temporary. From the way Timothy told *his* story, he positioned himself quite similarly before he got married, settled down, had kids, and accepted that his life in Chicago would be longer than just a short strategic stay. After those transitions, and after many more disappointing experiences in American congregations, Timothy's own resistance to all-Ghanaian congregations loosened, as it became a higher priority to find solid new trust networks for his life in Chicago.

As Franklin and I parted ways, I wondered if as time went by he would start to see things "grounded in home" as less restrictive and more comforting. I wondered if he would actually become more tightly connected with the Ghanaian community in Chicago—and perhaps even a Ghanaian church—in the future, assuming he ended up staying longer than planned, as so many did. I wondered if, in ten years, he would be in a similar position as Timothy: relaxing his resolve to "avoid gatherings of Africans" because the social connection that was possible in such communities was hard to find anywhere else.

Other nonattendees I interviewed tended to fall in one of two categories. They were either students, like Franklin, who had at least some social support among their classmates, were in a relatively more privileged position, and had confidence in their ability to realize their aspirations in the future; or they were working jobs with odd weekend hours that didn't allow them to go to church on Sundays.

Ama, whom I first met in Accra in 2009, and who later migrated to the United States herself, fell into the latter category. She was sponsored by a cousin and came to work, and the only job she could find was a live-in caregiver position in a home for adults with permanent mental and physical disabilities. She worked most weekends, so trying out new churches was difficult, and the job kept her in a small city where she had limited connections. The people she knew—her cousin and his wife, and another older Ghanaian couple who took her under their wing—were largely church-avoiders, for some of the same reasons expressed by Franklin. Although in Ghana she went to the Evangel Ministries headquarters, and after she moved she still frequently read the books and listened to the sermons of the founder, there was no Evangel Ministries branch nearby and she had no way to travel to the neighboring city where there was one.

Ama's social network was severely limited by comparison to the young, single members of Evangel Ministries in Chicago. Working long hours, having few existing ties beyond two older families, lacking transportation, and not being familiar with the ways in which American young people make new friends, she had few social ties even after two years of living and working in the United States. She felt this particularly acutely in the realm of romantic partnerships. She transitioned into her late twenties and her mother in Ghana repeatedly encouraged her to find someone there to marry, to solidify her position and start a family. As I kept up with her through the years, I sometimes asked her myself, "Have you met anyone?" She would laugh: "Where would I meet someone?" And in spite of my obligations to remain neutral as a scholar, I often thought to myself that what she needed was a good church—a place with a strong culture of connection, where she could expand her trust networks by making friends and possibly finding a partner.

On the one hand, the stories of Sylvia, Franklin, and Ama are important because they show the diversity of choices aspirational migrants from Ghana make about whether and where to go to church. Ethnicity and prior religious background do not determine their congregational memberships. A Ghanaian Presbyterian moving from Ghana to the United States today will not necessarily go to a Ghanaian or a Presbyterian church. New migrants from Ghana instead make choices about their religious memberships, often trying out different styles and traditions. On the other hand, even when they make different decisions, they tend to share one focus: the desire for a congregation with a good social feel. In nine cases out of ten, a congregation must have that to be considered a good one. These counterexamples thus ultimately support the main point: that within their church choices, finding a place of connection and trust is frequently the priority.

Leaving the Community

As discussed in the introduction, the imaginative and symbolic activity of personal trust is a balancing act between dual motivations: to enjoy the many constitutive benefits of personal trust—from emotional energy to social support—while also protecting oneself against the risk of others' mistakes, failures, or ill-will. This means that various bases of trust, even if effective, are rarely perfect or fixed. In the case of Evangel Ministries, the open nature of church membership made it an easy and accessible basis for personal trust, but it also made it easier for people to leave the community and thereby weaken their church-based trust networks. Being highly voluntary and portable, as compared to other bases like family, ethnicity, or social class position, was both the source of its particular appeal and its greatest limiting factor.

As a result, even though Evangel Ministries' members were for a time very involved in each other's lives, usually that period ended. Evangel could operate *like* a family during certain seasons of people's lives, but unlike a family it had no permanent claim on those who moved on. The community alternatively accepted losses of members and exerted social pressure on them to stay; but in the end, membership would always be voluntary by nature.

The first person I observed leaving the community was a woman in her forties named Evangeline. She was the congregation's first choir director. I found it easy to connect with her in my early weeks of participation, given our shared interest in music. She was married, but her husband did not come with her to Evangel Ministries. Instead, she came each week with her seven-year-old daughter. As we got to know each other better, she explained that her husband was planning on starting a church of his own soon, so he didn't want to get connected at Evangel only to leave shortly after.

Her husband's new church then started about six weeks later, and he told Evangeline he needed her to start the choir there, so she had to leave Evangel Ministries. From her perspective she had no choice but to say yes. Nevertheless, it was a hard transition to make.

She was emotional on the Sunday she led the music for the final time. At one point she teared up in the middle of a conversation and excused herself to the restroom. After the service, the choir convened and prayed for her in her new venture, and complimented her on how well she had led us. It was a drawn-out goodbye, as she accepted warm wishes and glowing sentiments from all the other members.

Although everyone said that since she wasn't leaving town, they would all still see each other, that didn't really happen. Evangeline was sad that day because her life was busy, as was everyone else's, and she knew that if they didn't go to church together they wouldn't have much free time to connect. She stayed in loose touch with Elijah, she told me a couple years later, but it wasn't the same as being weekly connected with the whole group.

When she first told me about her husband's plans to start a new church, it seemed strange to me that as a religious person he would rather stay home on Sunday mornings than go to Evangel Ministries with his wife, all for the sake of avoiding the inevitable moment of leaving. Yet later on it became clear he was protecting himself and the community against the break in trust that would happen after he connected, got involved, and then left to start a new church. Evangeline's leaving, although it was sad, was accepted by the group because it was couched in terms of her duty to her husband. If both of them were Evangel Ministries members and then broke off, there might be more questions about why they couldn't just invest in the community that already existed, especially since the congregation Evangeline's husband was planning to start was a Charismatic church with similar teachings and practices.

This type of leaving one congregation to start another one has been a major trend in Ghanaian Charismatic Christianity and a major source of tension within the movement. People looking from the outside talk about it in connection with corruption among pastors: they see it as rampant and as proof of the self-serving nature of Charismatic religious leaders. People on the inside of one or another church organization talk about how important it is to stay loyal—Evangel Ministries' founder has written half a dozen books on this topic. Yet the people who leave have real frustrations and/or real visions that to them feel undeniable. Daniel, the young man whose story is told in chapter 4, was one of them: starting a new Charismatic church seemed a natural next step in his trajectory of transformation. Likewise, Evangeline's husband was someone who found a sense of purpose in his life as a migrant when he took on the project of starting a church, a subject to which I return in chapter 7. He felt a loyalty of his own to the church organization in Ghana where he became born again, and he promised them he would take charge of a new Chicago branch.

People also at times left Evangel Ministries for other, more practical reasons. For example, from 2010 to 2014, Evangel in Chicago went through four different choir directors. After Evangeline was David, who stayed about six months and then left to join his wife who was in medical school in the Southeast. After David was Gift, who served for a brief time and then was replaced by a newcomer from Ghana who was more experienced in music and leadership. In addition, from 2010 to 2014, many of the core members present on my first day had moved away. This included Benjamin, who moved south; an older couple named Prudence and Kwame, who moved west; a young woman who moved back to her home in Zimbabwe; and another who finished medical school and left town. These cases were all different from Evangeline's because there was a natural reason for the departure: jobs, school, or family took them elsewhere. They were still instances of loss, however, when a relationship that was a major part of one's weekly routine was suddenly gone.

Lastly, in a few cases people left for more deliberate—and thus more hurtful—reasons. One couple who were very committed and close to the pastor when I came to the congregation in 2010 decided they needed to leave because of concerns they had about the larger Evangel Ministries organization.[11] Their decision did not go over well with the rest of the church. Deep relationships were suddenly damaged. In this case, there was no easy rationale for the community to accept it as a natural and right event, as there was in Evangeline's case, or in the cases of the many who left Chicago for work-related or economic reasons. It was an undisguised hard break.

Further, even among those who stayed within the congregation, there were limits to and variations on how much they trusted particular people. In a conversation with one informant named Anthony, for example, when I told him I was writing about trust within the Evangel Ministries congregation, he told me he does *not* trust everyone in the congregation just because they go to church together. There are some, he said, who are just "here for the logo," meaning they have joined the bandwagon of Evangel Ministries but aren't fully reliable or invested in the relationships. He seemed to see some members as having more self-serving motivations for their involvement in the church, and was less inclined to trust such people. Likewise, Benjamin told me that when talking about his most personal issues and goals, there were just a few people in the church he would go to. He trusted certain other members more than others—Timothy and Gift, for example—that he felt were more likely to be helpful and with whom he felt a closer connection.

Nonetheless, participation at Evangel was still a basis of trust networks for both Anthony and Benjamin, even if they did not trust everyone in the network on an equal level. There were certain people whom they trusted very much, whom they would never have met or trusted to such an extent apart from their association with Evangel Ministries. For both of them, this included the women they later married, and some of their closest friends. It also included many less intimate ties that might not stay with them throughout their lives, but still, for a time, collectively provided many emotional, social, and material benefits.

Even the strongest cultures of connection cannot guarantee everyone will trust perfectly all the time. The promise of finding a basis for personal trust networks in religious association does not mean that risk becomes irrelevant, that trust is never broken, or that personal trust is engaged in equally with everyone within the group. As Tilly (2010, 271) argues, "Neighborhoods, communities, markets, voluntary organizations, and ethnic groups often contain or overlap trust networks, but rarely constitute them." Evangel Ministries itself is not a perfectly bounded trust network; rather, membership in that group contains and overlaps existing trust networks, and provides a basis for new trust networks to form.

What this *does* mean, however, is that religious association, particularly within congregations with cultures of connection, provides a potential rationale for trust networks to develop among people who were formerly strangers. And the fact that this works in the way it does, even though the perfect and final elimination of risk is impossible, suggests that people seek out such rationales for trust in the face of obstacles. In spite of persistent risks, perpetual shifts, and regular breaks and failures, aspirational Ghanaians in America engage in imaginative and symbolic leaps of faith with others whom they know only through religious association; and this speaks to both the potential of religion as a basis of trust networks and the nature of trusting activity in general.

6

The Shape of Identity

VISIONS, REVISIONS, AND NEGOTIATIONS

THE LABEL "IMMIGRANT" can obscure as much as it reveals. It defines a person based on one step in a life-long journey, one moment of resettlement in a narrative arc. Yet research into the lives of transnational migrants is increasingly showing us how uncertain these resettlements can be, and how often external forces and personal decisions result in stalls, reversals, or step-by-step progressions within the process of immigrating. As one example, Anju Paul (2011) describes how migrants with limited amounts of capital make progressive moves through "a hierarchy of destination countries" (1842), starting with those that are easier to enter and moving up toward those—usually in the West—that have more restrictive immigration policies but are also believed to provide greater opportunities. As another example, Hagan and colleagues (2008) have shown how the increase in mass deportation from the United States has forced many undocumented migrants from Latin America into a state of circular migration. These migrants' moves involve stints in the United States, followed by deportations to their country of nationality, followed by returns to the United States, and so on.

In the case of the Ghanaians I interviewed, deportations were less frequent. Yet many if not most of them experienced stalls, reversals, or progressions in their migration trajectories. Stories like Benjamin's were common, where migrants initially came for a tertiary degree but were forced to drop out and either return home or find other kinds of work. Many others, like Elijah and Catherine, moved multiple times between locations across the United States and European countries like the United Kingdom. Still others came with plans to achieve certain professional goals before getting married and starting a family, but found their professional goals harder to obtain and the pull of family life stronger than they anticipated. To balance the desire for a family with the demands of their aspirations, many dealt with short- to long-term separations from spouses, partners, and children. Finally, in response to new challenges and opportunities, many of them developed different aspirations unique to their situations as transnationals, revising their rationales for moving abroad.

All these shifts were connected to choices about identity: which collectives they aligned themselves with and which ones they wanted to be part of. Their choices about identity were, of course, also constrained by how others viewed them and by the circumstances of their lives. Unexpected twists and turns—a major setback, the birth of a child, a new ambition—tended to revive the question of identity, by making certain identities easier or more difficult to hold onto. Similarly, moving into and through new social settings tended to bring identity questions to the fore.

In this chapter I focus on the readjustments I observed among Ghanaians in Chicago, who came with initial visions and were later compelled to engage in revisions of their goals and subsequent identity negotiations along the way. The stories highlight change over time: turning points, setbacks, sharp left turns, and new dreams for the future. While in this chapter I shift the focus slightly away from religious association to examine such changes, I do so to lay the groundwork for the arguments put forth in the next chapter—namely, that migrants' religious memberships can directly influence how they engage in the revisions of their goals and the negotiations of their identities; and that this often happens as part of a renewal or deepening of religious commitment, spurred on by the personal trust relations found within the church. Religious associations are, therefore, much more than settings where migrants cope with their circumstances or take a break from the social strains of being foreign. They are memberships that directly influence how they answer the question of identity, and that shape the trajectories of their personal and professional lives.

Defining Success

"I promised myself I would only go back with one of two things: money or knowledge." As described in chapter 3, Benjamin came to the United States with a particularly clear vision for his life. It was rich, ambitious, and specific. How he understood himself (i.e., his identity) and where he wanted to go in life (i.e., his vision) converged in the moment he crossed the ocean to pursue his goals. As someone who already lived comfortably and had a bachelor's degree before he came, he hoped to either become wealthy or become highly educated. He came under a student visa and enrolled in a program for his master's in business administration (MBA). His intent was to graduate and earn good money as a financial analyst, and/or go on for a Ph.D. and teach in a university.

When he said he would only go back with one of these two things, he wasn't talking about a final return—he was simply talking about a visit. I asked him if he had been back to Ghana since his initial move to Chicago, and he said no, he had been waiting to do that until after he had achieved one of these goals. He also said he had been waiting to get married until he had reached this "higher level." It seemed, then, he initially expected to meet these goals relatively soon after arriving in the United States—at least within a five- to ten-year period.

It was a major setback, then, when he found after one year that he could no longer afford his tuition. Other frustrations followed. Not wanting to return to Ghana having accomplished so little, he obtained a job driving a taxi, like many other West Africans in the city. The upside of being a taxi driver was that he could make his own hours, earn cash in hand by the end of the day, and not likely be questioned about his legal status by employers or co-workers. The downside was that it was difficult to earn enough money to save for school. It also symbolically placed him in a different social-class category than the one he was used to.

During one of our conversations he listed the job's annoyances. He explained that while you can make a lot of money driving a cab, it's still not "decent" money relative to the amount of work involved. As a driver, he they often worked 24-hour days.

"Do you know how cab-driving works in the city?" he asked.

I shook my head, no.

He explained that for a car to be used as a cab, the owner had to buy a medallion, which is a city's way of licensing and regulating the taxi industry. Medallions were expensive; according to Benjamin; you could "pay a mortgage" with the amount of money it cost. In New York, they could cost about $400,000, but in Chicago they were more like $250,000.[1] Except for a few people who could afford their own medallions, individual cab drivers did not own cabs but, rather, leased them. Benjamin's lease was about $95 a day, or about $650 a week. Leasing by the hour wasn't possible. Thus, for him to maximize his profits, it made sense for him to work as much as he could in each 24-hour period he leased his cab.

In Chicago, as West Africans gravitated to the taxi business, a few started to buy their own medallions and lease them to others, thus initiating West African–owned taxi companies. This increased the appeal of the work for the average newcomer to the area, since a Ghanaian company was likely to be even more understanding if one's immigration documents were not in order. The most obvious of these companies in Chicago was Gold Coast Taxi (see figure 6.1), named after Ghana's colonial-era title.

Yet for someone in Benjamin's position who did not own a medallion or a company, the work was grueling and the money was irregular. On certain weekend days he could gross up to $500, but there were many more weekdays when

FIGURE 6.1 A Gold Coast taxi, photographed on the street in Uptown.

he earned much less, and about half or more of his earnings would go to the daily lease and the gas he used. If he earned around $250 on a weekday, for example, he only took home about half of that amount.

The structure of the job also encouraged unhealthy habits. The incentives to cram as many fares as possible into a 24-hour period meant many drivers took few breaks to either exercise or eat well. They often ate in their cabs, and tended to subsist on cheap takeout meals. This was especially true if they lived alone and had no one else to cook for them. Benjamin told me this at a sandwich shop where he ate several times a week ("sadly," he mourned, "I never learned how to cook"). He noted that a lot of drivers ended up with high blood pressure as a result. He told me to just start looking into cabs as they went by, and I would see—the drivers were all in poor physical shape.

In spite of the fact that he was working as a driver, in general he tended to distance himself from those who drove taxis. In his view it was something he was doing temporarily, out of necessity, and it did not accurately reflect where he came from or where he was going. After complaining about the work and making sure I knew how out of sync cab driving was with his plans, he defined himself against those who were happy to drive a cab indefinitely because they were unable to dream bigger. He saw these other Ghanaians and Nigerians as choosing to drive taxis because, "They have too limited a definition of success." He claimed they believed they were successful only because they were doing basically the same thing here as they were doing "back there," but now making more money doing it. The implication was that these were lifelong low-wage laborers, whether they worked in Ghana or abroad, while Benjamin was not. "My definition of success," he said, "is a sense of fulfillment, to be able to practice what I learned in school."

In the meantime, he spent more and more time with the people at Evangel Ministries. As a devout and dependable single man in the congregation, he was inevitably the target of matchmaking efforts by the other members. He expected this; it was part of the role of a good church in the lives of Ghanaian migrants. Yet he resisted the matchmaking efforts of the women in the church, turning the hopeful sisters and friends down. This was because he didn't want to be matched on the basis of where he was currently in life. Being a cab driver, he was usually introduced to nurse assistants or maids.

"The perception is that we are all in the same bracket." Yet Benjamin did not see himself as part of that same "bracket"—he saw himself as heading toward a higher social class. He didn't want to get married to someone of a lower bracket while he was temporarily under-placed. Rather, he wanted to meet someone who was at the level or could get to the level he desired for the future. He mentioned Anna and Timothy as an example of the kind of life and marriage he wanted. They were both educated professionals with good jobs—"on the same level," he said. Until he could attract someone on that level, he wanted to avoid marriage.

This being his situation, his life and relationships within Evangel Ministries were his main outlet: choir rehearsal, going to the gym with his friend Gift from church, helping fellow church members move, and spending Sundays with the congregation. His ties to Timothy and Anna kept him connected to his larger ambitions, because he could see them living out the life he wanted and he could better envision it for himself. Meanwhile, his daily conversations with his mother and his routine of sending her money kept him rooted in Ghana, staying "local" to a place where he was more than just another foreign taxi driver. Those rituals and relationships helped him respond to setbacks and negotiate his identity as needed, as well as hold on to an optimistic definition of success.

Benjamin's aspirations and the subsequent rationale for his life in Chicago continued to change over the several years during which I periodically interacted with him. Much about his life was different after three years from our first interview. For one thing, he got married. Although he avoided the matchmaking efforts of the women in the church, he soon met a black American woman, Jeannette, who lived in his building. After a couple of years of dating, they were married at the office of the justice of the peace, because they were waiting for the right time to do the full church wedding.

When he told me this, I was curious to know if he had taken his new wife to Ghana to meet his relatives, given his earlier resistance to the thought of going back for a visit before he had been successful in terms of his original plans. He told me they took a two-week trip earlier that year. Jeannette enjoyed it, though he admitted it was a bit overwhelming for her—he had so many acquaintances, friends, brothers, cousins, aunts, uncles, and so on for her to meet. He seemed to have adjusted to the idea of being settled in Chicago with his new wife and reinitiating contact with his extended family, in spite of having strayed from his initial intentions.

Benjamin had also taken steps in a new professional direction. He was back in school, and was about to finish a more affordable degree in information technology. He and Jeannette were planning a move to Dallas, where he had a connection in the industry who spoke promisingly of his ability to get him a job. He was much happier about the shape his life had taken than he was in our first interview. He had a new rationale for his life in the United States: building a family with Jeannette and finding a white-collar job somewhere between his original high aspirations and the dead-end work of taxi driving. In each stage, his life demonstrated the many twists and turns a migrant trajectory can make; and how each of these shifts can spark a renegotiation of the questions of identity and aspiration.

The Educational Imperative

Perhaps more than any other reason, Ghanaians come to the United States for higher education. Even if they stay long past graduation, finding jobs and settling down, the initial impetus to move abroad is often the desire for a tertiary degree or qualification. This is a pull factor that implies a corresponding push factor in Ghana: they often cannot get the degree they want if they stay there. Many of them, especially those who live relatively comfortable lives in Ghana, would prefer not to move abroad if possible, but the paucity of educational supply relative to demand makes it necessary.

Anna's story of coming to the United States demonstrated this. Something she said in one of our early conversations surprised me initially: she never wanted to leave Ghana while growing up. This contradicted my implicit assumptions about the pervasiveness of the "American dream," as an idyllic vision of the United States widely shared by young people in contexts of heavy out-migration. To the contrary, living in the United States wasn't something Anna idealized; her parents had lived abroad in the past and had returned home because they were tired of being immigrants. She knew it was not all it was cracked up to be. Nevertheless, she *did* want to be a doctor, and problems in the system when she was ready to enter a university made going abroad her only reasonable choice.

When she was school-age in Ghana in the 1980s, most good education was to be found in private schools. Public schools were still of low quality, and the state government—which was struggling through a major recession while trying to recover from a long series of political coups—was making limited investments in schooling. The government was borrowing money heavily from other governments and development banks just to stay afloat, let alone expand its social programs.

This changed in the late 1980s. International organizations concerned about long-term development in Africa believed that expanding education would help rescue countries from the poverty-debt-conflict trap. Yet there was not enough money to expand all sectors of education in all areas. So in 1988, the World Bank published an influential document laying out a suggested agenda for education in Africa: prioritize universal primary schooling.[2] Their lending practices changed in line with this recommendation. Whereas in 1978 20 percent of World Bank education lending to Africa was earmarked for primary schools and 40 percent was earmarked for higher education, by 1992 these numbers were reversed, and primary schooling received a plurality of funding dollars.[3]

Since education funding in Ghana relied heavily on global lending, the situation on the ground shifted in response. The country demonstrated the hoped-for short-term gains in literacy and primary-school completion rates. Yet a new problem was created. More and more children were reaching the final grade of primary school, while fewer were able to finish secondary school, and even fewer could find spots in Ghanaian universities, colleges, or vocational schools. The shift in policy focus resulted in an educational bottleneck, where few students were able to progress into good tertiary-school programs even as more and more young people earned their primary and secondary certificates and wanted to continue on. Thus, in 2004, only about half of all qualified prospective undergraduates in Ghana were admitted to public universities.[4]

Growing up during this time, Anna went to good primary and secondary schools in southern Ghana that retained many elements of the British colonial system. When she entered high school, students at age nine or ten took an entrance exam and applied to different secondary schools. After another two years, they took an intermediary exam, which determined the program they were admitted to, whether liberal arts, sciences, or business. After this point, their instruction focused exclusively on one of these programs. There was an identifiable hierarchy in which sciences were the most prestigious and liberal arts were the least. According to Anna, it was nearly impossible to switch tracks from arts to sciences, once placed.

Being placed on the sciences track, Anna had reason to hope for admittance to a Ghanaian medical college. However, when she finished high school there was a university-wide strike that lasted for two years, which resulted in a university admissions backlog. Getting into college at home was therefore temporarily impossible, so she traveled overseas for her baccalaureate, doing a year and a half in Spain and the rest at a school in Oklahoma City.

For a while she still hoped to return and earn her medical degree at home, but this looked increasingly unlikely. Of the two medical schools in Ghana, one would not take her because of her international degree and the other would accept students only after a "trial year." There was also corruption within the admission process: "if they knew your dad or your family somehow and they didn't like them, they would just not take you." In the end, she decided to go to a medical school in Chicago.[5]

In a classic article, sociologist Everett Hughes (1945) coined the term "master status" for identities that shape how one is perceived and how one behaves in almost every area of life. In the United States, race and gender are usually cited as examples of a master status. For transnational Ghanaians, possession of higher education tends to operate similarly. Yet education is also different from the master statuses of race and gender in that it can be achieved, while the master statuses of race and gender are for the most part ascribed. The latter are imposed upon a person as one comes into society and are very difficult to alter or manipulate. If a master status can be achieved, however, a transformation of one's identity in the direction of greater social status and a higher-class position is possible. This makes the pursuit of schooling more than just one of many possible goals. Education becomes a type of imperative for obtaining a higher social status.

I saw lots of evidence of this in how members of Evangel Ministries talked about schooling: their conversations often focused on a person's hopes to obtain an advanced degree or a person's intentions to enroll in some kind of program or prerequisite course. Being in school was seen as the goal, and being out of school was portrayed as a temporary necessity until enough money could be saved or admission into a degree-granting institution could be obtained. The members were always very curious about my own education, and always responded with praise when I mentioned my higher degrees. Through such conversations, a status distinction was upheld between those who were working toward a higher education degree and those who were working at jobs requiring little specialized skill, like driving cabs or working in retail.

The corresponding statistics are also revealing: it is estimated that one in two Africans in the United States has some postsecondary education, and roughly 30 percent of highly educated Ghanaians live and work abroad.[6] In combination with others from Nigeria and Ethiopia, and other countries of sub-Saharan Africa, the majority of this group of new blacks has at least a high-school degree, and about 35 percent have a bachelor's or higher degree.[7]

Thus, when Anna had to decide whether to return to Ghana or continue working toward a medical degree abroad, she chose the latter. It was the same choice so many of her generation made when pushed. It wasn't because she idealized life in America. It was because higher education was important enough to outweigh other considerations. If getting her education meant she had to go abroad, that's what she would do.

Yet university education in the United States often brings new challenges. The chief among these is student debt. International students are not eligible for the federally subsidized loans on which so many U.S. citizens rely. They often take out loans from family members, or from private lenders with high interest rates. After graduation, the loan payments make it necessary to stay in the United States and work. As a physician, Anna's degree came with thousands of dollars in school debt; and since she couldn't be certain to find a job in Ghana well paying and stable enough to keep up with her payments, she and Timothy continued to stay and work in Chicago. Although they talked about wanting to go back, they couldn't feasibly do so until the loans were repaid.

Turning Points

After marrying and finding jobs, Anna and Timothy had two children. They were happy to start a family, but it also further complicated things. On the one hand, even taking care of two kids was very difficult in their lives in Chicago, as Timothy explained once when I asked him if they planned to have more children. He said they would if they went back to Ghana in the next five years. "Here, though," he said, "It is just too hard to take care of kids."

"Is that because of how expensive day care is?"

"Yes, and because they need so many things, and in Ghana there is always just family around to watch them.... It's just so hard raising kids here."

At the same time, however, their kids rooted them deeper in America, because they were growing up with American lifestyles and relationships. They had American friends at preschool; and they usually ate American food, instead of the time-consuming Ghanaian stews and starches that their parents rarely had the time or energy to make. As each year passed, it would be increasingly difficult to move the kids to Ghana, a place that was home to Anna and Timothy, but foreign to their children. Having a family was thus a turning point that tied them more firmly to an identity about which they felt ambivalent.

This explained why, when I asked Anna whether it was positive experience coming abroad, she replied it was 50 percent positive, 50 percent negative. The downsides counterbalanced the benefits. Both within and outside of the migrant community, people looked at her and Timothy and saw a success story. Yet even their trajectory together, with such a seemingly positive outcome, demanded they revise their initial expectations and negotiate their identities along the way.

Jeremiah was another person who came to Chicago for education and stayed longer than planned. When I met him he had an advanced degree in theology from a Catholic university and worked as a hospital chaplain. He was also the leader of a Ghanaian Charismatic Catholic group in the city, which met on Sunday nights at a local Catholic parish to engage in rituals of expressive prayer, healing, and spiritual rejuvenation, like other associations within the Catholic Charismatic Renewal.[8]

I met Jeremiah at the hospital where he worked, and he led me to the cafeteria. He wore glasses, a dark gray suit, and a blue tie. For about an hour we talked about his life in Chicago, his role in the church, and his views on the challenges Ghanaian migrants face. Although soft-spoken at first, he revealed his passion, intelligence, and thoughtfulness as our conversation progressed.

Like Anna and Timothy, he planned to go back to Ghana but was kept in Chicago by the burden of student debt. Yet unlike them, his wife and children were in Ghana already, so more of his income could be devoted to the long-term goals of paying off the debt and returning there himself. He lived alone in an apartment near work to save on expenses; and although he tried to visit his family as often as he could, the plane ticket cost several thousand dollars he could otherwise be putting toward his debt.

This was another common way of balancing various educational, work-related, and family-related aspirations. Often, long—but it was hoped temporary—stints of family separation were necessary for the sake of maximizing resources. Sandra's story in chapter 3 demonstrated this, too, as well as Sylvia's story in chapter 5. I observed many different variations on this theme, where children would be sent from the United States to Ghana without their parents, or vice versa; where spouses and partners would live in two countries for many years; and where aunts, uncles, and grandparents were relied upon heavily.

For many of those I interviewed, the decision of whether to raise their kids in America or in Ghana was perhaps the most pivotal issue in revising their goals. In spite of the apparent educational advantages of sending their kids to U.S. high schools, many in the community were as likely to prefer to keep their children in Ghana. They didn't necessarily want to raise American children. This was both because it was more expensive and they had less help from extended family members—that was the reason Anna and Timothy cited for waiting until their return to Ghana to have more children—and because they felt American youth were often morally untethered, disrespectful to elders, and disdainful of tradition.

Reflecting this, several others I interviewed who were college age and came from wealthy families grew up with the understanding that their parents didn't want them to spend too much of their lives in the United States, and thereby become Americanized. One of them, Akosua, grew up with her grandmother in

Ghana while her parents lived in the United States. Another one, Koku, was told by his father growing up that if he got into an Ivy League school in the United States, then he could go abroad for education; otherwise he would be sent to college in Ghana.[9]

Not everyone had this option, of course; some who hoped to wait until their return to Ghana to raise kids, for example, defaulted to raising their children in the United States, as their hoped-for return became increasingly pushed back. In still other families, parents disagreed about which was best. In all these cases, however, the decision of where kids should spend their school-age years was an important one. It was a central part of the process of revising goals and negotiating their family's identity.

"They Will Know Why I Came"

As my conversation with Jeremiah continued, I learned he had also made further revisions to his goals in the years since earning his theology degree that had less to do with family aspirations and more to do with his own sense of purpose in life. While living in Chicago and taking on the leadership of the Catholic Charismatic Renewal (CCR) prayer group, he gained increasing influence as a member of the local Ghanaian community and the global CCR network.

On a weekly basis, much of his energy and passion went into this work. He referred to the CCR as the "spiritual live wire" of the Catholic Church, and described its prominence in Ghana, as part of the broader shift among Ghanaians toward Charismatic Christianity. "Ghana has taken the lead in the Charismatic movement," he explained. A group of Ghanaians recently celebrated the fortieth anniversary of the Catholic Charismatic Renewal (CCR) in his home country. There were also now prayer groups like his in many states throughout the United States.

His group in Chicago was small, but it was closely connected to CCR networks in Ghana, and the Ghanaian leadership of the CCR visited Chicago just about a week before Jeremiah and I met. That visit involved a weekend's worth of events. On Friday, they had their usual evening prayer service, to which they invited outsiders. The next day, they held a retreat from nine A.M. until two P.M., which again was open to everyone in the community. Jeremiah and the other leaders of the Chicago group also met with the visitors from Ghana on Sunday morning before the regular Mass. Then the visitors went with them to church from one to three P.M., and spoke to the whole church community during the Mass. Afterwards, they went to the parish hall for an event they called the "Breaking of the Bread." For this social event, which lasted from three to six P.M., members of the prayer group bought tickets for $10 each, and brought many of their family and friends.

Jeremiah held other roles of leadership and community organizing, too. He was involved in the development of an International Prayer Conference Line. This was a conference-call prayer meeting that took place from eight to nine every Sunday evening, when Ghanaian Charismatic Catholics from all over the world would call the conference phone number and pray together. Finally, he was a part of the Ghanaian Council of Churches, a committee of Chicago-area church leaders that met regularly to discuss ways to bring Ghanaian churches together and support them in their efforts. Beyond his pastoral role in one local Catholic community, therefore, he held positions in broader leadership networks that covered the globe and went beyond Catholicism.

Although this work was not part of his original vision in coming to the United States—that vision was simply to earn his degree and return home—Jeremiah found a new sense of purpose in his connected leadership roles, which led him to revise his understanding of his migration and his plans for the future. He felt his work with the Ghanaian Council of Churches was a meaningful way to provide support and networking for Ghanaian pastors in Chicago, as well as to bridge the gap between Ghanaians in the homeland and those who had moved abroad.

The purpose of this group, he said, "Is also to speak with one voice." In other words, the group was positioned to speak back as a unified community to issues in the homeland. For example, he had recently been suggesting to the council that they should write an annual pastoral letter that could be sent back to Ghana, and could be used to express the views of the diaspora to the churches at home on both political and spiritual issues. He explained that it would be nonpartisan but expressing general concerns.

"What sorts of things are you most concerned about?" I asked.

"There have been some abuses from clergy at home. There are people trying to take advantage, false prophecy."

He decried the problem of "uneducated" pastors who went into the ministry primarily with the goal of becoming wealthy or famous—the illegitimate "one-man churches" mentioned often as a problem in the transatlantic community. According to Jeremiah, if Ghanaian church leaders abroad could speak to these issues in order to caution people to avoid false prophets, then it was their responsibility to do so.

As someone working in a medical context, he also had concerns about the faith-healing practices of many of Ghana's new Charismatic churches. The problem, he noted, was when people would go to religious leaders before they went to the doctor, and then those leaders would pray for healing without considering if it was actually a medical case and without sending them to the doctor. "Back at home," he explained, "every problem is viewed as spiritual." He contrasted this with the way every problem in the United States is viewed in scientific and medical terms. He felt strongly that both perspectives were one-sided, on their own.

This topic carried us into another important revision of his original goals, a new aspiration tied to his experiences with both American and Ghanaian culture. He wanted to establish a pastoral center and clinic in central Ghana when he eventually returned. This clinic would merge the best of American and Ghanaian insights on healing: it would address health problems holistically, and would be an unbiased place where people could get an assessment of the best course of action combining scientific and spiritual strategies. With this clinic, he said, "I want to strike a balance between science and the spiritual."

His experience with these two contrasting perspectives on healing made him want to integrate them in practical ways to the service of his home country. This meant that while at one point his continued stay in Chicago was a concession to the restrictions of his school loans, he now saw it as an opportunity to pursue his new dream, through both networking and fundraising.

Already he had hosted several fundraisers and convinced a family to donate a plot of land around Kumasi, Ghana's second-largest city, where the center could be built. There were some inherent obstacles to overcome, however. His desire for it to be a fully unbiased center limited his options. The most ready source of funding and support would be to pursue affiliation with an established church. As a Catholic with a degree in theology, he could probably get support from the Catholic Church, or at least gain employment in the church that would support the center. But he wanted it to be a welcoming place for all types of Christians and Muslims, and having strong Catholic connections would not help in this regard. He thus had to rely on private donors or any capital he could save himself.

Another obstacle was the difficulty of asking for donations: neither Ghanaians at home nor Ghanaians abroad wanted to be asked for money. "We have all come here for money," he said, referring to those in the United States, "and people think, 'Leave us alone, don't bother us.'"

Yet if he tried to raise money back in Ghana, he noted laughingly, people would be wondering why he left the place with all the money to come back and raise money there, and would think he was not that bright. For these reasons the funds had been coming in more slowly than he hoped. Nonetheless, it was a project he was devoted to, which added an additional rationale to his continued stay in Chicago.

Toward the end of our conversation, Jeremiah showed me some evidence of this vision: his business card with the name of the center written underneath his own name. The business card was also interesting for another reason: it was two-sided. On one side was his name and contact information in the United States, with an image of an American flag underneath it. On the other side was his contact information in Ghana, with the Ghanaian flag underneath. It seemed an appropriate visual identifier for a man living within a transnational family and working within global religious networks. It was physical evidence of his dual identity.

After showing me the business card, Jeremiah said something about his intentions that stuck with me for a long time afterward: "I want to focus on getting to phase one [of fundraising] while in the United States, so when I go back, people will know why I came here."[10]

As I pondered this statement in the following days, it seemed to reveal a link between Jeremiah's personal goals and his desire to provide a rationale—to both himself and to others—for migrating abroad. The holistic health center was a narrative that made sense of his sacrifices, supporting his own resolve and giving his move to the United States legitimacy in the eyes of their community. Early on in our conversation I would have guessed his rationale for being in the United States was based on education and improving his family's life. By the end, though, I saw how it had developed into something bigger than that. I also saw how this development was important for him in explaining his migration to himself and to others in his extended family and community.

As noted in chapter 3, the migrant community exerts social control on fellow newcomers in the United States to be successful, not only for their own sake but also for the sake of the wider group. People at home in Ghana expect those abroad to come back with meaningful and important accomplishments, and to use these things to enrich the lives of others. If a migrant or returnee is viewed as unsuccessful in this sense, then the value of their migration can be doubted.

The pressure to succeed is felt through the kind of gossip that Benjamin and Sandra talked about as a barrier to trust between migrants. Franklin, the young, recent arrival who—though religious—avoided Ghanaian churches altogether, complained about this pressure to succeed and be "this unique group." He was tired of the implied messages within the community that new blacks had to prove they were a "model minority."

There is also a wider debate over whether the millions who have left Ghana are doing right by their communities. I observed this debate play out vividly in some online discussions on websites dedicated to Ghanaian diaspora issues, where people's views were less restrained than they might be in person. Many comments reflected the intense pressure that migrants feel from their sending communities, and the worry that those in the homeland feel about losing their best and brightest to the United States and Europe.

One posted article talked about an upcoming event hosted by the Ghanaian National Council—the community organization that organizes the Ghanafest each summer, described in chapter 2—as well as other social events throughout the year. In response to the article, one reader bluntly posted, "I think you guys should come home and develop your motherland."

Another responder, after discussing how important it was that people of different ethnic groups get along with each other at these social functions, posted:

> As for you retired Ghanaians, when are you going home to Ghana? Are you afraid of the lack of serious medical care there or what? You are still dying here and in Canada at ages 60, 70 or 80 years old. While some in Ghana, make it to 100 or more, despite not having a massive, medical complex. Oh, about me, the US will be only be a 3 week vacation spot for me... starting this year and thereafter![11]

Another very heated discussion took place concerning a prominent member of the Chicago Ghanaian community who had recently been cited by a local city paper as one of the most influential African Americans in Chicago. The article had lauded him for his philanthropic work in both Chicago in Ghana, and many comments were then posted, praising him for being a shining example for the Ghanaian diaspora. Yet other posted comments were critical, calling into question whether his motivations were truly noble, and chastising him for staying in Chicago and marrying a non-Ghanaian.

One critic posted: "This 'professor' is never proud of Ghana. This hidden agenda to reach the top has a very weak foundation and soon he will come toppling down in shame. Find out if he is on good terms with his biological family." Another followed up on this, asserting, "We all know this con man. If in doubt reply and I'll give you the contacts of his sister in Ghana, his brothers in Japan, and half-sibling in Accra and they will confirm what an arrogant crook he is."[12]

These critics claimed he failed to care appropriately for his family and to be "proud of Ghana," and this failure far overshadowed the critics' respect for his personal accomplishments. Although plenty of others responded to these comments by saying that the critics were just envious of his success, no one questioned the underlying principle: that successful Ghanaians abroad should both remit money to their families and contribute to the development of the country more generally.

For Jeremiah, the holistic health clinic was an answer to this question of whether his migration would be a good thing for himself and for his homeland. If he were able to accomplish it, there would be no doubt as to why he went abroad. Further, the way Jeremiah identified himself in his language, clothing, and business cards showed how his aspirations for his life and his identity were intertwined. What he wanted to do—establish a clinic in Ghana that brought together the best aspects of American and Ghanaian approaches to health—reflected how he viewed himself in relation to Ghana and America. His vision for an unbiased and holistic treatment center linked his Ghanaian background and his American experience, and it identified him—as his business card did visually—with both societies.

Nationality, Ethnicity, and Race

These stories have dealt primarily with the question of whether and how much Ghanaians in the United States want to become "Americanized," both as individuals and as families, and how such choices are connected to revisions of their initial aspirations. Yet the relevant dimensions of identity formation are also more complex than a single Ghanaian versus American binary. For Ghanaians, nationality, ethnicity, and race are distinct rather than corresponding domains of belonging. Identification with each of these collectivities governs different aspects of their lives, and identities must be negotiated when and if they come into conflict.

In particular, ethnicity and nationality are not the same thing. Ethnicity is a category of belonging to one of a number of linguistic and cultural groupings, such as the Akans, Gas, or Ewes. For those I interviewed, ethnicity could influence aspects of how they married, formed families, and engaged in rituals surrounding meaningful life course events, such as birth, death, and transitioning to adulthood. Ethnic identity was also connected to one's home region, since these linguistic and cultural groups remain concentrated in certain geographical areas. Some research also suggests that ethnically charged regionalism plays a role in Ghanaian national politics.[13]

In transitioning abroad, my interviewees varied in how much importance they placed on such identities. As mentioned in chapter 2, in Chicago there were cultural associations for each of the major subgroups—Asantes/Akans, Gas, Ewes, and others—under the umbrella of the Ghana National Council. Yet most of Evangel Ministries' members were not involved in such groups. They tended to avoid cultural associations, both those connected to the Ghanaian national identity and those connected to ethno-linguistic identities.

David, who was the choir director at Evangel Ministries for much of the latter part of my involvement there, was a good example of this. He was my guide during my first Ghanafest, as described in chapter 2, whom I asked about the traditional dances there. He was the one whom Elijah teasingly suggested wouldn't know about the dances because he was too Americanized. David thus fit into the category of those who did not tend to pursue new relationships with others in the migrant community. He was happy with a more diverse set of social connections established through his degree program and his religious life. "If not for

Evangel," he told me once, "I would be in the dark on the Ghanaian community in Chicago."[14]

There were, however, ways in which David remained connected to his Ghanaian identity, and aspects of his ethno-linguistic identity still played a role in his life. David was one of the first Ghanaians I met who alternately used his Ghanaian name—Kofi—and his "Christian" name, David. It took me a while to catch on to this, which meant for the first few weeks at Evangel I couldn't figure out which was his "actual" name. Yet I soon learned that Ghanaians are typically given one name at birth that often reflects the day on which they were born; for example, *Kofi* means, "born on Friday." They are then given a Christian name drawn from the English and/or biblical lexicon. As they become adults, choosing which one to use more often can be a meaningful signifier of how they position themselves in relation to their Ghanaian identity. In David's case, his tendency to alternate regularly between them, depending on the social setting or context he was in, conveyed a playful but also strategic attitude toward the two sides of his experience.

There is another aspect to this as well, which was that one's traditional name also reveals one's ethno-linguistic group. Although many of these groups share the habit of naming children after the day of the week on which they were born, the names are usually spelled or pronounced slightly differently across groups. Thus, when David went by Kofi, other Ghanaians also knew he was an Ashanti (the largest of the Akan groups) whose parents spoke *Twi*, and whose people came from the central region.

In David's case, though, it was also even more complicated than that, because while his mother was Ashanti, his father was Ewe. His fiancée and later wife, Amanda, also came from a mixed family: her father was Ashanti and her mother was Ewe. Being from mixed families themselves, their different ethno-linguistic backgrounds weren't an obstacle to getting married, but the situation did bring some logistical challenges, as he explained to me one day at choir rehearsal. The Ashantis were matrilineal, but the Ewes were patrilineal; and across their two families there were those in their parents' generation who still held closely to these traditions.

At their wedding, for example, David's maternal uncle announced during his toast that he considered David his heir, and if his own son wanted anything he would have to go through David first. David took it in stride, not contradicting him at the time. In practical terms, however, David and Amanda adopted a more Western model of family formation and responsibility, even as they symbolically tried to appease certain members of the older generation.[15]

This example indicated some more general points about ethno-linguistic identity. Everyone was usually aware of where they and others belonged, since this was suggested by basic cues like names and regions of birth. Some among the older generations held onto certain cultural practices associated with these identities as well. Yet these identities were rarely primary; and when they competed with other domains of identity, their associated rules were often adapted in certain ways, as with David and Amanda's marriage and family life.

However, the challenges of negotiating racial categories in the United States were much more complicated, as shown in other research on recent black immigrants. On the one hand, some studies find a disjuncture between national identities—that is, Jamaican, Cuban, Nigerian, and so on—and the meaning of being black in America. Assertions of national identity can at times be used as a protection against identification with race and classification as African American (Waters 1999). Still other studies, however, show a counterimpulse to embrace an Afrocentric identity and reclaim blackness as a unifying heritage. From this perspective, "Afrocentrism maintains that because of its African genetic, spiritual, and cultural origins, blackness possesses an essential and immutable nature that transcends time, place, and all other axes of identity" (Abrams 2014, 8). Becoming black in the transition to the United States can therefore provide a new place of belonging, and a footing upon which to resist the hegemonic definitions of white culture.

In my own research, I observed a mixture of these two impulses. There were many who resisted being grouped with African Americans, particularly because of the implicit association with poverty and criminality. As recounted earlier, Anna described how strange it was for her to see poverty-stricken black urban neighborhoods for the first time; Franklin described the pressure within the community to maintain a sense of "uniqueness" in contrast to other blacks and immigrants; and many times at Evangel Ministries, public prayers over children focused on keeping them safe from the influence of gang culture, drugs, and other dangers associated with the urban underclass.

Yet there were also some who embraced an Afrocentric identity over time, often by coming to view African American political and economic issues as their own concern. Sylvia, for example, was raised by her Ghanaian aunt in a primarily African American congregation, had a diverse group of friends in college—both American and non-American blacks included—and later pursued a master's degree in social work. She had a strong awareness of racial injustice in the United States and focused much of her career on combating it, as a counselor in low-income schools. Her husband was a filmmaker, writing and directing films about politics, race, and social issues. The church they attended was deeply involved in social activism, focused on issues of racial equality and reconciliation.

Another member of Evangel Ministries, Anthony, regularly talked and posted articles on his Facebook page about the racial bias in the American criminal justice system, particularly following the shooting of black teenager Michael Brown by a white police officer in Ferguson, Missouri, in 2014. Although he was perhaps the most vocal on these issues of anyone I met, there were many times during and following my research at Evangel Ministries when the Facebook pages of my contacts in the community were filled with similar expressions of fear and concern over injustices toward blacks in America.

The balancing act of living between Ghanaian society, white America, and black America is well illustrated in the story of one young man, Jonathan, whom I interviewed while he was an undergraduate at an elite college. If being black in America has long been associated with the double consciousness described by W. E. B. DuBois (1906), as a condition of living between two worlds and being forced to see oneself through the eyes of a dominant culture, then being Ghanaian *and* black in America involves an additional layer of awareness of difference, based on being foreign. Although quite young, Jonathan was already adept at working through the contradictions and challenges of the double consciousness and in crafting a hybrid identity.

Jonathan was born in Ghana, and when he was very young his father moved to New York City, settling in the Bronx. A few years later, when Jonathan was ten, he and his mother and brothers joined his father. His parents worked long hours in poorly paying jobs, and his father was a pastor of a Ghanaian congregation. During these years the family was mostly embedded in relationships with other Ghanaians, and their life revolved around the Ghanaian church. When Jonathan wasn't in school or helping take care of his younger siblings, he was at church serving alongside his parents.

"Their closest friends were church members, and that was pretty much it. I would say ninety-nine percent were Ghanaians. The church was small to medium, between sixty and ninety people. I was learning how to play the piano to be involved more in the church. . . . So I was getting to that time where I had to pick up some responsibilities in the church, but I never got to the stage where, now you have to lead worship, or be part of the choir or sing, because I was still kind of young."

Shortly afterward, however, their lives were disrupted when his parents divorced. He was understandably hesitant to talk about this topic when I asked him to tell me more about the situation.

"It had to do with domestic issues, domestic violence, fighting with the church elders, those sort of issues," he said vaguely. He also said their divorce was due in part to the strains of their lives as immigrants. This echoed Sylvia's description of her aunt's divorce described in chapter 3, as something resulting from the pressure of living abroad.

Since his father was a pastor, the divorce also resulted in rifts within the church. His parents both left the church, and his father went on to start a new congregation of his own. Jonathan and his brothers stayed with their mother, who had to work even harder to support them through multiple minimum-wage jobs. Jonathan took on new responsibility for himself and his brothers. Like many firstborn sons of single mothers, he developed a sense of independence and responsibility far beyond most of his peers.

"My mother has had a lot to worry about," he said, "so usually for me I take care of myself and I try to help out my younger brothers. I worked over the summer but not during school. Which meant my mom had to work a lot."

During this time Jonathan's social universe shifted considerably. Because of her lack of time and the painful history, his mother didn't become involved in another religious congregation for many years. Many of her friendships to other Ghanaians in the community also weakened and her social networks became very limited, even up to the time when Jonathan was in college. Probing further into this part of the story, I asked him, "Who are your mother's closest friends?"

"I don't know if she actually has one. Cause she's been so involved in the household, she had to either take care of us or go to work, so I think because even within the church, she's moved around so many times that she's never had that set person, long-term person. Maybe another place she might have a good friend might be at work, she's a home health aide, so maybe when she was involved in the training program, she forged some friendships. Also, there are some people from her hometown back in Ghana who live in the area and who she speaks to regularly and is friendly with; but I don't know the extent to which she feels like she's actually close to them. So she always tells me, 'being the oldest, you're my everything, you're my son, you're my husband, you're my best friend.'"

The divorce also meant they moved to a new neighborhood, which was mostly black but diverse in terms of nationality. Living in this new area brought Jonathan into closer contact with black American culture, and he drifted away from his Ghanaian identity in his early teen years. "There weren't a lot of Ghanaians in that neighborhood, more Jamaicans. I played soccer with a Jamaican team. So from then until high school . . . I felt like I was losing my Ghanaian identity. Because I was learning French back in Ghana, and then I lost it in high school, and my native language, *Twi*, I pretty much lost it as well until I got to high school. And my parents were always working. So there wasn't any Ghanaian heritage that we lived by in the household."

Meanwhile, the independence he developed as the first son of a single mother helped him do well in school. He was a motivated student, and with very little encouragement he applied and was admitted to a high-quality magnet high school in Manhattan. "My mom had nothing to do with it, I just chose that school. That's maybe one part of the story, that my parents have never been involved in my education. Back in Ghana they definitely were growing up, but now it's more that I do the whole thing, they obviously do care whether I do well or not, but most of the time it has been me just taking the initiative."

The magnet school opened up new opportunities for him. While there he was encouraged to apply to the best colleges and seek out scholarships for low-income international students. The school was also fairly diverse. There was even a small group of other Ghanaians at that school who reconnected him with his Ghanaian identity.

"When I got to high school, I met a group of Ghanaians and that was my first time that I actually started enjoying speaking the language, and feeling comfortable about myself, about being Ghanaian. We found joy in playing soccer, and we hung out and I still speak to some of them. So it helped me come to the conclusion that I am Ghanaian and I should be proud of it. And then from there it's picked up, and I love doing it."

Throughout his early school years, then, Jonathan lived between Ghanaian culture and a broader Afrocentric culture, alternately living out one more than the other depending on his immediate social context. Moving on to an elite college, however, added a new element to his experience: being a minority in a predominantly white environment. Although he arrived feeling proud of his accomplishments and hopeful for his future, a racially charged incident between white and black students in his first semester opened his eyes to a new reality.

"I remember the racial incident happened... when I had just arrived and I had the romantic view of the college, that I would come here and I would basically escape from everything I knew.... I'm away from the ghetto, the hood, everything else ... so it was kind of like heaven in my head. And then that racial incident happened and I was like, oh my god, it's not a perfect world. It's one thing to kind of know about racism and hear people talk about it ... and it's another thing to actually live it and see it happening around you."

Quickly his blackness became something he had to think about daily. "Once that happened, especially during the evening when I would go to my TA session or anything, walking back to my dorm I was actually watching my back, like every couple of seconds. And it wasn't something I had to think about, I would just look behind me. Some of my black friends I spoke to also had the same kind of feeling."

The incident opened up the possibility that something similar would happen to him—he could now be the target of hostility because of a physical trait he could not change. He could not work hard enough to eliminate the possibility. In fact, he was learning as he advanced through his education that the harder he worked, the more likely it was he would find himself in settings where his blackness was out of place.

Meanwhile, he found it harder to establish a supportive community with the few other Ghanaian students there. They were generally from higher-class families, and many of them had never lived in the United States until coming to college. They did not share Jonathan's experience of growing up Ghanaian in a black multinational neighborhood in the Bronx. For them, their Ghanaian identity was never in question—they were in America temporarily for college and would certainly return to Ghana after graduating. Although they were of the same nationality, these students and Jonathan had divergent experiences owing to their different class positions and migration histories.

Jonathan did, however, connect with a wider array of African students through his involvement in an African student organization. This seemed to reinforce the broader Afrocentric side of his identity. He also had a meaningful off-campus service-trip experience just a few months before we talked, which helped him think more about where he fit in relation to the social categories surrounding him: white, black, Ghanaian, African, African American, immigrant, and so on.

In this program, he explained, "You have a group of students live with an immigrant family, and my family was Rwandan, and I heard about their history and their culture, I taught them about myself, they learned about my Ghanaian heritage as well. And for me, having an immigration background, it was basically living my life in a different light. When I stepped back, I got to better understand that there are a lot of racial dynamics that I was definitely not used to."

Interacting with others from Africa who were both similar to and different from him helped him think more clearly about what he was experiencing at college as a black African student. As part of the program he wrote several essays reflecting on his experience, and he described some of his conclusions to me in vivid terms.

"One way that I've come to picture it is that I am a second-generation Ghanaian, not first; also, the best way I can picture it is if you can take a blank sheet of paper and you put a dot on it, and that dot represents my American experience and it's slowly expanding, but then in the background it represents my Ghanaian side. So ultimately I am Ghanaian but becoming more and more American. And even within that dot expanding it's a mixture of black America and coming here to college and experiencing white America."

The image showed how he negotiated his identity, not along a one-dimensional line but within a two-dimensional plane. The dot expanded across the background, but even then it had more than one shade. There was room for more than two categories—that is, black versus white, immigrant versus native. Even white America became part of who he was through his education and the ties he formed in school. And all of this was reflected in his goals for his life—his visions—that he hoped would both capitalize on and reinforce the different sides of his identity.

For example, he volunteered frequently in ways that expressed his unique strengths. "I'm the treasurer for the African Student organization, and for some time I was also involved in the Black Student Union. I was part of the committee for the alumni relations, so I keep in touch with our alumni. I'm also involved in tutoring high school students on Tuesday evenings."

He further participated in a program whereby current students talk to incoming freshman about diversity, "discussing issues about race, gender, and all that sort of thing." And he was looking to do more such work in different contexts. "I am thinking about doing a program over summer where I would be able to teach in Kenya for two months, June and July . . . and I'm also talking to the headmaster at the school that I went to when I was younger to see if I could come and teach there in the month of August. So that would give me a chance to go back to Ghana." As for after college, he was still working that out. He was originally a pre-med student, but his experiences made him aware of new interests and strengths, so he was starting to lean more toward going to graduate school and doing research.

He did know what kind of environment he would find ideal to settle in: "A small city, not as big as New York City. As long as I can have something like that, where I can still practice my Ghanaian heritage and see people that are like me, but then it's diverse, I'm definitely okay with that. As long as it's not just me in a really different environment."

For him, settling permanently in Ghana was not the goal, even though his mother planned to go back as soon as her kids were settled. While his mother looked forward to a day when she could return home to her familiar Ghanaian social universe, Jonathan had started looking for something different. He wanted a lifestyle in which he could enact his Ghanaian side at times but also interact with people with diverse heritages.[16]

The range of his involvements and ambitions thus suggested a desire to pursue simultaneously his connections to the place where he was born and his adopted black identity. If identity reflects relationships, and people also actively seek out certain social settings and relationships that reflect their desired identities, then Jonathan's choices about extracurricular activities and social engagements, and his developing goals for the future, were central aspects of his own identity negotiation process.

The Embeddedness of Identity

These personal narratives show what many sociologists have argued: that identity is embedded in social networks and interactions. Scholars have shown this to be true in diverse social settings, from higher education (Lehmann 2014), to political party mobilization (Xu 2013; Auyero 2000), to immigrant cultural and religious associations (Biney 2011, 2007; Rudrappa 2004). Each of these stories have demonstrated this point, with a particular emphasis on how changes in social networks—such as Benjamin's new relationship with Jeannette, or Jonathan's move to a new high school with new classmates—were connected to shifts in identity.

Each of these narratives also subtly demonstrate the role of personal trust in this process. The relationships that mattered for their identities were characterized by personal trust. Otherwise, why would these ties matter for how they identified? Why would people in general engage in rituals with certain others, or see themselves through their eyes, if they did not trust them?

Charles Tilly (2005) makes this point clear when he states that, "individual and collective dispositions result from interpersonal transactions" (7); and later he defines "networks of identity and trust" as "sets of social ties providing collective answers to the questions, 'Who are you?' 'Who are we?' and 'Who are they?'" (57). By definition, such networks "grow up from a wide variety of activities" (57)—that is, they are grounded in social behaviors. If we want to understand, therefore, how a particular migrant or a group of migrants negotiate their identities in different settings over time, we have to look at their major relationships of trust and the activities associated with those relationships.

This chapter, therefore, took a slight shift in perspective away from religion and toward more general relational processes that shape identities and goals. It was important to underscore this general sociological insight in order to support the argument made in the next chapter: that these Ghanaians' religious memberships not only reflected their identities and concerns but also had the power to change them. Church friends joined the ranks of family members, classmates, neighbors, and romantic partners, as people who mattered for how Ghanaian Christians saw themselves and where they were going in life; and this was perhaps the best evidence that they were together engaged in the imaginative and symbolic activity of personal trust.

7

The Nature of Faith

BETWEEN BELIEVING AND BELONGING

THE IMAGINATIVE AND symbolic activity of trusting others is, as Georg Simmel (1955) describes it, like a religious "leap of faith." It is a step into the unknown, into the uncertainty of what another will or will not do, that not only interprets but also *imagines* certain cues as assurance of security. In one essay, Simmel reveals just how important he thinks this religious-like faith is: "That, in the face of reasonable proof to the contrary, we still can retain our faith in an individual is one of the strongest of the ties that bind society" (9).

The analogy between trusting others and religious faith goes both ways. The Simmel quote, in fact, comes from his essay on religion, and is immediately followed by the statement, "This faith, now, is of a most positive religious character." Simmel argues that the types of rituals and relationships we usually view as "religious" are not some kind of distinct phenomenon but, rather, the culmination or concentration of certain general social experiences. Even the most complex doctrines and moral prescriptions echo more general experiences of connection and cooperation; and as such, connection and cooperation can be understood to express aspects of social life with correlates in religion.

Put more concretely, this means that the imaginative muscles people exercise when trusting others are in a sense the same ones they use to believe in God or the gods, religious meta-narratives, moral guidelines, and religious organizations and institutions. This idea of faith as an imaginative muscle, which develops through regular use and social reinforcement, is vividly described in Tanya Luhrmann's (2012) study of American Evangelicals and their pursuit of intimate relationships with God. Her interviewees often talked about creating pictures of God or Jesus in their mind as an embodied, present being, chatting informally with them over coffee or accompanying them through everyday errands. They also relied on others in the community to support them through this process, and they shared tips and strategies for how best to practice these imaginative and intimate experiences—how to make space for God to "show up" (281).

This activity assumes similar risks as those present in any interdependent exchange with another human being: God might *not* show up, or it might not go as expected. In these examples, therefore, the faith required is more than an attestation of God's existence or of certain ideas about supernatural reality. It is an activation of their belief that puts them in a dependent position in relation to God. It is a belief *in*, as much as a belief *that*. It is the side of faith that is expressed as trust.

The trust networks that transnational migrants from Ghana find through religious memberships can be seen in a similar light. In many of the stories I heard in Ghana, becoming part of a new Charismatic organization started with human connections. For Daniel, it was a classmate at school; for Ama, it was the pastor with whom she had a special relationship; for John, it was the pastor who visited his house and invested in his musical education. This was true in the stories from Chicago as well: for Sandra, her husband's ties connected her to the church; for Benjamin, it was a fellow taxi driver who invited him in; for Elijah, it was a phone call from a close friend and former classmate that brought him into the new church project.

In each of these cases, the personal connection to a religious group (a newfound belonging) over time resulted in deepening religious commitment (a newfound believing). Scholars have identified similar processes across diverse religious and social movements, from the rise of communist activist organizations in China (Xu 2013) to the historical rise of Christianity itself as a dominant religious force (Stark 1996). In the case of most Charismatic Evangelical Ghanaians, however, greater religious commitment following integration into a church community didn't usually take the form of "conversion," if *conversion* is defined as a change in what they believe about God or spiritual realities. Most of them would have attested to the existence of God and basic Christian teachings before their religious transformations. Rather, the heightening of their religious commitment took the form of intensified belief *in* God and Christianity. In other words, it involved increasing degrees of trust in those beliefs. It was shown in their greater willingness to act in line with Evangelical principles and put themselves in a dependent position relative to both God and others in the community.

When this happened it had consequences for the processes described in chapter 6: the reenvisioning of their goals and negotiation of their identities. This was shown already in Jeremiah's story: after coming to the United States for a degree, getting a job, and sending his family back home to Ghana while he worked to pay off his school loans, he become increasingly invested in the Catholic Charismatic Renewal movement and in the Ghanaian Council of

Churches in Chicago. Because of his work with those groups, his time in the United States became about more than earning a degree and financial security. It was tied to larger spiritual projects, and a belief in the greater meaning of his time living in the United States.

These new goals, and his developing identity as someone bridging American and Ghanaian society to the benefit of others—vividly illustrated by his two-sided business card—were impossible to separate from his church-based relationships. His connections in the global Catholic Charismatic community and the network of Ghanaian church leaders in Chicago sustained his imagination for the future and his view of himself as a bridge builder, rather than someone simply trapped between familiar and foreign societies.

In this chapter I tell similar stories of how this process works. I focus first on the transformations that often followed becoming embedded in a religious community, whether in a migrant or a nonmigrant congregation. I then show how revisions of aspirations and identities in turn resulted from those religious transformations. I describe how many of my informants became more committed to religious belief after becoming involved in Evangel Ministries and other similar congregations; how their deepening religious commitments led them to make choices about their professional and personal lives they likely would not have made otherwise; and how those commitments led them to negotiate dual and/or conflicting categories of membership by rooting their own identities primarily in religion, and thereby transcending categories of ethnicity, nationality, and race.

The Charismatic Transformation, Revisited

As noted earlier, Benjamin was not very religious before moving abroad. In the years he was growing up in Ghana and attending the university, he would sometimes go to church on Sundays, but only because it was the thing to do with his family. According to him, he was not serious about it for himself, and his lifestyle reflected this, particularly his involvement in visa fraud while working at the tourism board, as described in chapter 3. "I would just impress you, then rob you." He shook his head, remembering that time, during one of our conversations.

He said that now, after coming to the church, he often prayed for forgiveness for his past actions. He even wondered at times whether some of his postmigration disappointments were necessary punishment for these former sins.

I asked him to talk more about how things changed for him.

"You mean, my transformation?" He asked.

I nodded.

"Hardship can force you to accept certain things."

At a certain point, he said, he realized he needed to change. He needed to tame his lifestyle—less drinking and partying—spend more time at church, give more to others, and pursue God.

This decision, he explained, was made with the help of the community at Evangel Ministries. When he first visited there, he was at a low point, having just been forced to drop out of the master's program that brought him to the United States. He was invited to visit by Kodjo, a man I also knew from the church, whom he initially met at Ghanafest in 2009. Benjamin didn't immediately accept Kodjo's invitation, but he did give him his phone number. Kodjo kept calling him, so finally he agreed to go.

"I liked the place, but wasn't that regular at first . . . but eventually I started to go regularly." After this initial hesitance, the "love of the people," which he described in chapter 5, led him to be a more regular attender.

I then asked him: "What do you think are the most important things that the church does for you?"

Sensing I might be hinting at material resources of some kind, he replied: "The church cannot give me money. Rather, it gives me some sense of belonging. I have made a lot of friends . . . and it can provide people to confide in."

"Who there are you able to confide in?"

"Mostly I will just talk to Kodjo." This fit with what I had seen—Benjamin spent a lot of time with Kodjo and his family. He treated Kodjo's kids like his own niece and nephew.

He then talked about a change in his outlook: "I am able to accept life the way it is. . . . It is hard to describe, because sometimes these things are very emotional, but I am now able to relate to life on a much more mature and optimistic note. I used to be very cynical, when things would not play out the way I wanted them to. Now I can meet people at church who are doing very well, but went through even worse things than I did in the past, and so I am encouraged." In this way, his newfound sense of belonging in the church led him to believe in better things for himself and his future.

I then asked: "Who would you go to if you had to make an important decision about work?"

"I would probably go to the guy in church that works for Deloitt, since he is quite successful in the field that I want to go into. He knows what recruiters are looking for."

I nodded—I knew the person.

"Would you ever consider going anywhere in the States other than Chicago?"

"Frankly I would not want to move. . . . I haven't really experienced anywhere else."

"If you did have to move, would you look for another Evangel Ministries there?"

"Yes, or another Charismatic church," he said decisively. Thus, after just nine months of being part of such a congregation, he now considered it an essential part of making life work, no matter where he ended up.

As noted in chapter 6, when I saw Benjamin again many years later, he was in fact planning a move out of state. He was married to Jeannette, the American woman he met in his apartment building. He was also finishing a degree in information technology and no longer driving a taxi. He brought Jeannette into the circle of Evangel Ministries, and the two of them received weekly marriage counseling from Elijah and Catherine. They both told me separately that this counseling was essential for figuring out how to make their cross-cultural marriage work. They were sad to leave Evangel, because it had become home to them. Arguably, without the renewed sense of optimism Benjamin developed in the context of the community there, he might not have been able to deal as well with the changes to his original goals, or to readjust his goals so successfully.

Benjamin's transformation thus involved several changes. The first change was the social one: the way his inner circle—his closest, most trusted friends—became populated by other members of Evangel Ministries in Chicago. The second change was the self-described "transformation" in his religious commitment and personal outlook. This wasn't a conversion into a new religion, since he always believed the basic tenets of Christianity. It was, rather, a change in how much religious ideals influenced his day-to-day life. As a result, he found a new sense of optimism that somehow, even though his time in the United States hadn't worked out as he planned, it would all turn out okay.

Others in the community had similar stories. Timothy talked about how he was less interested in collective religious practice as a teenager in Ghana and as a university student in the United States. He referred to himself at that time as a "knucklehead," who didn't realize the importance of faith. He also noted, too, that before coming to Evangel's Chicago branch, "any church I attended before, I didn't enjoy as much." In the trajectory of his narrative, coming to enjoy the Chicago congregation and smartening up about his faith were connected.[1]

Likewise, Sandra's religious life before coming to Evangel Ministries "wasn't very serious," she noted. "I would just go to church on Sundays and that's it." After marrying an Evangel Ministries pastor, and thereby getting deeply connected within Evangel's transnational networks, she felt a renewed interest in religion, however. This came through her dual appreciation for Evangel Ministries' welcoming atmosphere and its emphasis on spiritual growth.

She explained, "When you find yourself in a lazy environment, even if you are a hard worker, you will just get more lazy, but when you find yourself in a hard-working environment, then you will start working harder. At Evangel, they know how to work with you, they approach you, they bring you in."

Later in the same conversation, she said: "When I first came, I heard the pastor's wife teaching Sunday School, and I thought, 'Wow, you can't be here and be growing backward.' Then I heard the pastor teach, and I had never experienced teaching like that."[2]

From Sandra's perspective there was a difference between being a Christian who attends on Sundays and being "serious" and "hard-working." Transitioning from the former to the latter involved a deepened concern with spiritual growth, and more time and energy expended in the work of the church. It involved an increasing faith *in* her existing religion, rather than a change in faith *that* one or another religious teaching was true.

Reimagining the Journey

In many of these stories, the most common effect of religious membership on migrants' goals and decisions was simply enhancing their will to persist on their journey in spite of setbacks. Sandra put this the most bluntly of anyone, when she said the only reason why her husband allowed her to continue to stay in Chicago apart from him, with a new baby on the way, was that there was an Evangel Ministries branch there where she could go for support. Jeremiah, in chapter 6, also seemed willing to stay longer in the United States because of the new visions he developed through his church work, in spite of also living across an ocean from his spouse and children. Having a network of trusting relationships at church made a huge difference when they debated whether their current situation was endurable.

There were also moments, however, when enhanced religious belonging and believing after migration led people to fully abandon their original projects and start new ones, taking a major left turn and reimagining the purpose of their lives in the United States. The story of Evangeline and her husband followed this pattern.

When I first came to Evangel Ministries in Chicago, the musical portion of the Sunday service was a minimalist affair. After the opening prayers, a woman took the microphone from Elijah on the stage and led the group to sing along with recorded praise music. The lyrics were projected onto a screen to her right. We usually sang about four or five songs, ranging in tempo from bouncy, bass-driven anthems to swaying, melodic ballads.

Yet even though the implements were humble, the woman leading us, Evangeline, was full of passion. During bridges, breaks, or pauses between songs, she would riff freely with her hand raised and her eyes closed. Her voice would tremble with emotion. She was a soft-spoken woman in any other setting, but on the stage she had a compelling presence. The congregation stood, raised their hands, closed their eyes, and sang for all their worth right along with her. I remember one Sunday morning in particular, when the last song faded out, she started to preach spontaneously, giving a message to the congregation about pursuing God and being saved. She repeated several times over, "You can be saved!" The congregation reacted by clapping and affirming her: "Amen!" They said in response.[3]

I was drawn to Evangeline because of my own background in music, which seemed a ready way to make a connection. I introduced myself after a service several weeks after I started attending. When I said I also enjoyed singing and playing the piano, she immediately invited me to be part of the choir. I agreed, took her number, and starting going to rehearsals and singing with the group that very weekend.

As choir leader, Evangeline picked the songs for the week and emailed them to everyone in advance of rehearsal. Often, however, rehearsal was rescheduled or our plan was readjusted at the last minute. The very first weekend I participated, we were supposed to meet that Saturday afternoon. In the middle of the week I received a call from Evangeline, who told me that David—also a choir member at that time—was out of town and wouldn't be back in time. She decided we would therefore meet and rehearse before the service on Sunday at eight o'clock in the morning. Yet that Sunday, it was closer to nine before anyone arrived. We then found the building was locked, which was a periodic problem because we were renting a shared space in a performing arts center. Our rehearsal that weekend thus took place an hour before church in David's car.

This unpredictability produced a camaraderie, as we worked to solve such logistical challenges and find time for the choir work in the midst of members' busy, irregular schedules. I received many similar midweek calls from Evangeline about how the plan for the weekend had changed again. This also meant there were lots of opportunities to get to know each other better, when we were waiting on various delays and there was nothing to do but chat.

Evangeline lived in Chicago for about six or seven years before we met. Her home was in a high-rise apartment on the North Side of the city with her husband and one seven-year-old daughter, Sally. Sally also had interest in music, and was taking piano lessons and attending an arts-focused magnet school. When we met for rehearsal on Saturdays or on Sunday mornings before church, Sally was usually there, reading or helping with church setup. She rarely said much, though she was always observing. I sometimes wondered what her personality was like when she was at school with her peers. Was she more talkative there? Was that a place where she felt free to be herself, an American girl from Chicago, rather than at her mother's church of foreigners speaking *Twi* or heavily accented English? Or, was it the other way around?

One afternoon, Evangeline and I met at a bookstore café. We talked about music and about her life story as Sally read a Beverly Cleary book next to us. Evangeline was excited to tell me about her new project, a studio recording of original worship songs. She knew another Ghanaian in town who had a small home studio, and she was working with him to produce the record. She found out I had some past experience in writing and recording music, so during the first part of our conversation she asked me questions and discussed her own plans and ideas.

We then talked about how she and her husband came to Chicago. They were married in Ghana before either of them moved abroad. Her husband went first to Denmark for a master's degree, and then decided to move to Chicago at the urging of his brother. Evangeline explained that it was before the economy went bad, in reference to the 2008 recession. Her husband came to the United States hoping to find a position as a professional engineer, but was unsuccessful. Instead he found work teaching community college classes in earth science, math, and statistics.

When Evangeline later came to join him, she had a student visa to study business. Eventually they were awarded diversity visas through the "green card lottery," as she described it. She found a job working for an agency that surveyed urban areas and produced reports on environmental contamination in Chicago. Thus, both she and her husband found jobs, but not what they considered meaningful professions.

While we were talking about their experience, Sally tugged on her sleeve. "Mom, I'm hungry," she said.

Evangeline nodded and turned to me. "Can I go up and get her something?"

"Of course!"

When they came back from the counter, Sally had a cookie with a scoop of ice cream on top of it, and a big smile on her face. She squirmed back into her chair and started eating.

"Is she your only child?" I asked. I assumed so because I had never met any others at our many rehearsals and Sunday services.

Evangeline shook her head. "We have another one, who is also a girl."

Her eleven-year-old daughter lived with a friend in Ghana, "who is close, almost like a family member," she said.

"Have you been back there recently to see her?"

"No, I have not been back since we moved. But my husband was back there for a visit recently."

Her demeanor turned more melancholy with this topic, and I fumbled for something empathetic to say. "So do you miss Ghana very much?"

"Of course!" She said in her gentle way, laughing a bit.

She explained that although it wasn't easy to be separated from her daughter, it was the best decision they could make. As Jeremiah, Anna, and Timothy had all said, it was much more expensive to raise children in the United States. Evangeline and her husband worked hard just to send their younger child to a good school in the city and afford a two-bedroom apartment. There were also strong norms of relying on extended kin support for raising children in Ghana, so Evangeline found it more practical to leave her older daughter there with a trusted friend.

I looked again at Sally eating her ice cream and thought about the differences between her and her sister. Born just a few years apart, they were set on two very different trajectories. They did not know each other, really—nor would it be easy in the future to understand each other, I conjectured. Again, I found it hard to know what to say.

"Do you plan to say in the United States permanently?"

She shook her head. "It is not our plan. We want to get ourselves settled a bit, and then make some money and go back to Ghana, for sure."

I nodded, since this was usually the response I got to this question. But again, I thought about Sally and her sister. Whether and when their parents eventually returned to Ghana would have a major impact on their futures. Although it wasn't stated, I could sense—both in that conversation at the bookstore and in later chats—Evangeline was very aware of this, too. She knew that her daughters' lives hinged on the uncertainties of job opportunities, pay raises, rent hikes, and the number of classes her husband could teach as an adjunct each semester.

Our conversation rambled a bit from that point. We talked about where Evangeline was born, and how she met her husband at a small Christian Bible study. She explained why, as mentioned in chapter 5, her husband did not come to church with her. That very weekend he was attending a church conference in New York, as part of his planning process for starting the new branch in Chicago.

He is very conservative," she explained, "and likes staying with the church he is familiar with. This is part of why he doesn't want to come to Evangel. . . . If he gets involved there and then has to leave to help start a branch of the other church . . . you never know who you're going to hurt."

"Do you see any difference between the two churches?" I asked.

"There are some differences. . . . They all have the same beliefs, the same goal to make disciples, but different approaches . . . both are good, they're just different."

From her perspective, she said, Evangel was very committed to developing people's spiritual lives and knowledge of the Bible. "For the other church, while the spiritual side is there, they are more committed to developing the social side, encouraging their members to go further, get education, save your society, things like that."

She also told me how she became the choir director at Evangel Ministries. She didn't want to wait for her husband's church to start up to attend services, so when she heard Evangel Ministries had a branch in the area, she started going. At that time the church was very small, and its first leader, Reverend John, was doing both the preaching and leading the singing. One Sunday, most of the congregation was going to be absent the next week, so Rev. John asked Evangeline if she could lead the singing. It went well, and she soon took over the role.

She led the worship for about a year. She explained it was a weekly highlight in her life. It was the only setting where she could express her creative side—over time I came to see how artistic she was—and it was also a space where she felt strong and purposeful. Motivated by this experience, she started writing her own songs and planning to record them.

It was several weeks after our chat when Evangeline left to join her husband's new branch, and to lead the music program there instead. As noted in chapter 5, she rarely saw the folks at Evangel Ministries after this, though she and I kept in touch. Life got busy, and she became heavily involved with her husband's new church. Her role as a church musician continued to expand. She started to organize "worship nights," which brought Ghanaian musicians from around the city together to perform. She also kept working on her record. Over two years, the project moved closer and closer to production, and I was able to observe its development and final release via social media.

Several years later I was visiting Chicago, and Evangeline and I got together again to catch up. Sally again joined us. She looked much older, and had taken on a pre-teen seriousness. Meanwhile, Evangeline had a gift for me: the finished version of her record. She told me the story of getting to the final product in spite of several setbacks. Her friend with the recording studio unexpectedly moved to Texas and abandoned the project in the middle of it, and she was unable to track him down for several months. He was so unresponsive that she even talked with her husband about getting a lawyer. But eventually he gave her the materials to finish it somewhere else, and all ended well.

We talked again about goals for the future, and how they can change over time. Evangeline said she was thinking about writing a book, in addition to recording more music. She was interested in writing about motivation. She wanted to convey to others that it is important to have strong goals and a sense of purpose in life.

In the meantime, her husband's new church had grown. There were renting their own space in an office building not far from where we were sitting. We talked about how both of them had planned to do other things when they first came to Chicago, but then ended up in ministry.

"Life is too funny," she said at one point, shaking her head and laughing.

She explained what she meant: her husband had gone for years looking for engineering jobs, with no luck; after he started the church, he received several job offers in other cities. As soon as he committed to a new path, the doors he had been originally waiting for finally opened. Yet in the end he turned down the job offers. He decided adjunct teaching at the community college would leave him more time to devote to the church. By that point, his personal vision for his life was so grounded in his religious work that he was willing to sacrifice opportunities in engineering to pursue it.

After our conversation, I walked Evangeline and Sally down the street to the front door of their apartment building. Evangeline asked how the Evangel Ministries branch was doing. I reported that they had grown, though most of the original group was still there. They also found a permanent space. She was happy to hear it. She had not seen many of the members there in years, and she missed Elijah and Catherine in particular.

As I left them, I continued thinking about Evangeline's husband, and how committed he must have become to his new church to continue working as an adjunct instructor and turn down much better job opportunities elsewhere. It seemed he had reimagined his move abroad completely: he was now a church planter and global missionary, as opposed to another transnational job seeker. I wondered whether it felt empowering in a way to turn down those engineering jobs for the sake of something he considered more important. He had chosen to live by a new rationale, where meaning and community—believing and belonging—were prioritized above upward mobility. The new church gave him a space in which to do that.

"We Work to Live, We Don't Live to Work"

As part of my research, I interviewed a half-dozen Ghanaian pastors of churches in the Chicago area. I found that most of them, like Evangeline's husband, did not originally migrate abroad in order to start or lead a congregation. They were motivated by ambitions for schooling and careers. Yet along the way, they developed a vision to take advantage of their positions abroad to serve the church. In their narratives, they retrospectively reinvented their migrations in terms of a "calling" from God, while they acknowledged that when they first moved abroad they were not aware of this calling. As noted, organizations like Evangel Ministries relied on such strategically positioned figures to lead its branches abroad, especially when they already earned salaries by other means and could dedicate time to the church as volunteers.

Elijah himself was just such a case, and in his sermons he frequently talked about his experience of finding new purpose in his pastoral role. He did this to encourage the church members to think bigger about their ambitions, and to ask questions about meaning and purpose. As described in chapter 3, he was a participant at Evangel Ministries during its early days in the 1980s, but he was in medical college at the time to be a doctor, and he followed this ambition to a residency in England and a position in a small town in the American Midwest. According to him, he and Catherine would never have moved, except for a phone call from an old friend from medical school, and the sense that perhaps their migration to the United States could and should serve a greater purpose than material comfort for their family.

When they agreed to lead the new Evangel Ministries branch, it took about six months to find a new house and jobs for them both. The understanding from the beginning was that Evangel Ministries could not pay them, so they would need to continue to work full-time jobs in their respective medical professions. They both took pay cuts relative to what they earned in their former jobs, and the only position Elijah could find was on the opposite side of the Chicago metro area from Catherine's workplace.

With their full-time schedules and the long commutes, their lives were busy enough even before they added in the preparation of sermons and teachings, visits to sick or needy members, coordinating worship and outreach events, hosting visiting leaders from Evangel Ministries in Ghana, organizing meetings of the leadership committee, making phone calls to one-time visitors to encourage them to return, finding a space to meet, and paying rent. Elijah's Sunday routine was a grueling one: he would spend several hours at work doing early morning rotations as a physician at the hospital, drive roughly an hour to the church meeting, act as the master of ceremonies and preach a sermon of between one and two hours, socialize for an hour or two with members and visitors, have a meeting with the core leadership committee, and return home around dinnertime to feed, play with, bathe, and tuck in his young daughter. Catherine's day looked similar, minus the morning rotations. She taught the Sunday school class for adults before the main worship service, and then taught and took care of all the kids in another room during the sermon.

The hectic nature of their lives became clear to me one Sunday a few weeks after I started attending Evangel Ministries in Chicago. There was a visiting preacher from the larger organization there that morning, and as Elijah introduced him and talked about their warm memories from involvement in Evangel's early days, he mentioned the two of them were up talking until about three A.M.

the night before, and Elijah was then awake again at six to do his rounds at the hospital. He seemed amazingly energetic after only three hours of sleep.

When the visiting preacher came to the stage, he extoled the dedication of Elijah and Catherine to do what they were doing, noting how important it was to Evangel's success: "Something great has been going on," he said. "Evangel Ministries International has so many churches around the globe. So, when you are traveling almost anywhere, you can find a branch, and have home away from home." He continued that because of this, the members should be thankful and recognize what they were given in their leaders.

"You don't know how difficult it is to start a church!" He noted there were thousands of churches in Chicago, but "each of you are here, and that means something." Thus, the members should also be thankful for "my friend," Elijah. "He has always been a man of God as long as I have known him, through Scripture Union and church. Some professionals are here in the city to work and to make money, but your pastor is not in Chicago for the money. He would've had better money if he had stayed [where he was] . . . so be thankful for the messengers that God sends to you, because one day they may leave and you may realize that something is no longer there."[4]

The preacher thus told the congregation that their life together was a direct result of one couple's willingness to make sacrifices. Elijah and Catherine were aspirational migrants just like them, who were raised in small villages in central Ghana and worked hard to achieve success by moving abroad. They dealt with the same alienations, uncertainties, and risks as everyone else. Yet they were willing to give up some of the security they had obtained and take on additional risk in order to create a space of social and spiritual renewal for themselves and others.

Elijah himself regularly talked about how much he valued his work in spite of the sacrifices it required. He often said he didn't regret the pay cuts, the loss of security, or the added stress on his family. With his new position came so many benefits to him personally: studying books of theology or biblical exegesis, which enhanced his own spiritual growth; meeting new people, and hearing their stories; and getting to convey his enthusiasm about spiritual instruction to those around him. He also explained to me one day how this volunteer pastoral role affected his work as a physician:

"It's not common to see people who are full-time physicians also pastoring churches. . . . So it's changed my life significantly because it has also made me know that as a physician, my mortality rate is 100 percent. Everybody I see will eventually die. So over and above the physical treatment that we give, we should also look at the person from the spiritual perspective. Because there is a spirit and soul that go on to live forever. So I think it has really added a lot of substance to the work I do."[5]

Within the church, Elijah found an identity as someone who could significantly impact the spiritual well-being of others, and this sense of purpose carried over into other settings and interpersonal interactions. His work as a physician had additional "substance" because he now knew how to address both the physical and the spiritual health of his patients.

According to him, such acts of service to others made life meaningful. One of his favorite personal anecdotes was about his conversations with an uncle in his seventies. This man had lived a luxurious life with lots of money, expensive cars, and multiple wives and girlfriends, yet at the end of his life he told Elijah that all the things he worked for didn't matter to him anymore. He wished he had made the choice Elijah had, to dedicate his life to something greater within a church community. Elijah often said, after telling this story, that for himself he was happy he didn't have to wait until his seventies to realize the value of this.

Although Elijah preached from different books and biblical passages week to week, in a way his messages all came back to the same principle of putting God and the church first, and offered the same reassurance that if his listeners did so, they would find true fulfillment. It was not a promise they would become wealthy but, rather, they would experience what matters more than wealth.

"The word of God [the Bible] is God's plan for man's prosperity and abundant life," he taught one Sunday morning. He explained that prosperity in this sense did not just mean riches, but "wholeness." Later in the same teaching he said, "Don't pursue blessing in your life, blessing is a product of something."[6]

At other times he described "purpose" as the end goal of this process, by teaching fulfillment is found not in possessions but in purpose. "People in the past have dealt with existential issues, like *Who am I? Why am I here? What is my purpose on this earth?* We are blessed that the Bible reveals these things to us. . . Nobody is an accident, finding your purpose begins with knowing God."[7]

A natural and frequent extension of this was to be cautious about getting caught up in the search for material goods. One of his most frequently used teaching analogies was from a Deuteronomy 28:2: "And all these blessings shall come upon thee, and overtake thee, if thou shalt hearken unto the voice of the Lord thy God."

"It means you are going sixty miles per hour in one direction," he explained, "and the blessings are going a hundred miles per hour behind you. You are running away from the blessings, but they will overtake you. Don't go after the blessings!"

He said there is certainly nothing wrong with having a nice house, a good job, or a prestigious education; but if people make it their primary focus in life to pursue such things, they are likely to miss out on even greater goods in life—specifically, the joy of serving and connecting with others in relationship, and the confidence of living a virtuous life. "If you get all the nice things in life, the house, the car, the wife, the children, but miss the most important, then it doesn't help you," he said.[8]

Often when Elijah made such statements, he got a strong positive reaction from the congregation. The group would cheer, laugh, or say "Amen!" during his sermons, particularly when he talked about significant questions like finding purpose of life.

These messages might initially seem odd since he was counseling migrants not to prioritize what they had migrated in order to achieve. He was telling them not to go after things that they already decided to "go after" when they had moved abroad. Yet their strong positive response to his messages suggested that it was touching something deep and emotional within them. His words countered the disappointments and uncertainties staring many of them in the face. Here, Elijah promised, was a different answer to the question of what life was about, and one that did not need to be validated through elusive markers of immigrant success. A person's value was not tied to what they owned or achieved, but to their potential to live in relationship with others and with God, and to serve a larger collective project. This message was summed up in one of his most poignant statements, made again and again: "We work to live, we do not live to work!"

I could imagine this statement being made in a variety of contexts: a parent counseling an ambitious child to leave room for relaxation; a white-collar professional encouraging a colleague to wrap up early and go have a drink on a Friday afternoon; or even a faculty adviser suggesting the stressed-out graduate student could use a break. In *this* context, coming from one aspirational migrant to another, the connotation was to redirect their efforts and get free from the constant pressure to be professionally successful.

How did someone like Benjamin, for example, hear this message? Potentially, it suggested that even though he had not been able to meet his original professional goals, they were not what mattered most anyway. It provided a rationale for spending his weekends serving the church and the choir, rather than driving his taxi all day and night; and for embracing his relationship with Jeannette and their new future together, even though that future looked so different from what he had initially planned. The message suggested that a life spent chasing after education, a better job, and more money was not really a life, in spite of the messages the wider culture—both within and outside of the migrant community—might convey.

The statement could also imply a rejection of a particular set of North American and European values. Other aspects of Evangel Ministries' discourse backed up this interpretation. While Elijah and other leaders would at times speak positively about "white" civilization's ingenuity and hard work, they would as readily point out its spiritual failings—specifically, the overemphasis on individual autonomy and materialism. They would exhort participants to adopt the professionalism and discipline visible in Anglo-European culture, even while cautioning them against its spiritual blindness and misplaced priorities.

For example, in a long polemic against "mediocrity" in the church, one of the speakers at an Evangel Ministries regional camp meeting (see chapter 5) compared African soccer teams to the German team that won the World Cup that year: "Some of these guys that just won the World Cup title are not as talented as we are, but for them it is a science. An African with a soccer ball, eh . . . you see skill! But it's like we are content to just score one goal, two goals, three goals. But the Germans, they don't stop till the whistle is blown. . . . These guys who are less talented use statistics, they know that when they aim for the goal, 80 percent of the shots made in this area go in, 25 percent of the shots over here go in, and so on." He later said even more strongly that the willingness to settle for mediocrity is an "African spirit," using a version of global history to support this claim:

> Don't be angry if people say, "Oh, you're from Africa?" Because to them it is one big dusty place. . . . Did God create Europe first? No! But how can it be that [people think] they came and discovered you? For hundreds of years they kept coming with ships. . . . Then when they got there, they realized, we've suffered! Let's not do that again. So they invented planes so they could fly there instead. Yet in Africa, we have cars that can't even go straight! You must not be limited by your temperament. . . . Mediocrity leads to deception, and it is an African affliction, I have no apologies.

He then gave an opposing example of a new "mega-church" in Nigeria that was transcending the pull of mediocrity: "The engineering of the building was amazing; there was a university, and it could pass for any street in Korea or New York." While narrating the problem as an "African" one, he encouraged his listeners that it could and should be overcome.[9]

Yet if mediocrity was an "African affliction" in the discourse of Evangel's leaders, then materialism was an American and European one. Leaders made repeated claims about Western countries' rampant blindness to spiritual realities and backwards priorities. They claimed Western materialism was spreading throughout global society and too often found its way into the thinking of aspirational migrants from Africa.

In one sermon, Elijah was talking about how what happens in the spiritual world affects what happens in the physical world. He noted that while Africans have historically viewed almost everything as spiritual, even to the point of being too "superstitious," in modern America there is the opposite problem: "We live in an age where if you talk about spiritual things, people think you are weak-minded, or from the jungle somewhere."[10]

At other times, Elijah connected materialism to greed, which could and often would affect his listener's lives directly: "They have this American greed. . . . A youth pastor ran a scam, then got out and became an investor, and he changed his name and got people to invest all of their money in the scam. Then it all collapsed. People lost their entire retirement savings. He didn't think about anybody! People will betray you. Jesus was betrayed by someone close to him. Sometimes it is very difficult to trust people. We have to make sure we do not become that."

Here, he connected the biblical story of Jesus being betrayed by his disciple, Judas, to the everyday experiences of his listeners. The possibility of betrayal was very real in their lives, which made it hard to trust. He implied that part of this risk also came from an American materialism, which made people overly focused on their own success and thus more likely to take advantage of others. When he said, "We have to make sure we do not become that," he warned his listeners against becoming too invested in such things, to the point where they are unable to "think about anybody" but themselves. As he noted on earlier in the same sermon: "If you are overly engrossed in the things of this world it will make you unfruitful. In America you are a number, but in the church you are more."[11]

Elijah and other Evangel Ministries leaders returned to this message again and again because they knew their listeners, as aspirational migrants, were already to some extent invested in certain narratives of material success. Elijah told me he saw this as a particular challenge of his ministry: "So many who are able to come here are looking for success, and they become too preoccupied to do God's work."[12]

Similarly, a visiting preacher at a camp meeting addressed this issue directly, taking on a strong fatherly tone:

> Part of my responsibility is to heal you from your future disappointments. People travel from Africa because they want a certain glory. They think, if only I can land myself in America and get some dollars, I will have arrived. They think, once I get to the airport, my prosperity has begun! They come for education; but are there no universities back home in Kenya, in Nigeria, in Ghana? They think, but if only I can attend Harvard, Yale . . . [but] money cannot answer all the world's problems. If you want a life of beauty for yourself, and glory means beauty, make sure Christ is in you. They say that experience is the best teacher, but I beg to differ. There are certain experiences that you will die before you have a chance

to learn what the experience could teach you. There are some hurts and disappointments in life you do not need![13]

This message was salient for his listeners because they already knew what he was talking about. Most of them had experienced this kind of disappointment, when their airport optimism was eroded in the face of the reality. Evangel Ministries' message presented an alternative to doggedly holding onto their original beliefs and desires. It was an opportunity to adopt a different set of motivations.

Ultimately, many took on this new way of thinking. In at least some of the life histories I collected and observed—Jeremiah, Benjamin, Evangeline's husband, and Elijah—believing in this message resulted in major shifts of direction and priorities. This discourse was thus more than just rhetoric. In the context of these particular moral emphases, the new and renewed sense of belonging and believing changed the course of many lives.

Transcending Categories

As discussed in chapter 5, during my time at Evangel Ministries in Chicago I noticed a paradox: the church members were all Ghanaian or West African, but a common message conveyed by Evangel Ministries' leadership was that Evangel Ministries was not a Ghanaian church. The leaders often emphasized its international focus and its vision to bring in diverse groups of people. And they didn't just talk about this—they took steps to codify it. There were rules, coming direct from the organization's headquarters, prohibiting open expressions of Ghanaian culture during formal services, such as singing songs in *Twi* or wearing Ghanaian cloth. There were also repeated exhortations, especially at the yearly camp meetings of the North American branches, to run the church in a more professional and polished way so as to make the church more appealing to Americans.

Of course, Evangel Ministries' members frequently still spoke in *Twi* with each other informally. Such habits were hard to break. Sometimes, though, one member would jump in and remind another of the rules. I remember going to Ghanafest with the group in 2010 and listening to an older woman in the church, Prudence, rant about a problem with her car mechanic in a stream of *Twi*. Although I was the only non-*Twi* speaker present, and I was not the person she was talking to, another member jumped in and said, "You are spoiling the church!" It was a reference to what a visiting leader had said about how speaking *Twi* in church limits and "spoils" its potential.

The tone was playful, though, so Prudence didn't take offense. She just laughed and threw her arm around my shoulder. "I know," she said, "But what I have to say is too precious to say in English." In this way, she reassured both of us that she was not intending to alienate the sole non-Ghanaian present, nor undermine the inclusive emphasis of the church. She was just speaking out of a momentary frustration.[14]

There were other incidents, however, in which the tensions between the organization's goals and the local congregation's culture were not so easy to resolve. Elijah and the other leaders of the organization sought to establish a multicultural space of worship, but in practice at Evangel Ministries this priority was often outweighed by the routines, exchanges, and feelings of solidarity that made Evangel feel like a "good church" to its Ghanaian core members. The weighing of these two concerns was complicated, because many of the members *themselves* were also invested in the idea that Evangel could be more than a Ghanaian church, and they believed that following the organization's rules would serve that purpose.

This resulted in tension one Sunday morning within the choir. Following a lively service, the seven choir members who sang that morning had an impromptu meeting to discuss possible improvements to the quality of music and our professional presentation on stage. Getting the music program on its feet was a struggle that summer, since it was difficult to amass a large enough group and there were very few members who owned instruments or had the skill to play them. This particular Sunday, though, we had the biggest group ever singing in the choir; we sounded more professional because we had spent more time in rehearsal, and there were more people than usual in the seats. Everyone was feeling the momentum.

The members started offering ideas for building on our success. One person suggested we coordinate our clothing on stage so it would look more professional. Doris, a woman in her thirties wearing a skirt suit in full traditional Ghanaian fabric, suggested we could all wear traditional dress one Sunday. The choir director at the time, David, responded, "Actually, the traditional cloth is not really allowed, the Reverend said that."

Another younger member of the choir nodded her head and said it was true.

"Really?" Doris said, looking stunned, "Is not allowed on stage, or not allowed in church? For everyone?"

"Well, that's why I wear this," David said, gesturing to his suit and tie. He was stumbling over his words, clearly feeling awkward, but explained that it was so the church wouldn't sent the message "subliminally" that it was just for one kind of person.

"I didn't know," Doris said, now clearly offended.

"I know, and it's not really . . . we've made exceptions." David replied, still feeling awkward.

"Well, this is what I have," Doris huffed. "So if the church wants to buy me new clothes, then okay."

"I guess I came on too strong with it," David said, backpedaling further, and then changing the subject, "but it's okay, we will just coordinate through the week."

Nothing more was said on the issue, at least that I overheard. After this exchange, Doris only sang with the choir one or two more times while I was at Evangel Ministries. I was sadly not surprised; it was an embarrassing moment for everyone present, and it made Doris's wardrobe and her ignorance about the rules the subject of intense scrutiny.[15]

Yet this exchange was also revealing on multiple levels. First, it showed again how the agenda of the Evangel Ministries organization to build an international church could conflict in practice with what migrants like Doris looked for in their religious community. Second, it demonstrated the class dynamics at work in these tensions: that being able to purchase American clothes and carry oneself in an Americanized way, as mandated by the leadership and as David was able to do, hindered the ability of other migrants with fewer resources and less knowledge of the organization to fully participate in the rituals of the community.

Third, it showed through David's reaction that some members believed in the rules because they believed in the importance of transcending the church's Ghanaian identity, even if actually achieving that goal was a long way off. Over time and through additional observations, I concluded that part of the reason for this was the desire to transcend limiting categories of nationality, ethnicity, and race in general, as a partial solution to the challenges of negotiating identity, discussed in chapter 6. They were looking to achieve what Marti (2015, 1048) refers to as "ethnic transcendence"—developing a religious identity that "supersedes their ethnic and racial differences."

This objective came out particularly strongly at regional camp meetings. At the camp meeting during which I had bristled at being commanded to purchase a collection of sermon tapes by Evangel Ministries' founder (see chapter 5), I was also called out at an earlier session for a very different reason. The guest preacher from Ghana, John, asked everyone in the group who was not Ghanaian to come up front and stand before the rest of the congregation. There were nine of us: four Americans including myself (two white, two black), two people from Liberia, a woman from Sudan, another woman from Zimbabwe, and one more woman from Cameroon. We stood in front of a group of about fifty people.

John asked each of us to say our names and introduce ourselves. He then exhorted the church to embrace the diverse people in their midst, as we continued to stand at the front of the congregation for about 45 minutes. He asked the congregation to pray over us. Each of us standing in the front was surrounded by a clump of those from the larger group, who asked God to bless us and make us feel welcome within Evangel Ministries. This act openly affirmed their value for diversity.

Throughout the camp meeting, John returned to this principle of embracing diversity again and again, sometimes using harsh language to chasten those who continued to speak in *Twi* and wear Ghanaian clothes in the church.

"Our harvest field is the world," he said during one session. "A pastor cannot restrict himself to Accra; a pastor cannot restrict himself to Africa . . . but you don't always have to go to where people are to go into the world; it is also ministering to people from all over the world right where we are."

He admonished the crowd, "We have restricted our ministry. You have been pastoring a Ghanaian church, and Evangel Ministries International is NOT a Ghanaian church, it is an international church." He then clicked his tongue in frustration. "Some of our churches right now . . . African Americans cannot even come. The pastor's wife gets up, speaks in *Twi*," he said a few words in *Twi*, acting out this scenario, and the crowd laughed loudly.

He then asked the woman operating the projector to bring up a picture showing Matthew 13:31–32 on the projector screen, which stood to the far left of the stage. The passage read, "He [Jesus] presented another parable to them, saying, 'The kingdom of heaven is like a mustard seed, which a man took and sowed in his field; and this is smaller than all other seeds, but when it is full grown, it is larger than the garden plants and becomes a tree, so that the birds of the air come and nest in its branches."

John read this passage out loud to the group. "Does it become a tree because Evangel is going green?" He joked, "Because we are becoming eco-friendly?"

There was hearty laughter again from the crowd.

"No, it is because we grow and become a place where birds can lodge. Your church should be a place where a French person can come and lodge freely. . . Not just African birds, black birds. The church is not for black birds alone!"

As he was preaching, John's expressiveness escalated to a high point at this final statement about "black birds." He communicated with the crowd using his whole body, adding emphasis with sweeping arm gestures and an intense, direct gaze. As he concluded, much of the crowd was on its feet.

"That is why your church as it is, we cannot accept it," He said. "You may know some churches that are just Ghanaians, but that is not this church. Ban *Twi* speaking, ban *Ga* speaking; it is immature of you if there are people there who cannot understand it. If you want to have praises in *Twi*, you can come to my house before church; but the church itself is international. There are international languages, and *Twi* ain't one of them, baby!" The laughter turned to cheering as he nearly shouted this last point.[16]

John's discursive rejection of the "church as it is"—that is, Ghanaian in composition—and the overwhelmingly positive response from the crowd surprised me at the time. I later became convinced it was based in their desire to worship in a religious community that could transcend a single ethnic or national category. Although many of them attended Evangel Ministries, a mostly Ghanaian church, because it offered them a culture of connection that many multicultural American congregations seemed unable to provide, they still believed in the possibility of multicultural religion, especially if it could be built on the basis of the connected community they enjoyed.

Talk of inclusivity thus presented a different way of addressing the issues of identity negotiation discussed in chapter 6. It subjected categories based on race, ethnicity, and nationality to the category of being a born-again Christian. The message of inclusivity was also a message of freedom: being a "black bird" did not define Reverend John's listeners at the camp. They would be limiting themselves if they assumed they belonged to a community that was only Ghanaian or only black. Rather, they belonged to and could build a community that transcended those categories.

This was made clear in another conversation with Elijah, when I asked him, "Do you think it is important to Evangel Ministries to hold onto some aspects of Ghanaian culture, or is that just kind of a secondary thing?"

"We would wish that is a secondary thing," he said. "It's very difficult, but we would wish it was a secondary thing . . . definitely there will still be traces of the Ghanaian culture. What we try to do is to distill as much of it as possible, especially the unnecessary parts, so we can welcome as many people who will be able to worship with us. Because at the end of the day, somebody will say that blood is thicker than water, but spirit is also thicker than that. So what binds us together is the spirit of God. It transcends culture, transcends race, transcends language. And the more we are able to develop in God, the more we are able to cross racial, cultural, and language barriers."

"Is that one of the reasons why the services and the songs are all done in English?"

"Absolutely, that is it."

"So people can come, and everyone can understand?"

"That's right," he said. "Because we feel that we are in America, and almost everybody who is from Africa, who has some kind of a job in America, speaks English. You have to do that to survive. And in Ghana, some of the songs are in *Twi*, the local language, because that is the language that most people speak. But if you are here, then we also want to adapt ourselves to the wider culture in which we find ourselves."[17]

There were many powerful words used in his explanation: *transcend, blood, survive,* and *adapt*. Elijah believed he could relax his commitment to his Ghanaian identity in favor of a more universal one—that of the religious community—and that this was possible for the congregation to do as a group.

From this viewpoint, the earlier statements that initially appeared incongruous with reality—that the heavily Ghanaian Evangel Ministries was "not a Ghanaian church"—and the exchange that embarrassed a woman for not owning American fashions were connected to something larger: the transcendence of identities that held people back.

Belonging and believing within the religious community thus provided a rationale for negotiating identity in a new way, just as it provided a rationale for making certain kinds of revisions to migrants' original goals. As demonstrated in Elijah and Catherine's life together, the aspiration to serve the church became more important than professional ambitions. At the same time, their religious commitments became more central to their identities than the available categories of "Ghanaian," "American," "black," "African," or "immigrant." In fact, they strongly believed those other identities should be secondary to the religious identity of being "born again." This came out in Elijah's poignant statement: "Blood is thicker than water, but spirit is even thicker than that." It was a very real symbolic rejection of the binaries of nativity, ethnicity, and race.

Expanding Identities

The story of Sylvia, the woman who attended a non-Ghanaian congregation and married an American she met there, also showed the potential of religious identities to transcend categories. As told in chapter 5, when she was a teenager she went with her aunt to a non-Ghanaian, African American church; and when she became an adult she attended a predominantly white, but still somewhat diverse, congregation of young professionals. Although her churchgoing trajectory looked different from Evangel Ministries' members, her outlook on church and its role in her life was actually quite similar. While Evangel Ministries worked to transcend categories through its discourse and practices in the context of a Ghanaian community, Sylvia transcended categories by getting connected personally with diverse others in the context of a nonmigrant church. Because she was able to do this—something others like Anna and Timothy hoped to do, but could not because they didn't find the right church—her story demonstrates a uniquely integrative, bridge-building experience.

As was true of many others, Sylvia's religious membership started with an invitation from another—in her case, a co-worker. For a while after they met, he would invite her to clubs, parties, and other social events, but she usually declined. She explained, "I was so private that I usually put him off." When he invited her to church with him one day, though, she accepted. "I felt bad saying no, since it's church, what could go wrong?"

She was surprised to find herself drawn in. "I liked it for many different reasons. It stands for social justice and racial reconciliation, and there was an intentionality about building community. It was actually more like in my Ghanaian culture where people often just show up at your doorstep to hang out, and there's no objection to being open. I also enjoyed the pastor, and thought he taught us well. It was pretty diverse, though more Caucasian, but a growing African American group, maybe some Latino."

She became very involved in this church and found close friends—and eventually her husband—among its diverse membership. As noted in chapter 6, she and her husband shared a concern for racial justice in the United States. While building a biracial family, she developed strong sympathies with the African American community. When they moved to a new city, the congregation that best fit their biracial experience was a mostly African American Episcopal Church with a strong historic social justice vision. It was very similar to the church she went to as a teenager with her aunt.

She summed up her thoughts about the process of selecting the new church in this way: "At different times in your life you look for certain things, and the community there seemed embracing. Going back to something familiar, I had forgotten how much I know about the service and how comforting it is. I don't know if I'm gonna need that a year from now, or four years from now, but right now it is good.... When you move to a new place, you might not have friends or know where things are, but one thing I think I can find is a church and go worship."

Her words said a lot about what religious association meant for her, even as they echoed the sentiments expressed by many others. Church choice was fluid: at different times in her life different things were important, and so she felt free to pick and choose a place of worship accordingly. At the same time, finding an "embracing community" was crucial. Moves to a new place, because they could be lonely and disorienting, often triggered the impulse to "find a church and go worship." Church was a setting of comforting, familiar rituals and a way to connect.

Sylvia was also unusual in that she was unsure about whether she would eventually settle in Ghana. Most of my informants at least intended to do so one day, but when I asked Sylvia about whether she wanted to return, she said, "Possibly. It's something I'm thinking about."

When she and her husband visited Ghana for three weeks the previous Christmas, she said, "It felt different, like I'm still part of my family, and yet also part of something new with this other person, which is something I haven't felt before." For right now, then, they planned to live in the United States indefinitely.

Sylvia's experience and class position certainly helped her to successfully navigate a congregation where she was in the minority. A more recent immigrant like Sandra, for example, would likely have had a harder time making true connections there. Nevertheless, her story illustrated a particular way in which religious association could assist in expanding identities across racial and national categories, by connecting immigrants into nonmigrant networks. Given the closeness of the friends she made there, and the fact that one of them became her husband—a relationship of the deepest levels of personal trust—it seems she, too, found religion to be a basis of trust. In her case, the bonds of trust transcended categories; and over time they shaped what kind of a family she entered into, where she lived, and how she thought about the question of returning to Ghana.

Certainly, none of these personal stories are yet over. We do not know where Elijah, Catherine, Benjamin, Sylvia, or any of the others will settle in their later years. We don't know whether their children will be raised in America or in Ghana, what sorts of jobs they will pursue, whether they will have financial stability or distress, or how much they will identify with mainstream America, black America, Africans in America, or Ghana. We therefore cannot know for certain in each case what the long-term implications of their religious commitments will be.

Yet their stories do show that religious trust networks and spiritual transformations can powerfully shape identities and aspirations. In order to understand the long-term outcomes of this aspirational migrant group, therefore, we have to pay attention to religion. We must recognize how religious membership provides a basis for the imaginative and symbolic activity of personal trust and the development of new connections characterized by such trust. We must acknowledge that such networks matter greatly for what happens in the days, weeks, months, and years following those initial steps off the airplane. These are the social ties, established between former strangers, in which many migrants engage in their most meaningful activities, and answer the questions, *Who are we? Who are they?* And, *What really matters in life?*

8

Conclusion

RELIGIOUS BASES OF TRUST AND INTEGRATION

IN THIS BOOK I have used the personal stories of aspirational migrants from Ghana in Chicago to illustrate how and why religious membership can serve as a basis of social trust, specifically of the personal type enacted within relationships. I started by asking, How do Christian aspirational migrants from Ghana choose a church upon arrival in the United States? And, How do their church choices affect the development of their identities and goals for their migrations? By looking closely at their experiences with religious membership, I concluded that Ghanaians' church choices frequently express a desire to establish new social bonds characterized by personal trust. Their resulting religious-based trust networks also influence how they negotiate their identities and reenvision their personal goals over time.

I have defined personal trust as an activity engaged in within social networks, in which people imaginatively come to a state of positive expectation about each other, and thereby become willing to take on the risks of cooperating on important projects.[1] Imagination, in this sense, is not exactly make-believe; but it is a willful suspension of doubts, an inclination to focus on the reasons to trust rather than the reasons to withhold trust. The relevant metaphor, borrowed from Georg Simmel, is a leap of faith. It is a step into the unknown, a choice—sometimes conscious, often not—to see another as trustworthy until proven otherwise. Trusters use symbols with shared meanings, such as religious identity or race, to assess whether to make such imaginative leaps. People look for others to trust, and they use imagination and symbolic cues to deal with the inherent risk.

When religious membership serves as a basis of such trust, this means three things. First, it means that, at the outset, religious communities provide spaces for interactions where symbolic cues supportive of trust can be used to make leaps of faith. This is the role, for example, of things like dress, language, and objects used in the congregational space, which can be taken as indicators of trustworthiness. Second, it means that memberships in religious organizations themselves can be used as symbolic indicators of trustworthiness, as when two strangers meet and learn they are both part of the Charismatic movement in general or of Evangel Ministries in particular. Finally, it means that practices associated with organized religion, particularly in congregations like Evangel Ministries with a strong culture of connection, can be constitutive of personal trust between participants. They are practices of sociability that bring benefits to the people involved, and they express and enable the activity of personal trust.[2]

Painting offers a good analogy for this third point. On one level, we would describe painting in the following way: the painter is taking a paintbrush, dipping it into paint, and applying it to a canvas. On another level, we would say he is creating a painting. Both are true; the former describes the necessary mechanics and the latter emphasizes the broader significance of the activity. Likewise, an act like giving a ride to church is *both* an enactment of personal trust and a practice typical of a congregational culture of connection (see chapter 5). Such practices are the necessary mechanics, but the broader significance is that personal trust and cooperation are happening.

Religious practices don't always take on this meaning, but they often do, particularly within the distinctly American model of the religious congregation that is voluntary and functionally diffuse, and is echoed in the Charismatic Evangelical model in Ghana (see chapter 2). In congregations that emphasize intense sociability, trusting activity often becomes frequent and significant enough between members that those relations become trust networks—that is, social ties characterized by the activity of personal trust. This can happen for those who move across borders and those who don't; but for the former, it can be a particularly important basis of trust when other bases are threatened, limited, or broken down.

To be clear, my argument is not that religion for Ghanaians at home and abroad is *only* or even *primarily* about social dynamics. Such a claim would reduce religion in general and Ghanaian Charismatic Christianity in particular to a search for social connection. By contrast, a full account must leave room for personal spirituality, belief, and private devotion. Tweed's (2006) definition of religion described in chapter 2, which I have found useful since it stresses the collective work of making homes and crossing boundaries, also accounts for the role of superhuman forces and the need to enhance joy and confront suffering. There are multiple sides to any human institution as complex as religion, and I have not tried to account for them all. Instead, I have argued in a more limited way that, among transnational Ghanaians who are already at least nominally Christian, finding bonds characterized by personal trust is a major priority in choosing among various church options.

Although this study was limited to Ghanaian Christians, it is likely that other types of religious communities could offer a similar basis of trust for migrants. There is evidence that West African Muslim associations have cultures of intensified social connection similar to Ghanaian Charismatic churches, as in the example of the Murids from Senegal, a Muslim brotherhood living in New York (Abdullah 2013). Buddhist and Hindu temples also often adopt a more congregational style of association in North America, in response to the different needs of their immigrant members (Yang and Ebaugh 2001). The relationship between social trust and integration is likely a relevant issue for these groups, as well.

One question naturally follows from this argument—namely, how finding a basis of personal trust in religion relates to their integration into American society. Some readers of this book, when they learn about the amount of time and energy Evangel Ministries' members invested in their migrant church, might wonder if intensified involvement in such churches could hinder migrants' ability to successfully integrate. Indeed, the question of whether ethnic religious congregational life is "good" or "bad" for immigrant integration in America runs through years of scholarship.

One perspective (Breton 1964) sees ethnic religious activity in conflict with integration. If migrants invest most of their time and energy in ethnic religious institutions, and those institutions are segregated from other spheres of American life, then migrants should be less likely to succeed in the economy (because of the conflicting demands on their time) and less likely to enjoy the benefits that flow through diverse networks (because everyone they know well is also an immigrant).

I wrestled with this question myself during a poignant moment on a Sunday as I said goodbye to Evangel Ministries, at the end of my first summer of participant observation. I was moved because the congregation threw a party with a cake for me after church. The choir bought me a greeting card signed by all the members. Benjamin's inscription hit me hard: "To my first white lady friend."[3] I was honored. I was also struck by what it said about the nature of his social experience in Chicago. That experience revolved around a job and a church community that was almost entirely African, in spite of his efforts to avoid being too immersed in the migrant community; this was so, such that after a year and a half of living in Chicago, he had no other white friends.

Does having no white friends, and spending much of his weekend investing in church work rather than earning as much money as possible, hinder Benjamin's integration into American life? Perhaps. Does Evangel Ministries' leadership take unfair advantage of their members' tenuous, in-between circumstances when they exhort them to pour their energy into church life rather than work? Maybe. Does Evangeline's husband's decision to turn down good jobs in engineering in order to stay in Chicago and pastor an African church mean that he and his children will be materially worse off than they could be? It might seem so.

Yet these questions as worded are also problematic in their implications. They portray integration in terms of a transition from foreign to familiar, and put the onus on immigrants themselves to make the "right" choices in their religious lives to assist in this process. They carry an underlying normative assumption about what migrants' priorities should be, and thereby cast doubt on whether immigrants are acting in their own best interest when they spend their time, money, and energy in collective worship.

This problem has correlates in other studies of religion. Exploring religious practice among a handful of inmates in a Philadelphia prison, Dubler (2013) criticizes the stereotypes of the "poor man of religion" and the "bad man of religion." The former is a character who turns to religion out of desperation and adopts simplistic creeds that work against his best material interest; the latter is a character who uses religion to manipulate others for his own gain. Dubler argues that because of these stereotypes, the religiosity of black men in prison is often portrayed as either a psychological crutch or a coercive tool.

Such stereotypes also show up in depictions of African Charismatic Christianity, both at home and abroad. In Ghana, those who follow the historic mainline churches, such as the Roman Catholic or the Anglican Church, often view new Charismatic organizations with some skepticism, as chronicled in chapter 4. For example, several Anglican young men I interviewed in Accra were very critical of the many "one-man churches" started in recent decades. By implication, these churches are led by the bad men of religion and attended by the poor men of religion. Scholarly work on African Christianity also tends to highlight material needs as motivations for conversion, reinforcing the poor man image. Gifford (2004) argues that the success of Accra's mega-churches relies on their promises of health and wealth in the here and now. These churches claim to be able to provide what people need in a material sense, and this is why they are attractive.

There is also a third stereotype, however, that is employed in relation to African migration and integration: the strange man of religion. This character is foreign in every respect, engaging in bizarre spirituality with incomprehensible fervor. He is not so much manipulative or misled but, rather, operating according to a different logic. This stereotype showed up in a *New York Times* article on African Pentecostalism in America, which identified one Nigerian pastor as "coming for your soul." Later, the article referred to the pastor's aspirations as "outsized"; and the whole article read as a report on an interesting curiosity.[4] In such depictions, both the strange man and poor man stereotypes are lurking. The African pastor is portrayed as both out of step with American culture and foolishly invested in a losing project.

Yet these stereotypes misconstrue the actual experiences, desires, and choices of transnational Ghanaians. For example, there were significant structural and cultural forces contributing to the fact that Benjamin had no white friends. To explain his racially limited social networks as a result of his involvement in an all-Ghanaian congregation would be extremely short-sighted, because it would ignore the reality of the historical power relations between Africa, North America, and Europe, and the nature of the racial order in the United States. There are far more Americans without any black friends than there are new immigrant blacks without any white friends.

These stereotypes also ignore what many transnational Ghanaians do to overcome such barriers, as when Anna and Timothy looked for a racially diverse church and Elijah thought carefully about what he might be able to change about the congregation's practices to make Americans feel welcome. If these efforts are in the end unsuccessful, and Evangel's members thus do not access what could be a potential avenue for facilitating positive social integration, is the problem with the ethnic church or with the racial order and its associated dynamics of distrust?

Fortunately, many scholars have countered the strange man of religion stereotype by showing how collective religious practice has historically made newcomers *less* strange, integrating them through a type of voluntary membership that is and has long been quintessentially American.[5] Through religious practice, the foreign becomes familiar; but it also *transforms* familiar social contexts in turn. In other words, we can observe a type of integration operating within religious memberships that encourages, and indeed depends on, transformation in both new communities and their receiving institutions.

From the foundation of this rich evidence of religion's integrative potential, my goal has been to step back and ask what transnational Ghanaian migrants actually want from their migrations and their religious lives. Research under the banner of congregational studies has highlighted the extensive social functions of migrant congregations (Ebaugh 2000); I wanted to also show how migrants enter into such congregations in the first place and whether they actually prefer "ethnic" churches to other possibilities. I found that new social connections are not just a side effect of religious activity, but are in fact something Ghanaian migrants prioritize when choosing among church options. I found they wanted deep social connections, and I found these connections to be characterized by the activity of personal trust. I also found that many of them would rather find such connections in congregations that are truly diverse and inclusive. They would rather *not* go to Ghanaian churches, all things being equal.

Thus, on the one hand, my findings support other scholars' insights into how ethnic congregations assist integration, in spite of the fears surrounding the strange man and poor man stereotypes. Yet my findings also point to another salient connection between religion and integration for those who attend nonmigrant churches. Sylvia, for example, found trusting relationships within a diverse congregation. Her positive experience within that community, and the new ties to close friends and eventually her husband she found there, solidified her place in the United States and her desire to build a life here.

Of course, many Ghanaians did not have such a positive experience in nonmigrant churches. Anna and Timothy, for example, were unable to connect to new trust networks within American congregations, and this echoed their experiences of alienation in other settings. If it is true, as claimed by Jeremiah in chapter 5, that about a third of Ghanaians attend Ghanaian churches, another third attend non-Ghanaian churches, and another third don't attend anywhere, then it is also clear that many of those who attend Ghanaian churches would prefer to be attending non-Ghanaian churches, if not for the difficulty of finding trusting relationships in such places.

Religious membership for Christian Ghanaian migrants is thus largely positive for their integration into American life; however, it is not even as integrative as they would like. Whether or not Sylvia's experience is repeated depends upon the kind of cultures that develop within specific congregations, and whether or not they are able to maximize the integrative potential of shared religious association by facilitating personal trust between diverse groups. When there is distrust along lines such as race, nationality, and class, this becomes difficult, and many migrants ultimately gravitate to homogenous religious spaces. Yet the problem is not strange men practicing strange religion; it is how congregational cultures reflect symbolic categories of distrust and keep strangers out. What hinders integration in this case is implicit resistance to transformation within receiving institutions, rather than resistance on the part of newcomers themselves.

Far back in history, Weber (1946 [1904]) identified religious membership as a basis for social trust and integration. Yet if this potential in American religious life is eroded by racial and ethnic distrust—a general threat to our society that sadly seems to be advancing rather than retreating—then something significant will be lost. Either that basis will have to be recovered or new possibilities will have to be imagined.

Ultimately, imagining new possibilities happens on personal and structural levels. Integration depends on class position, political processes, resource distribution, and culture, but it also hinges on trust—little leaps of faith that defy risk and imagine the other in a positive light. Such leaps are difficult to make. If we cannot make them, however, we will never enjoy the personal goods of trust reciprocated or the collective goods of a strong society. The answer is to reject the symbolic categories of the racial order and take little leaps with the other, whether in religious or in other social spaces. In my experience within a Ghanaian transnational community, I found America's newest residents quite willing to take such leaps. I hope that by conveying my experience through this book, I can encourage others to reciprocate.

Research Methodology

The ideas and experiences that led to the writing of this book started long before the actual research. In 2007, while a beginning graduate student, I was invited to work as an assistant on two demographic research projects in Malawi, East Africa: the Malawi Religion Project (Adams and Trinitapoli 2009) and the Malawi Longitudinal Study of Families and Health. I worked with these projects for two summers, while also collecting and analyzing data on the growth of Pentecostal churches (Manglos 2010), the role of religious leaders in brokering collective resources (Manglos 2011), and the psychological impact of faith healing in the context of the generalized AIDs epidemic (Manglos and Trinitapoli 2011).

One afternoon while driving with one of the Malawian research staff, I saw a large church called Winner's Chapel. I asked the man what it was. He said he thought it was "the Nigerians," and explained that it was a Pentecostal church. This intrigued me. I knew that local Pentecostal churches were sprouting up quickly around the country—the middle school in Balaka, for example, had about a half-dozen of these churches meeting in different classrooms on a Sunday morning—but I didn't know there were also Pentecostal churches coming from other parts of Africa. After a bit of reading, I learned that West Africa, and Ghana and Nigeria in particular, were major centers of global Pentecostal outreach. I decided to write a proposal to spend the next summer in Accra, Ghana, doing research on the sources of Charismatic-Pentecostal growth. I soon learned that while "Pentecostal" was the preferred terminology in Malawi, "Charismatic" was the term more often used in Ghana.

At the time I was particularly interested in the connection between religious switching and changes in social networks. Working within the framework of social capital theory, I wanted to know whether young people who switched to Charismatic-Pentecostal churches gained more bridging capital—or in other words, whether their networks expanded to include more socioeconomic and ethnic diversity, and whether this could be a source of upward mobility for members.

This summer of research in 2009 became the first component of the data used in this book. Like many scholars before me, I was impressed by the popularity of the new

Charismatic churches, the excitement surrounding their meetings and events, and the larger-than-life quality of their leaders. It was clearly a major cultural phenomenon. I was also impressed by how quickly they were planting new branches around the world. This sparked a new curiosity: How do Ghanaian Charismatic rituals and routines translate into diverse new contexts in the West and in other parts of the Global South?

I decided to focus on Evangel Ministries International, for several reasons. First, by chance I had a contact—a relative of a friend—who was a member there (Ama, from chapter 2). Second, Evangel Ministries had branches in the United States and a branch in Malawi, and at the time I was considering doing research across three sites to address the question mentioned earlier (although I never ultimately collected research in Malawi on the topic).

This first of four phases of research involved attended the Evangel Ministries headquarters for four weeks on Sunday mornings and Tuesday nights. I took shorthand notes during the services, and also during each day's activities more generally, focusing on casual conversations and my observations about how the organization operates. All these shorthand notes were then typed up at the end of day. These daily fieldnotes also often included reflections on what I thought and felt in response to the day's events.

During the weekdays I worked in the office at the Regional Institute of Population Studies (RIPS), on the campus of the University of Ghana in Legon, a suburb of Accra. I shared an office with the graduate students in the RIPS program, where lots of lively discussions about Ghanaian culture generally and religion specifically took place. I also lived in the dorms—called hostels in Ghana—with Ghanaian students, and spent most weekends socializing with Ama and her friends.

I collected formal interviews with eleven people during this time. Six of these were Evangel Ministries' members, one was another Charismatic young man (Daniel, from chapter 2), and four were Anglican young people. I collected the latter to get the perspective of religious outsiders to the movement. I recruited Evangel Ministries' members by approaching them after church and asking if they would like to be interviewed. I recruited the Anglican interviewees through the personal contacts of Daniel, who was a graduate student in the RIPS program. He also accompanied me to many of the other interviews, in order to introduce me and help me navigate the city. All of the interviewees were proficient English speakers.

I used open-ended interview protocols, focusing on how they came to be a part of their religious tradition (whether Charismatic or Anglican); whether, in the case of those who were Charismatic, their moves into their church changed the nature of their social lives; and what their views were on the growth of Charismatic churches in Ghana. I also started each interview by asking and probing for a general life history. I obtained written consent in all cases, and audio-recorded and transcribed these interviews verbatim. All these interviews were covered by ethics board protocols at the University of Texas at Austin and the Noguchi Memorial Institute at the University of Ghana.

There were also five people with whom I had more informal ethnographic interviews, including Ama. In these cases, we did not schedule a separate interview, our conversation was not recorded, and they did not fill out a consent form. However, we did have one or several conversations covering the same topics, and these ended up being recorded in my fieldnotes. They were also aware of the project I was doing and, in the case of Ama, later gave consent to the use of her story.

The second of the four phases of research took place in Chicago. As told in the introduction, I selected this site because it was a city with an Evangel Ministries branch, and it was also a place I knew well and had personal connections. I contacted the branch through the phone number listed in the directory on the main Evangel Ministries International website. Again, as reported earlier, I reached the head of the U.S. branches, who recommended I attend the next week and talk to the pastor. This began two months of in-depth participant observation at the branch.

The first phase of research in Ghana was more exploratory, so I didn't identify myself to the organization's leadership. I wanted to wait until I had a better understanding of my project. After the research at the Chicago branch began, I explained to Elijah exactly who I was and what I was doing, and requested permission to keep going. Although I don't know exactly who he talked to about this, he told me several days later that his leaders said it was fine, but they requested I not use the actual names of the organization or the people in it. He said the organization did not want too much "media attention" (although, of course, in Ghana they got plenty of it by this time).

I spent the first three weeks of this period simply participating, which meant joining the choir and attending Sunday morning and Wednesday night services. There were also a few events throughout the summer that involved more extensive participation, including the Ghanafest (see chapter 3) and the summer camp meeting of Midwest branches (see chapter 5). Finally, there were several birthday parties or other celebrations throughout the summer that I attended with the community.

After the first few weeks I began to approach members I already knew to set up separate one-on-one interviews. Doing so was often difficult because of their busy schedules, so many of the interviews took place before or after services. A few took place at coffee shops, restaurants, or interviewees' homes. Again, I collected a combination of formal interviews that entailed a separate one-on-one meeting, the use of the interview protocol, and written consent; and informal ethnographic interviews, which were done by convenience, covered many of the same topics, and were recorded in my fieldnotes. As with Ama, if I used stories from any of the latter, during the writing phase I gained the person's permission later to use the material in the book. Although a few of these interviews were audio-recorded, most were not. I decided after the first few interviews that it was more effective to do interview reconstructions from handwritten notes. This kept the conversation more informal and made me less preoccupied with the operation of the recorder.

During this period I did formal interviews with twelve of Evangel Ministries' members and informal interviews with another fourteen members. Of the latter, five were members of other Midwest branches of the church whom I met at the camp meeting. The rest were all members of the Chicago branch. Notably, not all were Ghanaian. Of the Chicago branch group, one woman was Zimbabwean and another was African American, born and raised in Chicago. Of the group I interviewed from other branches, one woman was Liberian.

The protocol for the formal interviews focused first on personal history, with particular attention to their migration trajectory. I asked specifically about how they came to decide to go abroad and what their aims were at the time. I then asked about their religious upbringing, if any, in Ghana before migration, and then about how they came to be involved in Evangel Ministries. I probed about what it was that drew them there and what they liked about it now. Finally, I asked them to tell me about their experiences as foreigners in the United States and what they hoped and planned for the future, and specifically whether they saw themselves settling in the United States or back in Ghana.

Because Evangel Ministries conducted all its services in English, was built on professional networks within the diaspora (see chapter 5), and emphasized its global rather than Ghanaian character (see chapter 7), members tended to come from a higher socioeconomic class than other Ghanaian churches in Chicago, or the Ghanaian migrant community more generally. Thus, the group represented in this book is definitely more educated and wealthier than average. However, as should be clear by the combination of stories recounted in the text, there was still some diversity among those I interviewed and got to know, and many of them still struggled to make ends meet and find good jobs in the United States. Although they were usually better off than most, their stories still revealed the wider social and economic challenges facing transnational Ghanaians.

By the time this second phase was done, my research focus had shifted. This was when I started to formulate the question of how transnational Ghanaians chose a church upon arrival, as a window on how they made choices about their social networks, identities, and future goals in response to the challenges of migration. Their choices about church seemed weighted with significance, as a way to exercise agency within their own integration process. In order to answer this question, though, I needed comparative data with those who chose other churches or who didn't attend any churches at all. I also needed more data on what the relevant options were in the context of Chicago.

The third phase of research, therefore, was devoted to extending my data in this way. For the second summer (2011), I continued participating at Evangel Ministries in Chicago, and collected a few more interviews with new members there; but I also pursued more interviewees through a snowball quota sampling method. I asked several of Evangel's members for contacts with others in town who went to different churches, and I put out queries through my own networks in Chicago to see if anyone knew any Ghanaians in the city who would be willing to do an interview.

My goal in terms of the quota was to get at least several interviews within three categories: attendees and leaders of other Ghanaian churches; attendees of non-Ghanaian churches; and nonattendees. I did not make particular efforts to select on any other characteristics, except that all were first-generation movers to the United States and were at least nominally Christian. Like the Evangel Ministries congregation, they tended to be more educated and wealthy than the average among Ghanaians at home or abroad, but there was also some diversity in their ages, level of privilege, professions, and length of time living in the United States.

I collected twelve formal interviews and one informal ethnographic interview with those attending other Ghanaian churches, of which five were pastors; one formal interview a woman (Sylvia) attending a non-Ghanaian church; and one formal interview with a man (Franklin) who didn't attend anywhere. Overall, it was difficult to identify informants in the latter two categories through these networks, so I supplemented later on in the final phase (see later). However, I found it to be common among those who attended Ghanaian churches to have attended other types of churches in the past. Such narratives became quite useful to the book's argument about church choices. There were nine such cases in the interviewee sample. During this phase I also collected formal interviews with two new members of Evangel Ministries and informal interviews with three new members. By the end of this phase of research, my focus on church choices, trust networks, and the negotiation of identities and aspirations had for the most part become clear. Both the second and third phases of research were covered by an ethics review board protocol at the University of Texas at Austin.

The last phase of the research was more protracted and less intensive, but no less important for informing the book. My focus was to supplement the interviews with nonattenders and attenders of non-Ghanaian congregations, and to continue following up periodically with my closest connections at Evangel Ministries. In 2013, I sampled five Ghanaian students through my teaching networks, three of whom attended non-Ghanaian churches and two of whom didn't attend anywhere. These interviews followed a similar protocol as those described earlier. They were also reconstructed from handwritten notes, and were covered by an ethics review board protocol at Williams College. This resulted in formal in-depth interviews with a total of forty-four informants and ethnographic interviews with another twenty-two people.

During the following two years, I also kept in regular contact with some of my informants through social media, phone, and email. These continuing relationships were invaluable for me to consistently verify the conceptualization of the project and to observe how their lives in the United States developed over time. I took fieldnotes on these periodic conversations when relevant to the subject of the book. From 2013 to 2015, this data collection was covered under an ethics review board protocol at the University of Notre Dame.

Through this multiphase process of research, I was able to develop a dataset of narratives that were uniquely transnational and diverse in representation, and in certain cases extended over a period of six years. The book relies on these narratives combined with my fieldnotes from twenty-five weeks of in-depth participation at Evangel Ministries.

Getting this degree of narrative richness was important in two ways. First, it helped me reach a deeper level with certain people to understand the development of their experiences, desires, and choices over time. My two research questions (see the introduction) were, in the most simple terms, about *what people want* in relation to religious membership and migration, and how what they want changes in time. In order to get to a point of confidence in answering such a personal question, it was crucial to cultivate such relationships that would last beyond the point of in-depth participation.

Second, the personal knowledge I shared with these newfound friends and acquaintances allowed me to bring greater emotional depth to the book, highlighting their voices while also revealing my own thoughts and feelings when helpful. In any ethnographic reporting, a balance must be struck between honesty about the researcher's position in relation to the subject matter and fairness in the representation of others. As Cobb and Hoang (2015) have recently argued, ethnographies always make a choice about whose voice is amplified. Following feminist standpoint theory (Haraway 1988) and a Bourdieusian theory of reflexivity (Bourdieu and Wacquant 1992), ethnographers have increasingly engaged in a process of self-reflection about their own positions relative to their informants in their reporting. Yet there is a risk of falling into a scholar-centered ethnography, where the scholar herself becomes the central voice in the narrative. Cobb and Hoang thus argue for a protagonist-centered ethnographic approach that puts the voices of informants first.

While I consider this an important corrective, I am also far from ready to jettison the insights of standpoint theory. It does not need to be an either/or question. The narratives in this book are not mine, but I was deeply engaged in the experience of learning about them and living life, for a time, with my friends and acquaintances in the Ghanaian community. In that sense we co-created the insights in this book, and this is especially true for those three or four people with whom I shared deeper friendships. I therefore prefer to identify my method as *relationship-driven ethnography*. My aim was to be co-protagonist with the central cast of characters, showing up when necessary, receding when not. I used many others as models, including ethnographies by Desmond (2007), Brown (2001), Tweed (1997), and Scheper-Hughes (1992).

Throughout the research I was always honest with people about my work. I often discussed the book informally with those whom I got to know well and talked about my research more generally. That said, I have no doubt there were times and places in which people shared information in the context of a personal relationship, without considering whether or not they wanted it to be in the book. Standard models of informed consent do not cover such instances. I therefore used my own judgment to evaluate the personal information obtained, and to decide whether or not it needed to be reported. I left out anything that seemed sensitive and was not necessary to the book's argument. In cases where sensitive information was important to include, I made sure it was shared in the context of explicit informed consent (i.e., a formal interview) or I followed up with informants to ask their permission to include it.

My analytic strategy for the ethnographic data closely followed that of Jack Katz (2001), as a move from a detailed description of *how* church choice and religious association works for Ghanaian migrants to an explanation of *why* they make the choices they do. Of his seven aspects of good data for moving from "how" to "why," I focused on the following: using data strategically to parallel turning points in informants' lives (#2); and using rich and varied stories (#3) to rule out rival hypotheses, such as the idea that shared ethnicity as such is the main draw of Evangel Ministries to its members, or the idea that religious-based ties matter very little as compared to other bases of social connection. I also brought out emotionally poignant moments (#7) to connect my informants, myself, and my readers together in an experience of being "humbled by transcending concerns that structure persistent patterns in their lives" (Katz 2001, 447), specifically the need to trust others and be trusted in turn.

By collecting observations of where people went to church, what they considered to be a good church, and what they did in such churches, and from these making an argument about the importance of personal trust and its nature as a symbolic and imaginative activity, I have also engaged in a type of abductive analysis (Tavory and Timmermans 2014). This means I recorded research evidence while noting particularly surprising events and statements—such as the patterns of church-switching my informants engaged in, or their statements about attending Evangel Ministries *in spite of* rather than because of its being a Ghanaian church—and worked creatively backward toward a theory that could explain both the patterns and the variations in the stories I collected. The goal of abductive analysis is not to attain the single complete explanation—as if there were a single complete explanation for any observed social action—but to craft a compelling and viable explanation and bring it to the research community for debate. Such as been my goal with the book's argument about personal trust.

Notes

CHAPTER 1

1. The classic work on the Polish community by Thomas and Znaniecki (1996) vividly depicts the social experience of these earlier waves of migrants, particularly those from Western and Southern Europe that came in large numbers in the late 1800s and early 1900s. For a summary of the historical waves of migration to the United States, see also Portes and Rumbault (2014, 1–47). Given the fluidity of racial categories and fears about the threat of new immigrants, there were some European immigrant groups like the Irish who in the early twentieth century were portrayed by some as nonwhite or not-quite-white (Orser 1998). Nevertheless, the intensity with which being European has come to be associated with whiteness in the global racial order means today's immigrants from Africa, Asia, and Latin America are more often and more sweepingly categorized as nonwhite than were earlier waves of immigrants in the United States.
2. These estimates are from the Pew Research Center, based on 2013 U.S. Census data, www.pewresearch.org/fact-tank/2015/10/07/a-shift-from-germany-to-mexico-for-americas-immigrants/.
3. For summaries of the development of the 1965 Immigration Act and its impact on the demographics of the immigrant population, see Lee 2015; Reimers 1983; and Keely 1971.
4. Pew Research Center, data as of 2015, www.pewresearch.org/fact-tank/2015/11/02/african-immigrant-population-in-u-s-steadily-climbs/. See also Halter and Showers Johnson (2014) for an overview of this growth in West African migrants to the United States.
5. The literature on African migrants shows they tend to be more educated than most other foreign-born groups, as well as the native-born black population; also, they tend to have high levels of English proficiency, and tend to maintain fairly strong

social and economic ties to those back home, although they do not tend to see equal returns to education in their earnings (Boon and Ahenken 2012; Thomas 2010; Bennett and Lutz 2009; Read and Emerson 2005; Dodoo 1997).

6. International Organization for Migration 2009; Akyeampong 2000.
7. Erik Badia, Tim O'Connor, and Rich Schapiro, "Kwasi Enin Says His 'Passion' Got Him Accepted at Every Ivy League School," *New York Daily News*, April 1, 2014, www.nydailynews.com/new-york/education/whiz-kid-wins-ivy-league-jackpot-article-1.1742417.
8. Even in the immediate news frenzy surrounding Enin's accomplishment, there were objections to how his admission success was framed in terms of his race and immigrant status. See Benjamin Dinovelli, "Defending Kwasi Enin," *Daily Princetonian*, April 6, 2014, http://dailyprincetonian.com/opinion/2014/04/defending-kwasi-enin/. The broader struggles of black students within college settings has been notably expressed by the "I, Too, Am Harvard" movement of students, creating awareness of the ways in which they are often misunderstood or misjudged by other students. See Bethonie Butler, "'I, Too, Am Harvard': Black Students Show They Belong," *Washington Post*, March 5, 2014, https://www.washingtonpost.com/blogs/she-the-people/wp/2014/03/05/i-too-am-harvard-black-students-show-they-belong/?utm_term=.5991678d343d. This movement has inspired replications by black students in other universities, including Oxford and Notre Dame.
9. These forced identity choices occurring within the environment of higher education are eloquently described in the novel *Americanah* by Chimimanda Adichie. They were also major themes within the five interviews with Ghanaian university students I conducted as part of my research study.
10. Beginning most notably with Henry M. Stanley's 1878 book *Through the Dark Continent*, the association of Africa with darkness has plagued the European and American cultural consciousness. Today, using this term directly has fallen out of favor because of its Eurocentric history, but for many Americans, Africa remains "dark" in the sense that they know little about its distinct history or the varied landscapes, people groups, and societies.
11. Dodoo 1997.
12. Empirical research demonstrating the factors along which assimilation is now segmented includes the following: Avenarius 2012; Iceland and Scopitili 2008; Garip 2008; Warner 2007; Portes 2007; Esser 2004; Guarnizo, Portes, and Haller 2003; Hagan 1998; Dodoo 1997; Portes and Grosfoguel 1994.
13. Albanese 2012, 10–13; Cadge and Ecklund 2007; Warner 1998, 1988; Herberg 1983 [1955].
14. For case studies of groups from Asia, see Chong 2009; Chen 2008; Kurien 2004; Yang 1999; for those from Latin America, see Rey and Stepick 2013; Mooney 2009; Johnson 2007; Tweed 1997; for those from Africa, see Abrams 2014 and Biney 2011, as well as edited volumes by Adogame and Spickard 2010 and Olupona and Gemingnani 2007.

15. Abrams 2014; Glick Schiller and Çaglar 2008; Tettey 2007; Glick Schiller, Çaglar, and Guldbrandsen 2006.
16. These statistics are from my own analysis of 2008 Afrobarometer data, which is a publicly available survey dataset conducted in multiple countries across the continent (www.afrobarometer.org). There are also substantial numbers of Muslims in Ghana, at about 16 percent of the total population, but in order to limit dimensions of variation in my sample, I focus only on Christians in this study.
17. See the book's Research Methodology section; also see Manglos 2011, 2010.

CHAPTER 2

1. For this portion of the historical narrative I rely heavily on works by Robinson (2004) and Insoll (2003) on the spread of Islam in Africa, as well as local histories by Wilks 1993; McCaskie 1986, 1983; Yarak 1986; Fynn 1971; and Arhin 1967.
2. Wilks 1993.
3. For more on the history of the Asante Empire and its interactions with neighbors, as well as with the European powers, see Manglos-Weber 2015; Wilks 1993; McCaskie 1986, 1983; and Fynn 1971.
4. This religious historical overview relies on Isichei 2004; Meyer 2002, 1992; Allman 1991; Smith 1945.
5. See also Pakenham 1992 and Chamberlain 1974.
6. I analyze the complex internal and external pressures that led to the collapse of the Asante Empire in an earlier work, focusing on their implications for the relationship between social trust and political authority; see Manglos-Weber 2015.
7. Some good summaries of the relationship between out-migration and education can be found in the following works: Effah and Senadza 2008; Akyeampong 2000; Peil 1995; Dodoo 1997. For a general discussion of this trend on the African continent, see also Davidson 1995, 318–323.
8. Robert Bates (2008) argues that the incentive structures for postcolonial state leaders in Africa following the transition to independence led to widespread state failure and civil unrest across the continent. This narrative fits the case of Ghana, which was plagued by coups, uprisings, and economic collapses through the 1970s and 1980s. For more on the politics of reform in the 1980s and 1990s in Ghana specifically, see Herbst 1993.
9. See Wheatley and Rodriguez (2014) and Rodriguez and Paredes (2014) for summaries of these recent bureaucratic trends and the criminalization of immigrants.
10. See Massey and Sanchez (2010) for an analysis of the rise of anti-immigrant sentiment in the United States.
11. These data are from the World Bank, World Development Indicators Database, data.worldbank.org.
12. These data are from the American Fact Finder page of the U.S. Census website, http://factfinder.census.gov/faces/nav/jsf/pages/index.xhtml.

13. For this description of the Ghanaian migrant population in the United States, I rely on my own data, as well as the following works: Halter and Showers Johnson 2014; Opoku-Dapaah 2012; Biney 2011; Akyeampong 2000; Peil 1995.
14. See Lehrer 1998 for an example.
15. For some examples of social capital theorists who consider trust a central concept, see Burt 2005: 112–125; Nooteboom 2007; Newton 2001; Putnam 2000, 134–139.
16. This description relies primarily on the work of Fredricksen (2012) and Möllering (2001), though it is echoed in other characterizations of trust as well: Barbalet 2009; Mizstal 2001; Lewis and Wiegert 1985. Barbara Mizstal (1996) describes trust as both habitus and passion—terms that point to its embodied, enacted, and emotional nature, and that fit closely with an imaginative and symbolic view of trust.
17. For this insight I am indebted to the article "Black Like Them" by Malcolm Gladwell, originally published in *The New Yorker*, April 29, 1996, http://gladwell.com/black-like-them/.
18. In this statement I am relying on the insights of Smith (2015, 62ff) on the multiplicity of human motivation, and how the presence of two or more seemingly incommensurable motivations can lead to variation, which is ultimately acted upon.
19. See the edited volume by Warner and Wittner (1998) for a number of studies to this effect, as well as works by Levitt 2007; Chen 2008; Yang 1999; and Chong 1998.
20. Foner and Alba (2008) compare and contrast how European and American scholarship places very different emphases on the integrative versus separatist effects of immigrant religion.
21. Bulut and Ebaugh 2014; Winchester 2008; Williams and Vashi 2007; Bartkowski and Read 2003.
22. Evangelical Charismatic Christianity is a branch of Protestant Christianity closely related to Pentecostalism. These churches tend to focus on personal emotional experiences of God; they teach that people are saved through an unmediated, personal, and trusting relationship with God; and they emphasize the importance of evangelizing this message to people of other religions and Christian traditions. Churches identifying as Charismatic are now the largest religious group in Ghana, and have influenced many of the older denominations, as exemplified in the Charismatic Catholic Renewal movement. For more on Charismatic Christianity in Ghana, see chapter 4; also see Soothill 2007; De Witte 2005; Gifford 2004, 1994; van Dijk 2004; Meyer 1998, 1992; Hackett 1998. Regarding the global growth of Charismatic and/or Pentecostal Christianity, see Anderson 2007; Miller and Yamamuri 2007; Meyer 2004; Robbins 2004; Martin 2002; Freston 2001; Poewe 1994.
23. See Gifford (2004) for a thorough description of the movement and its discursive culture.
24. For research into the embrace of Christian institutions by Africans on the continent, see Magesa 2004; Isichei 2004; Comaroff and Comaroff 1991; Fields 1982.

For studies of the role of Christian conversion among slaves in the New World, see Sensbach 2005; Lincoln and Mimaya 1990.
25. Edwards 2014; Perry 2013; Marti 2012; Shelton and Emerson 2012; Emerson and Smith 2001; Emerson, Smith, and Sikkink 1999.
26. See Barron 2016; Cobb, Perry, and Dougherty 2015; and Perry 2013.
27. Mooney 2013; Cadge et al. 2013.

CHAPTER 3

1. Arthur 2009; Lindberg and Morrison 2005; Morrison 2004; Owusu 1996, 1989.
2. The low point of Ghana's economy was in 1982, when it reached a growth rate of *negative* 6.9 percent annually (World Bank, World Development Indicators). This was the result both of a global downturn driven by the energy crises of the 1970s and of mismanagement of the economy by Ghana's leaders (Herbst 1993).
3. Emmanuel Hansen 1989, "The State and Food Agriculture," as quoted in Owusu 1996, 312.
4. U.S. Department of State, Number of Visa Issuances and Adjustments of Status in the Diversity Immigrant Category, www.travel.state.gov/content/visas/english/immigrate/diversity-visa/diversity-visa-program-statistics.html.
5. My field notes from July 17, 2009, recount an incident of being pulled over for speeding by a police officer while driving home late at night with two Ghanaian friends. The police officer implied that without payment of a bribe, he would have to exercise his right to report the incident and take us to the station. The woman I was with secretly recorded what he said on her phone. She then told him that she had done so, and that her father was an important figure in the news media, at which point he promptly sent us on our way without reporting the incident.
6. On the Ghanaian culture of migration, see also Coe 2012 and Peil 1995. On the concept of a culture of migration, see Massey et al. 1993.
7. U.S. Department of State, Information on Obtaining Student Visas, http://travel.state.gov/content/visas/english/study-exchange/student.html.
8. U.S. Citizenship and Immigration Services, Students and Employment, March 11, 2016, https://www.uscis.gov/working-united-states/students-and-exchange-visitors/students-and-employment
9. Ibid.
10. These statistics are compiled by American Student Assistance and are published on their website, www.asa.org/policy/resources/stats/. All statistics are sourced from the *Chronicle of Higher Education*, the Federal Reserve Board of New York, and the Federal Reserve Bank of New York.
11. Kim Clark, "How Can International Students Get Financial Aid?" *U.S. News and World Report*, September 8, 2008, www.usnews.com/education/blogs/college-cash-101/2008/09/18/how-can-international-students-get-financial-aid.
12. Field notes, July 5, 2010.

13. *Kente* cloth is woven fabric that is wrapped around the body and is worn by chiefs and queen mothers of the Akan people group, although its influence as ceremonial clothing has spread more broadly across West Africa. The designs are highly symbolic, with colors symbolizing attributes such as peacefulness and wealth, and it is still often donned for ceremonial occasions both in Ghana and among Ghanaian community groups abroad.
14. See Best 2013, 35ff.
15. Best (2013) narrates this history in the context of the Great Migration of former slaves from the rural American South to the urban North. See also Lincoln and Mimaya 1990, 117–126.
16. Alison Fisher, "The Battle for Uptown," *AREA Chicago* 13, http://areachicago.org/the-battle-for-uptown/.
17. As cited in Maly and Leachman 1998.
18. For a helpful overall of the rise of the intersectional approach and its importance for sociological theory, see McCall 2005.

CHAPTER 4

1. Author interview with "John," July 9, 2009.
2. By focusing on the social benefits drawing young people to Charismatic churches in Ghana, my intent is not to imply religious practice in Ghana is "only" or "really" about social dynamics as opposed to spiritual ones. Quite the opposite—I am convinced by reading the work of other authors that there are distinct strains of spirituality and imagination operating within Ghana's Charismatic churches as well (Daswani 2012; Biney 2011, 2007; Tettey 2007). Nevertheless, I choose to focus on the social aspects in this book for two main reasons. First, as an outsider who is a sociologist rather than a theologian, I am more comfortable observing and reaching conclusions about social dynamics than spiritual ones. My bent as an ethnographer is to make arguments about what I can observe, and that includes where people go to church, what those churches are like, and how people interact with others in those churches. Second, I became convinced in my research that the growth of Charismatic Christianity in Ghana is not so much a spiritual conversion movement, in the sense that it involves a change in one's beliefs or perceptions of the spiritual, as it is a social movement of younger generations—already Christian in most cases—toward congregational forms that better suit their social lives and concerns (see also Manglos 2010 for a similar argument in the case of Pentecostalism in Malawi). Because of this, my object throughout this study is patterns of religious association, and my argument pertains to that object rather than to religion in Ghana writ large.
3. Director, Professor Francis Nii-Amoo Dodoo. Since my visit there in 2009, a new director, Professor Samuel Nii Ardey Codjoe, has been appointed. See http://rips-ug.edu.gh/.
4. Field notes, June 28, 2009.

5. This history is based in the work of Birgit Meyer (2004, 2002, 1998, 1992) on German missionaries among the Ewe, and the work of Elizabeth Isichei (2004, 1995) on the early spread of Christianity on the continent.
6. Miller and Yamamuri 2007, 18.
7. This apt term was coined by Andrew Chesnut (2003) in his work on Pentecostal-Charismatic Christianity in Brazil.
8. For histories of the rise of Pentecostal churches and Charismatic renewal movements in Ghana, see Biney 2011; Asamoah-Gyadu 2010; Gifford 2004; Omenyo 2002.
9. Both the spread of Pentecostalism and the success of locally originated conversion movements like Harris's are described in detail in the work of Anderson 2007, 2001; and Martin 2002.
10. Manglos and Weinreb, 2013.
11. See Robbins 2004; Meyer 2004; and Martin 2002 for summaries.
12. Field notes, July 5, 2009.
13. Field notes, October 18, 2014.
14. Field notes, July 1, 2009.
15. Author interview of "Annie," July 26, 2009.
16. Population Reference Bureau, "The World's Youth 2013 Data Sheet," www.prb.org/DataFinder/Topic/Rankings.aspx?ind=19.
17. World Bank, World Development Indicators Database. data.worldbank.org.
18. Author interview of "Daniel," June 30, 2009.
19. Author interview of "George," July 19, 2009.
20. "O Come All Ye Faithful," *The Economist,* November 1, 2007, www.economist.com/node/10015239.
21. Author interview of "Mary," July 16, 2009.
22. Field notes, July 28, 2009.

CHAPTER 5

1. Name has been changed.
2. Field notes, June 6, 2010.
3. Field notes, July 28, 2010.
4. In a different religious setting—a community of Orthodox Jews—Tavory (2013) nonetheless identifies similar meanings within congregational rituals, which are compelling precisely because they refer publicly to the intimate details of congregants' lives—in this case cited here, their financial situations—and thus codify the intimacy congregants feel within the group, as well as their sense of being central and necessary to the enactment of the ritual itself.
5. Field notes, July 15, 2011.
6. Field notes, July 11, 2010.
7. Field notes, July 16, 2010.
8. Author interview with "Sylvia," May 14, 2011.

9. In this paragraph, Franklin references Ousmane Sembène, the Senegalese director, producer, writer, and actor who lived from 1923 to 2007 and produced dozens of books and popular films in French and Wolof.
10. Author interview with "Franklin," July 27, 2011.
11. Although I heard many more details about this situation as it occurred, I have chosen not to include them here to protect the people involved.

CHAPTER 6

1. I did not verify the cost of the taxi medallions he quoted, primarily because in the context of his story, what they actually cost matters less than how he perceives and describes the system. These numbers are those he gave in the interview on July 1, 2010.
2. World Bank, 1988. See also Aikman 2011 and Emoungu 1992.
3. Samoff and Carrol 2004.
4. Effah and Senadza, 2008.
5. Author interview of "Anna," August 3, 2010.
6. Teferra 2008.
7. These statistics are from my own analyses of data from the New Immigrant Survey, collected in 2003–2004; see http://nis.princeton.edu/.
8. The Catholic Charismatic Renewal (CCR) is a movement within the Catholic Church aptly described by Thomas Csordas (2007, 296) as, "based on a born-again spirituality of a 'personal relationship' with Jesus and direct access to divine power and inspiration through 'spiritual gifts' or 'charisms,' including faith-healing, prophecy, and speaking in tongues." Structurally, the CCR developed through small prayer groups and communities within the Catholic Church, although at times conflicts between the emphases of the CCR and the Catholic hierarchy have resulted in congregational splits and upheaval. For more information on its history, relationship to the wider Catholic organization, and spread worldwide, see Gooren 2012; Csordas 2007, 1997; and Hervieu-Leger 1997.
9. Author interview with "Akosua," February 11, 2013; author interview with "Koku," February 19, 2013.
10. Author interview with "Jeremiah," June 7, 2011.
11. Posted June 28, 2010, https://www.ghanaweb.com.
12. Ibid.
13. For more on this point, see Arthur 2009; Kelly 2005; Morrison 2004; Frempong 2001.
14. Author interview with "David," July 31, 2010.
15. Field notes, January 8, 2011.
16. Author interview with "Jonathan," February 16, 2013.

CHAPTER 7

1. Author interview with "Timothy," August 3, 2010.
2. Author interview with "Sandra," June 15, 2011.
3. Field notes, June 20, 2010.
4. Field notes, July 11, 2010.
5. Author interview with "Elijah," June 20, 2010.
6. Field notes, August 1, 2010.
7. Field notes, July 25, 2010.
8. Field notes, August 1, 2010.
9. Field notes, July 15, 2010.
10. Field notes, July 4, 2010.
11. Field notes, June 12, 2011.
12. Author interview with "Elijah," July 5, 2010.
13. Field notes, July 18, 2010.
14. Field notes, July 31, 2010.
15. Field notes, July 11, 2010.
16. Field notes, July 15, 2010.
17. Author interview with "Elijah," June 20, 2010.

CHAPTER 8

1. As noted in the introduction, this conceptualization of personal trust integrates the work of Georg Simmel (1990, 1955), Mario Small (2009), Blaine Fowers (2015), and Charlies Tilly (2005). The following theoretical pieces have also been helpful in crafting this description of trust: Fredericksen 2012; Archer 2010; Barbalet 2009; Mizrachi, Anspach, and Drori 2007; Uslaner 2002; Newton 2001; Möllering 2001; Mizstal 1996; Fukuyama 1995.
2. The empirical connection between religious participation and trust is shown in Seymour et al. 2014.
3. Field notes, August 8, 2010.
4. Andres Rice, "Mission from Africa," *New York Times,* April 8, 2009, www.nytimes.com/2009/04/12/magazine/12churches-t.html.
5. See the chapters in the edited volume by Warner and Wittner (1998), as well as works by Warner (2007, 2000); Yang (1999); Yang and Ebaugh (2001); Foley and Hoge (2007); Chen (2008); and Mooney (2009).

References

Abdullah, Zain. 2013. *Black Mecca: The African Muslims of Harlem*. New York: Oxford University Press.

Abrams, Andrea C. 2014. *God and Blackness: Race, Gender, and Identity in a Middle Class Afrocentric Church*. New York: New York University Press.

Adams, Jimi, and Jenny Trinitapoli. 2009. "The Malawi Religion Project: Data Collection and Selected Analyses." *Demographic Research* 21: 255–288.

Adogame, Afe, and James V. Spickard, eds. 2010. *Religion Crossing Boundaries: Transnational Religious and Social Dynamics in Africa and the New African Diaspora*. Leiden, The Netherlands: Brill.

Aikman, Sheila. 2011. "Educational and Indigenous Justice in Africa." *International Journal of Educational Development* 31: 15–22.

Akyeampong, Emmanuel. 2000. "Africans in the Diaspora: The Diaspora and Africa." *African Affairs* 99: 183–215.

Albanese, Catherine. 2012. *America: Religions and Religion*, 5th ed. New York: Wadsworth.

Allman, Jean Marie. 1991. "'Hewers of Wood, Carriers of Water': Islam, Class, and Politics on the Eve of Ghana's Independence." *African Studies Review* 34(2): 1–26.

Ammerman, Nancy Tatom. 2005. *Pillars of Faith: American Congregations and Their Partners*. Berkeley: University of California Press.

Anderson, Allan. 2001. *African Reformation: African Initiated Christianity in the 20th Century*. Trenton, NJ: Africa World Press.

Anderson, Allan. 2007. *Spreading Fires: The Missionary Nature of Early Pentecostalism*. New York: Maryknoll.

Archer, Margaret S. 2010. "Routine, Reflexivity, and Realism." *Sociological Theory* 28(3): 272–303.

Arhin, Kwame. 1967. "The Structure of Greater Ashanti (1700–1824)." *Journal of African History* 8(1): 65–85.

Arthur, Peter. 2009. "Ethnicity and Electoral Politics in Ghana's Fourth Republic." *Africa Today* 56(2): 45–73.

Asamoah-Gyadu, J. Kwabena. 2010. "Mediating Spiritual Power: African Christianity, Transnationalism and the Media." In *Religion Crossing Boundaries: Transnational Religious and Social Dynamics in Africa and the New African Diaspora*, ed. James V. Spickard and Afe Adogame, 87–103. Boston: Brill.

Auyero, Javier. 2000. *Poor People's Politics*. Durham, NC: Duke University Press.

Avenarius, Christine. 2012. "Immigrant Networks in New Urban Spaces: Gender and Social Integration." *International Migration* 50(5): 25–55.

Barbalet, Jack. 2009. "A Characterization of Trust, and Its Consequences." *Theory and Society* 38(4), (Special Issue: Emotion and Rationality in Economic Life): 367–382.

Barron, Jessica M. 2016. "Managed Diversity: Race, Place, and an Urban Church." *Sociology of Religion* 77(1): 18–36.

Bartkowski, John P., and Jen'nan Ghazal Read. 2003. "Veiled Submission: Gender, Power, and Identity among Evanglical and Muslim Women in the United States." *Qualitative Sociology* 26(1): 71–92.

Bates, Robert H. 2008. *When Things Fell Apart: State Failure in Late-Century Africa*. New York: Cambridge University Press.

Bellah, Robert N., Richard Madsen, William M. Sullivan, Ann Swidler, and Steven M. Tipton. 1985. *Habits of the Heart: Individualism and Commitment in American Life*. Berkeley: University of California Press.

Bennett, Pamela R., and Amy Lutz. 2009. "How African American Is the Net Black Advantage? Differences in College Attendance among Immigrant Blacks, Native Blacks, and Whites." *Sociology of Education* 82(1): 70–100.

Best, Wallace D. 2013. *Passionately Human, No Less Divine: Religion and Culture in Black Chicago, 1915–1952*. Princeton, NJ: Princeton University Press.

Biney, Moses. 2007. "Singing the Lord's Song in a Foreign Land: Spirituality, Community, and Identity in a Ghanaian Immigrant Congregation." In *African Transnational Religions in America*, ed. J. Olupona and R. Gemignani, 259–278. New York: New York University Press.

Biney, Moses. 2011. *From Africa to America: Religion and Adaptation among Ghanaian Immigrants in New York*. New York: New York University Press.

Bongmba, Elias K. 2007. "Portable Faith: The Global Mission of African Initiated Churches (AICs)." In *African Immigrant Religions in America*, ed. J. Olupona and R. Gemignani, 102–123. New York: New York University Press.

Bonilla-Silva, Eduardo. 2013. *Racism without Racists: Color-Blind Racism and the Persistence of Racial Inequality in the United States*, 4th ed. Lanham, MD: Rowman & Littlefield.

Boon, Emmanuel, and Albert Ahenkan. 2012. "The Socio-economic Contribution of African Migrants to their Home and Host Countries: The Case of Ghanaian Residents in Flanders, Belgium." *International Migration and Integration* 13: 343–363.

Bourdieu, Pierre. 1987. *Distinction: A Social Critique of the Judgment of Taste*. Cambridge, MA: Harvard University Press.

Bourdieu, Pierre, and Loic Wacquant. 1992. *An Invitation to Reflexive Sociology*. Chicago: University of Chicago Press.

Brenneman, Robert. 2011. *Homies and Hermanos: God and Gangs in Central America*. New York: Oxford University Press.

Breton, Raymond. 1964. "Institutional Completeness of Ethnic Communities and the Personal Relations of Immigrants." *American Journal of Sociology* 70(2): 193–205.

Brown, Karen M. 2001. *Mama Lola: A Vodou Priestess in Brooklyn*. Berkeley: University of California Press.

Bulut, Elif, and Helen Rose Ebaugh. 2014. "Religion and Assimilation among Turkish Muslim Immigrants: Comparing Practicing and Non-Practicing Muslims." *Journal of International Migration and Integration* 15(3): 487–507.

Burt, Ronald S. 2005. *Brokerage and Closure*. New York: Oxford University Press.

Cadge, Wendy, and Elaine H. Ecklund. 2007. "Immigration and Religion." *Annual Review of Sociology* 33: 359–379.

Cadge, Wendy, Peggy Levitt, Bernadette N. Jaworsky, and Casey Clevenger. 2013. "Religious Dimensions of Contexts of Reception: Comparing Two New England Cities." *International Migration* 51(3): 84–98.

Chamberlain, Muriel. 1974. *The Scramble for Africa*. London: Longman.

Chen, Carolyn. 2005. "A Self of One's Own: Taiwanese Immigrant Women and Religious Conversion." *Gender and Society* 19: 336–357.

Chen, Carolyn. 2006. "From Filial Piety to Religious Piety: Evangelical Christianity Reconstructing Taiwanese Immigrant Families in the United States." *International Migration Review* 40: 573–602.

Chen, Carolyn. 2008. *Getting Saved in America: Taiwanese Immigration and Religious Experience*. Princeton, NJ: Princeton University Press.

Chesnut, Andrew. 2003. "Pragmatic Consumers and Practical Products: The Success of Pneumacentric Religion among Women in Latin America's New Religious Economy." *Review of Religious Research* 45(1): 20–31.

Chong, Kelly. 1998. "What It Means to Be Christian: The Role of Religion in the Construction of Ethnic Identity and Boundary among Second-Generation Korean Americans." *Sociology of Religion* 59(3): 259–286.

Chong, Kelly. 2009. *Deliverance and Submission: Evangelical Women and the Negotiation of Patriarchy in South Korea*. Cambridge, MA: Harvard University Press.

Chong, Kelly. 2008. "Coping with Conflict, Confronting Resistance: Fieldwork Emotions and Identity Management in a South Korean Evangelical Community." *Qualitative Sociology* 31(4): 369–390.

Cobb, Jessica Shannon, and Kimberly Kay Hoang. 2015. "Protagonist-Driven Urban Ethnography." *City & Community* 14(4): 348–351.

Cobb, Ryon J., Samuel L. Perry, and Kevin D. Dougherty. 2015. "United by Faith? Race/Ethnicity, Congregational Diversity, and Explanations of Racial Inequality." *Sociology of Religion* 76(2): 177–198.

Coe, Cati. 2012. "Cultures of Migration: The Global Nature of Contemporary Mobility." *Journal of Ethnic and Migration Studies* 38(6): 913–931.

Coleman, James. 1990. *Foundations of Social Theory*. Cambridge, MA: Harvard University Press.

Collins, Patricia Hill. 2009. *Black Feminist Thought: Knowledge, Consciousness, and the Politics of Empowerment*. New York: Routledge.

Collins, Randall. 2005. *Interaction Ritual Chains*. Princeton, NJ: Princeton University Press.

Comaroff, Jean, and John L. Comaroff. 1991. *Of Revelation and Revolution: Christianity, Colonialism, and Consciousness in South Africa*. Chicago: University of Chicago Press.

Csordas, Thomas. 1997. *The Sacred Self: A Cultural Phenomenology of Charismatic Healing*. Berkeley: University of California Press.

Csordas, Thomas. 2007. "Global Religion and the Re-Enchantment of the World: The Case of the Catholic Charismatic Renewal." *Anthropological Theory* 7(3): 295–314.

Daswani, Girish. 2012. "Global Pentecostal Networks and the Problems of Culture: The Church of Pentecost in Ghana and Abroad." In *Global Pentecostal Movements: Migration, Mission, and Public Religion*, ed. Michael Wilkinson, 71–90. Leiden, The Netherlands: Brill.

Davidson, Basil. 1995. *Africa in History*. New York: Touchstone.

Desmond, Matthew. 2007. *On the Fireline: Living and Dying with Wildland Firefighters*. Chicago: University of Chicago Press.

De Witte, Marleen. 2005. "The Spectacular and the Spirits: Charismatics and Neo-traditionalists on Ghanaian Television." *Material Religion: The Journal of Objects, Art, and Belief* 1(3): 314–334.

Dodoo, Francis Nii-Amoo. 1997. "Assimilation Differences among Africans in America." *Social Forces* 76(2): 527–546.

Dubler, Josh. 2013. *Down in the Chapel: Religious Life in an American Prison*. New York: Farrar, Strauss, and Giroux.

Du Bois, W. E. B. 1903. *The Souls of Black Folk*. New York: Bantam Classic.

Ebaugh, Helen Rose. 2000. "Structural Adaptations in Immigrant Congregations." *Sociology of Religion* 61(2): 135–153.

Edwards, Korie L. 2014. "Role Strain Theory and Understanding the Role of Head Clergy of Racially Diverse Churches." *Sociology of Religion* 75(1): 57–79.

Effah, Paul, and Bernadin Senadza. 2008. "Ghana." In *Higher Education in Africa: The International Dimension*, ed. Jane Knight and Damtew Teferra, 208–237. Boston: Center for International Higher Education.

Emerson, Michael O., and Christian Smith. 2001. *Divided by Faith: Evangelical Religion and the Problem of Race in America*. New York: Oxford University Press.

Emerson, Michael O., Christian Smith, and David Sikkink. 1999. "Equal in Christ, but Not in the World: White Conservative Protestants and Explanations of Black-White Inequality." *Social Problems* 6(3): 398–417.

Emoungu, Paul-Albert. 1992. "Education and Primitive Accumulation in Sub-Saharan Africa." *Comparative Education* 28(2): 201–213.

Esser, Hartmut. 2004. "Does the "New" Immigration Require a New Theory of Intergenerational Integration?" *International Migration Review* 38(3): 1126–1159.

Fields, Karen E. 1982. "Christian Missionaries as Anticolonial Militants." *Theory and Society* 11(1): 95–108.

Foley, Michael W., and Dean R. Hoge. 2007. *Religion and the New Immigrants: How Faith Communities Form our Newest Citizens*. New York: Oxford University Press.

Foner, Nancy, and Richard Alba. 2008. "Immigrant Religion in the U.S. and Western Europe: Bridge or Barrier to Inclusion?" *International Migration Review* 42(2): 360–392.

Fowers, Blaine. 2015. *The Evolution of Ethics: Human Sociality and the Emergence of Ethical Mindedness*. New York: Palgrave Macmillan.

Frederiksen, Morten. 2012. "Dimensions of Trust: An Empirical Revisit to Simmel's Formal Sociology of Intersubjective Trust." *Current Sociology* 60(6): 733–750.

Frempong, Alexander K. D. 2001. "Ghana's Election 2000: The Ethnic Undercurrent." In *Deepening Democracy in Ghana: Politics of the 2000 Elections*, ed. J. Ayee, 141–159. Accra: Freedom Publications.

Freston, Paul. 2001. *Evangelicals and Politics in Asia, Africa, and Latin America*. New York: Cambridge University Press.

Fukuyama, Francis. 1995. *Trust: The Social Virtues and the Creation of Prosperity*. New York: Free Press.

Fynn, John Kofi. 1971. *Asante and Its Neighbours 1700-1807*. Evanston, IL: Northwestern University Press.

Gambetta, Diego, and Heather Hamill. 2005. *Streetwise: How Taxi Drivers Establish Customers' Trustworthiness*. New York: Russell Sage Foundation.

Garip, Feliz. 2008. "Social Capital and Migration: How Do Similar Resources Lead to Divergent Outcomes?" *Demography* 45(3): 591–617.

Gifford, Paul. 1994. "Recent Developments in African Christianity." *African Affairs* 93(373): 513–534.

Gifford, Paul. 2004. *Ghana's New Christianity*. Bloomington: Indiana University Press.

Glick Schiller, Nina, and Ayse Çağlar. 2008. "'And Ye Shall Posses It, and Dwell Therein': Social Citizenship, Global Christianity, and Non-Ethnic Immigrant Incorporation." In *Citizenship, Political Engagement, and Belonging: Immigrants in Europe and the United States*, ed. D. Reed-Danahay and C. Brettell, 203–225. New Brunswick, NJ: Rutgers University Press.

Glick Schiller, Nina, Ayşe Çağlar, and Thaddeus C. Guldbrandsen. 2006. "Beyond the Ethnic Lens: Locality, Globality, and Born-Again Incorporation." *American Ethnologist* 33(4): 612–633.

Gooren, Henri. 2012. "The Catholic Charismatic Renewal in Latin America." *PNEUMA: The Journal for the Society of Pentecostal Studies* 34(2): 185–207.

Gordon, Milton. 1964. *Assimilation in American Life: The Role of Race, Religion, and National Origins*. New York: Oxford University Press.

Guarnizo, Luis E., Alejandro Portes, and William Haller. 2003. "Assimilation and Transnationalism: Determinants of Transnational Political Action among Contemporary Migrants." *American Journal of Sociology* 108(6): 1211–1248.

Hackett, Rosalind I. J. 1998. "Pentecostal/Charismatic Appropriation of Media Technologies in Ghana and Nigeria." *Journal of Religion in Africa* 28(3): 258–277.

Hagan, Jacqueline. 1998. "Social Networks, Gender, and Immigrant Incorporation: Resources and Constraints." *American Sociological Review* 63: 55–67.

Hagan, Jacqueline, Karl Eschbach, and Nestor Rodriguez. 2008. "U. S. Deportation Policy, Family Separation, and Circular Migration." *International Migration Review* 42(2): 64–88.

Halter, Marilyn, and Violet Showers Johnson. 2014. *African & American: West Africans in Post-Civil Rights America*. New York: New York University Press.

Haraway, Donna. 1988. "Situated Knowledges: The Science Question in Feminism and the Privilege of Partial Perspective." *Feminist Studies* 14(3): 575–599.

Herberg, Will. 1983 (1955). *Protestant, Catholic, Jew: An Essay in American Religious Sociology*. Chicago: University of Chicago Press.

Herbst, Jeffrey. 1993. *The Politics of Reform in Ghana, 1982-1991*. Berkeley: University of California Press.

Hervieu-Leger, Danielle. (1997). "'What Scripture Tells Me': Spontaneity and Regulation with the Catholic Charismatic Renewal." In *Lived Religion in America: Toward a History of Practice*, ed. D. Hall, 22–40. Princeton, NJ: Princeton University Press.

Hochschild, Adam. 1999. *King Leopold's Ghost: A Story of Greed, Terror, and Heroism in Colonial Africa*. Boston: Houghton Mifflin.

Horn-Udeze, Bettina. 2009. "'Here in Europe It's Like a Secret Cult': A Nigerian Migrant's Narration of Initiation into the System of Migration." In *Transcultural Modernities: Narrating Africa in Europe*, ed. E. Bekers, S. Helff, and D. Merolla, 377–390. Amsterdam and New York: Editions Rodopi.

Hughes, C. Everett. 1945. "Dilemmas and Contradictions of Status." *American Journal of Sociology* 50(5): 353–359.

Iceland, John and Melissa Scopiliti. 2008. "Immigrant Residential Segregation in U.S. Metropolitan Areas, 1990–2000." *Demography* 45(1): 79–94.

Insoll, Timothy. 2003. *The Archaeology of Islam in Sub-Saharan Africa*. Cambridge: Cambridge University Press.

International Organization for Migration. 2009. Migration in Ghana: A Country Profile. Geneva, Switzerland: International Organization for Migration.

Isichei, Elizabeth. 1995. *A History of Christianity in Africa*. London: Society for Promoting Christian Knowledge.

Isichei, Elizabeth. 2004. *The Religious Traditions of Africa: A History*. Westport, CT: Praeger.

Johnson, Paul C. 2007. *Diasporic Conversions: Black Carib Religion and the Recovery of Africa*. Berkeley: University of California Press.

Katz, Jack. 2001. "From How to Why: On Luminous Description and Causal Inference in Ethnography (Part 1)." *Ethnography* 2(4): 443–473.

Keely, Charles B. 1971. "Effects of the Immigration Act of 1965 on Selected Population Characteristics of Immigrants to the United States." *Demography* 8(2): 157–169.

Kelly, Bob. 2005. "The 2004 Elections in Northern Ghana." *Review of African Political Economy* 32: 455–461.

Kurien, Prema. 2004. "Multiculturalism, Immigrant Religion, and Diasporic Nationalism: The Development of an American Hinduism." *Social Problems* 51: 362–385.

Kurien, Prema A. 2012. "Decoupling Religion and Ethnicity: Second-Generation Indian American Christians." *Qualitative Sociology* 35: 447–468.

Lee, Catherine. 2015. "Family Reunification and the Limits of Immigration Reform: Impact and Legacy of the 1965 Immigration Act." *Sociological Forum* 30(S1): 528–548.

Lehmann, Wolfgang. 2014. "Habitus Transformation and Hidden Injuries: Successful Working-Class University Students." *Sociology of Education* 87(1): 1–15.

Lehrer, Eli. 1998. "We Want to Depend on Ourselves." *American Enterprise* 9(6): 34–37.

Levitt, Peggy. 2001. *The Transnational Villagers*. Berkeley: University of California Press.

Levitt, Peggy. 2007. *God Needs No Passport: Immigrants and the Changing American Religious Landscape*. New York: New Press.

Levitt, Peggy, and Nina Glick Schiller. 2004. "Transnational Perspectives on Migration: Conceptualizing Simultaneity." *International Migration Review* 38(145): 595–629.

Lewis, J. David, and Andrew Weigert. 1985. "Trust as a Social Reality." *Social Forces* 63(4): 967–985.

Lichterman, Paul. 2012. "Religion in Public Action: From Actors to Settings." *Sociological Theory* 30(1): 15–36.

Lincoln, C. Eric, and Lawrence H. Mimaya. 1990. *The Black Church in the African American Experience*. Durham, NC: Duke University Press.

Lindberg, Staffan I., and Minion K. C. Morrison. 2005. "Exploring Voter Alignments in Africa: Core and Swing Voters in Ghana." *Journal of Modern African Studies* 43: 565–586.

Luhrmann, Tanya. 2012. *When God Talks Back: Understanding the American Evangelical Relationship with God*. New York: Knopf.

Magesa, Laurenti. 2004. *Anatomy of Inculturation: Transforming the Church in Africa*. Maryknoll, NY: Orbis Books.

Maly, Michael T., and Michael Leachman. 1998. "Rogers Park, Edgewater, Uptown, and Chicago Park, Chicago." *Cityscape* 4(2): 131–160.

Manglos, Nicolette D. 2010. "Born Again in Balaka: Pentecostal vs. Catholic Narratives of Religious Transformation in Rural Malawi." *Sociology of Religion* 71(4): 409–431.

Manglos, Nicolette D. 2011. "Brokerage in the Sacred Sphere: Religious Leaders as Community Problem-Solvers in Rural Malawi." *Sociological Forum* 26(2): 334–355.

Manglos, Nicolette D., and Jenny Trinitapoli. 2011. "The Third Therapeutic System: Faith Healing Practices in the Context of a Generalized Aids Epidemic." *Journal of Health and Social Behavior* 52: 107–122.

Manglos, Nicolette D., and Alexander Weinreb. 2013. "Religion and Interest in Politics in Africa." *Social Forces* 92(1): 195–219.

Manglos-Weber, Nicolette D. 2015. "Innovations in Trust: Patrimonial and Bureaucratic Authority in the Asante Empire of West Africa." *Political Power and Social Theory* 28: 217–240.

Marshall, Ruth. 2009. *Political Spiritualities: The Pentecostal Revolution in Nigeria*. Chicago: University of Chicago Press.

Marti, Gerardo. 2012. *Worship Across the Racial Divide: Religious Music and the Multiracial Congregation*. New York: Oxford University Press.

Marti, Gerardo. 2015. "Conceptual Pathways to Ethnic Transcendence in Diverse Churches: Theoretical Reflections on the Achievement of Successfully Integrated Congregations." *Religions* 6: 1048–1066.

Martin, David. 2002. *Pentecostalism: The World Their Parish*. Oxford: Blackwell.

Massey, Douglas S., Joaquin Arango, Graeme Hugo, Ali Kouaouci, Adela Pelligrino, and J. Edward Taylor. 1993. "Theories of International Migration: A Review and an Appraisal." *Population and Development Review* 19: 431–466.

Massey, Douglas, and Nancy Denton. 1998. *American Apartheid: Segregation and the Making of the Underclass*. Cambridge, MA: Harvard University Press.

Massey, Douglas S., and Ilana Redstone Akresh. 2006. "Immigrant Intentions and Mobility in a Global Economy: The Attitudes and Behavior of Recently Arrived U.S. Immigrants." *Social Science Quarterly* 87(5): 954–971.

Massey, Douglas S., and Magaly Sanchez. 2010. *Brokered Boundaries: Immigrant Identity in Anti-Immigrant Times*. New York: Russell Sage Foundation.

McCall, Leslie. 2005. "The Complexity of Intersectionality." *Signs: Journal of Women in Culture and Society* 30(3): 1771–800.

McCaskie, T. C. 1983. "Accumulation, Wealth and Belief in Asante History. I. To the Close of the Nineteenth Century." *Africa: Journal of the International African Institute* 53(1): 23–43.

McCaskie, T. C. 1986. "Accumulation, Wealth and Belief in Asante History: Ii the Twentieth Century." *Africa: Journal of the International African Institute* 56(1): 3–23.

Meyer, Birgit. 1992. "'If You Are a Devil, You Are a Witch and, If You Are a Witch, You Are a Devil.' The Integration of 'Pagan' Ideas into the Conceptual Universe of Ewe Christians in Southeastern Ghana." *Journal of Religion in Africa* 22(2): 98–132.

Meyer, Birgit. 1998. "Make a Complete Break with the Past': Memory and Post-Colonial Modernity in Ghanaian Pentecostalist Discourse." *Journal of Religion in Africa* 28(3): 316–349.

Meyer, Birgit. 2002. "Christianity and the Ewe Nation: German Pietist Missionaries, Ewe Converts and the Politics of Culture." *Journal of Religion in Africa* 32(2): 167–199.

Meyer, Birgit. 2004. "Christianity in Africa: From African Independent to Pentecostal-Charismatic Churches." *Annual Review of Anthropology* 33: 447–474.

Miller, Donald E., and Tetsunao Yamamuri. 2007. *Global Pentecostalism*. Berkeley: University of California Press.

Mizrachi, Nissam, Renee R. Anspach, and Israel Drori. 2007. "Repertoires of Trust: The Practice of Trust in a Multinational Organization Amid Political Conflict." *American Sociological Review* 72(1): 143–165.

Mizstal, Barbara. 1996. *Trust: The Search for the Basis of Social Order.* Malden, MA: Blackwell.

Mizstal, Barbara. 2001. "Normality and Trust in Goffman's Theory of Interaction Order." *Sociological Theory* 19(3): 312–323.

Möllering, Guido. 2001. "The Nature of Trust: From Georg Simmel to a Theory of Expectation, Interpretation, and Suspension." *Sociology* 35(2): 403–420.

Mooney, Margarita. 2009. *Faith Makes Us Live: Surviving and Thriving in the Haitian Diaspora.* Berkeley: University of California Press.

Mooney, Margarita. 2013. "Religion as a Context of Reception: The Case of Haitian Immigrants in Miami, Montreal, and Paris." *International Migration* 51(3): 99–112.

Mooney, Margarita A., and Manglos-Weber, Nicolette D. "Prayer and Liturgy as Constitutive-Ends Practices among Black Immigrants." *Journal for the Theory of Social Behaviour* 44(4): 459–480.

Morrison, Minion K. C. (2004). "Political Parties in Ghana through Four Republics: A Path to Democratic Consolidation." *Comparative Politics* 36(4): 421–442.

Newton, Kenneth. 2001. "Trust, Social Capital, Civil Society, and Democracy." *International Political Science Review* 22(2): 201–214.

Nooteboom, Bart. 2007. "Social Capital, Institutions, and Trust." *Reivew of Social Economy* 65(1): 29–53.

Offutt, Stephen. 2015. *New Centers of Global Evangelicalism in Latin America and Africa.* New York: Cambridge University Press.

Olson, Daniel. 1989. "Church Friendships: Boon or Barrier to Church Growth?" *Journal for the Scientific Study of Religion* 28(4): 432–447.

Olupona, Jacob, and Regina Gemignani. 2007. *African Immigrant Religions in America.* New York: New York University Press.

Omenyo, Cephas. 2002. *Pentecost Outside Pentecostalism: A Study of the Development of Charismatic Renewal in the Mainline Churches of Ghana.* Zoetemeer, The Netherlands: Boekencentrum.

Opoku-Dapaah, Edward. 2012. "Ghanaian Sects in the United States of America and Their Adherents within the Framework of Migration Challenges since the 1970s." *African and Asian Studies* 5(2): 231–253.

Orser, Charles E. 1998. "The Challenge of Race to American Historical Archaeology." *American Anthropologist* 100(3): 661–668.

Owusu, Maxwell. 1989. "Rebellion, Revolution, and Tradition: Reinterpreting Coups in Ghana." *Comparative Studies in Society and History* 31(2): 373–397.

Owusu, Maxwell. 1996. "Tradition and Transformation: Democracy and the Politics of Popular Power in Ghana." *Journal of Modern African Studies* 34(2): 307–343.

Pakenham, Thomas. 1992. *The Scramble for Africa: White Man's Conquest of the Dark Continent from 1876-1912.* New York: HarperCollins.

Patillo, Mary. 2007. *Black on the Block: The Politics of Race and Class in the City*. Chicago: The University of Chicago Press.

Paul, Anju Mary. 2011. "Stepwise International Migration: A Multistage Migration Pattern for the Aspiring Migrant." *American Journal of Sociology* 116(6): 1842–1886.

Peil, Margaret. 1995. "Ghanaians Abroad." *African Affairs* 94(376): 345–367.

Perry, Samuel. 2013. "Racial Habitus, Moral Conflict, and White Moral Hegemony within Interracial Evangelical Organizations." *Qualitative Sociology* 35(1): 89–108.

Poewe, Karla. 1994. *Charismatic Christianity as a Global Culture*. Columbia: University of South Carolina Press.

Portes, Alejandro, and Ramon Grosfoguel. 1994. "Caribbean Diasporas: Migration and Ethnic Communities." *ANNALS, American Academy of Political and Social Sciences* 533: 48–69.

Portes, Alejandro, and Ruben G. Rumbaut. 2001. *Legacies: The Story of the Immigrant Second Generation*. Berkeley: University of California Press.

Portes, Alejandro. 2007. "Migration, Development, and Segmented Assimilation: A Conceptual Review of the Evidence." *ANNALS, American Academy of Political and Social Sciences* 610: 73–97.

Portes, Alejandro, and Ruben G. Rumbaut. 2014. *Immigrant America: A Portrait*, 4th ed. Berkeley: University of California Press.

Putnam, Robert D. 2000. *Bowling Alone: The Collapse and Revival of American Community*. New York: Simon & Schuster.

Read, Jen'nan Ghazal, and Michael O. Emerson. 2005. "Racial Context, Black Immigration and the U.S. Black/White Health Disparity." *Social Forces* 84(1): 181–199.

Reimers, David M. 1983. "An Unintended Reform: The 1965 Immigration Act and Third World Immigration to the United States." *Journal of American Ethnic History* 3(1): 9–28.

Rey, Terry, and Alan Stepick. 2013. *Crossing the Water and Keeping the Faith*. New York: New York University Press.

Riesebrodt, Martin. 2010. *The Promise of Salvation: A Theory of Religion*. Chicago: University of Chicago Press.

Robbins, Joel. 2004. "The Globalization of Pentecostal and Charismatic Christianity." *Annual Review of Anthropology* 33: 117–143.

Robinson, David. 2004. *Muslim Societies in African History*. Cambridge: Cambridge University Press.

Robinson, Eugene. 2011. *Disintegration: The Splintering of Black America*. New York: Anchor Books.

Rodriguez, Nestor, and Cristian Paredes. 2014. "Coercive Immigration Enforcement and Bureaucratic Ideology." In *Constructing Immigrant Illegality: Critiques, Experiences, and Responses*, ed. C. Menjivar and D. Kanstroom, 63–83. New York: Cambridge University Press.

Rudrappa, Sharmila. 2004. *Ethnic Routes to Becoming American: Indian Immigrants and the Cultures of Citizenship*. Piscataway, NJ: Rutgers University Press.

Samoff, Joel, and Bidemi Carrol. 2004. "The Promise of Partnership and Continuities of Dependence: External Support to Higher Education in Africa." *African Studies Review* 47(1): 67–199.

Scheper-Hughes, Nancy. 1992. *Death Without Weeping*. Berkeley: University of California Press.

Sensbach, John. 2005. *Rebecca's Revival: Creating Black Christianity in the Atlantic World*. Cambridge, MA: Harvard University Press.

Seymour, Jeffrey M., Michael R. Welch, Karen Monique Gregg, and Jessica Collett. 2014. "Generating Trust in Congregations: Engagement, Exchange, and Social Networks." *Journal for the Scientific Study of Religion* 53(1): 130–144.

Shelton, Jason E., and Michael O. Emerson. 2012. *Blacks and Whites in Christian America: How Racial Discrimination Shapes Religious Convictions*. New York: New York University Press.

Simmel, Georg. 1990. *The Philosophy of Money*. London: Routledge.

Simmel, Georg. 1955. "A Contribution to the Sociology of Religion." *American Journal of Sociology* 60(6): 1–18.

Small, Mario Luis. 2009. *Unanticipated Gains: Origins of Network Inequality in Everyday Life*. New York: Oxford University Press.

Smilde, David. 2007. *Reasons to Believe: Cultural Agency in Latin American Evangelicalism*. Berkeley: University of California Press.

Smith, Christian. 2003. *Moral, Believing Animals: Human Personhood and Culture*. New York: Oxford University Press.

Smith, Christian. 2015. *To Flourish or Destruct: A Personalist Theory of Human Goods, Motivations, Failure, and Evil*. Chicago: University of Chicago Press.

Smith, Edwin W. 1945. "Religious Beliefs of the Akan." *Africa: Journal of the International African Institute* 15(1): 23–29.

Soothill, Jane E. 2007. *Gender, Social Change, and Spiritual Power: Charismatic Christianity in Ghana*. Amsterdam, The Netherlands: Brill.

Stark, Rodney. 1996. *The Rise of Christianity*. Princeton, NJ: Princeton University Press.

Stevens, David W. 2004. "Spreading the Word: Religious Beliefs and the Evolution of Immigrant Congregations." *Sociology of Religion* 65(2): 121–138.

Tavory, Iddo. 2013. "The Private Life of Public Ritual: Interaction, Sociality, and Codification in a Jewish Orthodox Congregation." *Qualitative Sociology* 36(2): 125–139.

Tavory, Iddo and Stefan Timmermans. 2014. *Abductive Analysis: Theorizing Qualitative Research*. Chicago: University of Chicago Press.

Teferra, Damtew. 2008. "The International Dimension of Higher Education in Africa: Status, Challenges, Prospects." In *Higher Education in Africa: The International Dimension*, ed. Jane Knight and Damtew Teferra, 44–79. Chesnut Hill, MA: Boston College Center for International Higher Education.

Tettey, Wisdom J. 2007. "Transnationalism, Religion, and the African Diaspora in Canada: An Examination of Ghanaians and Ghanaian Churches." In *African*

Transnational Religions in America, ed. Jacob Olupona and Regina Gemignani, 229–258. New York: New York University Press.

Thomas, Keven J. A. 2010. "Household Context, Generational Status, and English Proficiency among the Children of African Immigrants in the United States." *International Migration Review* 44(1): 142–172.

Thomas, William I., and Florian Znaniecki. 1996. *The Polish Peasant in Europe and America: A Classic Work in Immigration History.* Urbana, IL: University of Illinois Press.

Thornton, Jonathan K. 1998. *Africa and Africans in the Making of the Atlantic World, 1400–1800.* New York: Cambridge University Press.

Tilly, Charles. 2005. *Trust and Rule.* New York: Cambridge University Press.

Tilly, Charles. 2006. *Identities, Boundaries, and Social Ties.* Boulder, CO: Paradigm.

Tilly, Charles. 2007. "Trust Networks in International Migration." *Sociological Forum* 22(1): 3–24.

Tilly, Charles. 2010. "Cities, States, and Trust Networks: Chapter 1 of Cities and States in World History." *Theory and Society* 39: 265–280.

Tweed, Thomas A. 1997. *Our Lady of the Exile: Diasporic Religion at a Cuban Catholic Shrine in Miami.* New York: Oxford University Press.

Tweed, Thomas A. 2006. *Crossing and Dwelling: A Theory of Religion.* Cambridge, MA: Harvard University Press.

Uslaner, Eric M. 2002. *The Moral Foundations of Trust.* New York, Cambridge University Press.

Van Dijk, Rijk. 2004. "Negotiating Marriage: Questions of Legitimacy and Morality in the Ghanaian Pentecostal Diaspora." *Journal of Religion in Africa* 34: 438–467.

Warner, R. Stephen. 1988. *New Wine in Old Wineskins: Evangelicals and Liberals in a Small-Town Church.* Berkeley: University of California Press.

Warner, R. Stephen. 1994. "The Place of the Congregation in the American Religious Configuration." In *New Perspectives in the Study of Congregations,* ed. James P. Wind and James W. Lewis, 54–99. Chicago: University of Chicago Press.

Warner, R. Stephen. 1997. "Religion, Boundaries, and Bridges." *Sociology of Religion* 58(3): 217–238.

Warner, R. Stephen. 1998. "Immigration and Religious Communities in the United States." In *Gatherings in Diaspora: Religious Communities and the New Immigration,* ed. R. Stephen Warner and Judy G. Wittner, 1–34. Philadelphia: Temple University Press.

Warner, R. Stephen. 2000. "Religion and New (Post-1965) Immigrants: Some Principles Drawn from Field Research." *American Studies* 41: 267–286.

Warner, R. Stephen. 2004. "Enlisting Smelser's Theory of Ambivalence to Maintain Progress in Sociology of Religion's New Paradigm." In *Self, Social Structure, and Beliefs: Explorations in Sociology,* ed. Jeffrey C. Alexander, Gary T. Marx, and Christine L. Williams, 103–121. Berkeley: University of California Press.

Warner, R. Stephen. 2007. "The Role of Religion in the Process of Segmented Assimilation." *ANNALS, American Academy of Political and Social Science* 612, Religious Pluralism and Civil Society: 102–115.

Warner, R. Stephen, and Judy G. Wittner, eds. 1998. *Gatherings in Diaspora: Religious Communities and the New Immigration*. Philadelphia: Temple University Press.

Waters, Mary C. 1999. *Black Identities: West Indian Immigrant Dreams and American Realities*. Cambridge, MA: Harvard University Press.

Weber, Max. 1946. *From Max Weber: Essays in Sociology*. Translated by H. H. Gerth and C. W. Mills. New York: Oxford University Press.

Wheatley, Christine, and Nestor Rodriguez. 2014. "With the Stroke of a Bureaucrat's Pen: American State 'Reforms" to Manage Its Undocumented Population, 1920–2012." In *Hidden Lives and Human Rights in America: Understanding the Controversies and Tragedies of Undocumented Immigration*, ed. L. Lorentzen, 157–178. Westport, CT: Praeger.

Wilks, Ivor. 1993. *Forests of Gold: Essays on the Akan and the Kingdom of Asante*. Athens: Ohio University Press.

Williams, Rhys H., and Gira Vashi. 2007. "'Hijab' and American Muslim Women: Creating the Space for Autonomous Selves." *Sociology of Religion* 68(3): 269–87.

Winchester, Daniel Alan. 2008. "Embodying the Faith: Religious Practice and the Making of a Muslim Moral Habitus." *Social Forces* 86(4): 1753–1780.

World Bank. 1988. *Education Policies for sub-Saharan Africa: Adjustment, Revialization, and Expansion*. Washington, DC: World Bank.

Wuthnow, Robert. 1998. *After Heaven: Spirituality in America since the 1950s*. Berkeley: University of California Press.

Wuthnow, Robert, and Conrad Hackett. 2003. "The Social Integration of Practitioners of Non-Western Religions in the United States." *Journal for the Scientific Study of Religion* 42(4): 651–667.

Xu, Xiaohong. 2013. "Belonging before Believing: Group Ethos and Bloc Recruitment in the Making of Chinese Communism." *American Sociological Review* 78(5): 773–796.

Yang, Fenggang. 1999. *Chinese Christians in America: Conversion, Assimilation, and Adhesive Identities*. University Park: Penn State University Press.

Yang, Fenggang, and Helen Rose Ebaugh. 2001. "Transformations in New Immigrant Religions and their Global Implications." *American Sociological Review* 66(2): 269–288.

Yarak, Larry W. 1986. "Elmina and Greater Asante in the Nineteenth Century." *Africa: Journal of the International African Institute* 56(1): 33–52.

Zolberg, Aristide. 2006. "Managing a World on the Move." *Population and Development Review* 33: 222–353.

Index

Page numbers followed by *f* indicate figures. Numbers followed by n indicate notes.

abductive analysis, 193
Aburi, Ghana, 47
acceptance, 106
Accra, Ghana, 6, 71–74
Accra Mall, 88
Achimota College, 15
Acme Vision International Ministries, 31, 32*f*
Adichie, Chimimanda, 196n9
Africa, 196n10. *See also specific countries*
    Christianity, 30, 74–78, 183–184, 187, 198n24
    Pentecostalism, 183–184, 187
    sub-Saharan, 138
    West Africa, 30, 74–78, 187
African Americans, 119–120, 148
Africans
    immigrants, 2–3, 6, 195n1, 195n5
    students, 152
African spirit, 170
African Student organization, 153
Afrobarometer, 197n16
Afrocentrism, 148, 151
Age of Sail, 13
Akan people, 12–16, 17*f*, 147, 200n13
Akyeampong, Emmanuel, 19
Americanah (Adichie), 196n9

American Community Survey, 19
American Evangelicals, ix, 123–124, 155–156
Americanization, 49, 51, 99, 140–141, 146–147
American Student Assistance, 199n10
Ammerman, Nancy, 104
Anglicans and Anglicanism, x, 15, 31, 74–75, 79–81, 183
Anglo-European culture, 169
animism, 83
anti-immigrant sentiment, 26, 197n10
apartment hotels, 59
Apostolic Church International, 31, 32*f*, 75
Asante Empire, 13–15, 197n3, 197n6
Ashanti Region, 37, 147
Asia, 30
associational patterns, 20
Asuza Street Revival, 75
Atlantic World, 13
Atta-Mills, John, 46–47
Austin (Chicago, IL), 53

Baptists, 73
Bates, Robert, 197n8
beginnings, 58–64

Belgium, 14
belief, 155–179
Bellah, Robert, 30–31
belonging, 155–179
Berlin Conference of 1884–85, 14–15
Bible, 15, 82, 85, 114, 168
Bible studies, 31, 83, 163
Bismarck, Otto von, 14
blackness, 74, 148, 151
blacks, 150, 152
   immigrants, 26, 64–65
   marginalization of, 33–35
   students, 196n8
   violence against, 57–58
Black Student Union, 153
Bonilla-Silva, Eduardo, 25–26
born-again conversions, 82–87
Born Again Movement, 30, 82, 84–86
Boston, Massachusetts, 20
Brazil, 201n7
Brenneman, Robert, 111
Breton, Robert, 29
bribery, 38, 199n5
Brong Ahafo Association, 50
Bronzeville (Chicago, IL), 53
Brown, Michael, 148–149
Buddhism, 5, 28–29, 182
Butler, Bethonie, 196n8

Cabrini-Green projects (Chicago, IL), 53
camp meetings, 111–118, 170, 174–175, 189
Cape Coast Castle, 13, 14f
Caribbeans, 65
categories, 172–177
Catholic Charismatic Renewal (CCR) movement, 141, 198n22, 200n2, 202n8
Catholics and the Catholic Church, 15, 74–75, 84–85, 143, 183
CCR (Catholic Charismatic Renewal) movement, 141, 198n22, 200n2, 202n8

Charismatics and Charismatic Evangelical Christianity, 30–33, 75, 79, 187–188, 198n22, 200n2, 201nn7–8
   congregations, 34
   draw of, 68–71, 80–82, 85–87, 89
   personal transformation, 82–87, 157–160
   rituals, 110–111
Chen, Carolyn, 30
Chesnut, Andrew, 201n7
Chicago Evangel Ministries, 9, 44–49, 91–95, 124
   choir, 9–10
   choir directors, 128–129, 160–165
   congregational culture, 104–111, 172–173, 176–177
   growth of, 165, 175
   leaving the community, 127–130
   members, 146, 190
   offerings, 110
   schedule of services, 106–109
   structure of support, 106, 108–109
   Sunday services, 100–104, 107, 109–110, 160
   trust, 129–130
   Wednesday services, 103, 109–110
   worship nights, 164
Chicago, Illinois
   black population, 52
   Ghanaian community, 18–22, 146–147
   Gold Coast Taxi, 133, 134f
   history, 52–53
   racial dynamics, 18–19, 52–58
   Uptown, 58–59, 60f, 61f, 133, 134f
children, 62, 140–141, 162–163
Cho, David Yonggi, 87
choir directors, 128–129
Christianity
   in Africa, 6, 13–14, 183, 198n24
   Charismatic Evangelical, 30–31, 68–71, 75, 79–89, 110–111,

157–160, 187–188, 198n22, 200n2, 201nn7–8
  Evangelical, 9, 30, 66, 123–124
  expansion of, 74–78, 156, 201n5
  immigrant, 28
  Pentecostal-Charismatic, 30, 110–111, 201n7
  practices and principles, 90–130
  Protestant, 198n22
  in West Africa, 74–78
Christian missionaries, 15, 47, 75
church(es)
  church hopping, 90, 123
  good churches, 118–121
  of the moment, 78–82
  non-Ghanaian, 118–121
church camps, 111–118, 170, 174–175, 189
church choice, 30–35, 120–121, 126, 183
church family, 113–114
church leaders, 142, 165–172, 183–184
Church of Pentecost, 75
class dynamics, 174
classmates, 48, 98
Cleveland, Ohio, 21
clothing, 93–94, 136, 165, 169, 173
Codjoe, Samuel Nii Ardey, 200n3
Coleman, James, 24
Collins, Patricia Hill, 64
Collins, Randall, 110–111
colonialism, 14–15, 47
commitment, 110, 113–114
commodities, 13
community building, 120, 177–178, 180–186
competitiveness, 36–65, 125, 170
congregational culture, 99–100, 104–111, 117, 172–173, 176–177, 181
  leaving the community, 127–130
  memberships, 126
  mixed-race congregations, 33
congregationalism, 30
congregational models, 5–6, 28

congregational studies, 108–109, 184–185
congregation-avoiders, 121–126
Connecticut, 21
connection: culture of, 104–111, 114, 116–117
constitutive-ends practices, 118
conversion, 82–87, 110–111, 156, 201n9
corruption, 38, 138, 170–171
courtship and dating, 44–45, 80
credit, 63
Csordas, Thomas, 202n8
Cuban diaspora, 29
culture
  congregational, 99–100, 104–111, 117, 172–173, 176–177, 181
  of connection, 104–111, 114, 116–117

Dallas, Texas, 21
darkness, 196n10
demographics, 81
Denton, Nancy, 18
Department of Homeland Security (DHS) (US), 16–18
deportations, 131–132
Deuteronomy, 168
DHS (Department of Homeland Security) (US), 16–18
Dinovelli, Benjamin, 196n8
disappointment, 39–43
distrust: problems of, 25–26, 57–58
diversity, 33–34, 174
diversity visas, 38, 162
domination, 64
Dodoo, Francis Nii-Amoo, 200n3
DuBois, W. E. B., 53, 149

early marriage, 45
education, 150–151, 197n7
  as imperative, 136–139
  missionary schools, 15, 47
  postsecondary, 138
  university or higher, 3, 40, 138–139

emigration, 16–18. *See also* immigrants and immigration; migration
emotional energy, 110–111
England, 13
Englewood (Chicago, IL), 53, 56–57
Episcopalians, 119–120
Ethiopia, 138
ethnicity, 98–100, 125–126, 146–153, 174, 184–185
ethnic transcendence, 172–177
ethnography, 192
ethno-linguistic identity, 147–148
Europe, 13–15, 195n1
Evangelical Christianity, 9, 66
   American, 123–124
   Charismatic, 30–33, 68–71, 75, 79–89, 110–111, 157–160, 187–188, 198n22, 200n2, 201nn7–8
evangélicos, 30
Evangel Ministries International, 8–9, 34, 48, 101, 163, 188
   birth and growth of, 45–46
   branches, 21
   camp meetings, 111–118, 170, 174–175, 189
   Chicago branch, 9, 44–49, 91–95, 100–111, 124, 127–130, 146, 160, 172–175, 190
   church colleagues, 1–2, 7–8
   community, 97
   congregation, ix, x, 1–2, 21, 31, 46
   congregational culture, 100, 104–111, 176–177, 181
   draw of, 67–71, 77–80, 87–89, 91
   English-only policy, 93, 172
   ethnic composition, 95, 98
   as family, 113–116
   fellowships, 87
   gatherings, 103
   as global, 95
   as a good church, 94–100, 118, 172–173
   headquarters, 72
   history of, 45–46, 74–76
   as international church, 175
   leaving, 127–130
   legitimacy, 77–78, 98
   North American branches, 115
   pastors, 92
   reasons for success, 78
   sermon tapes, 115–116
   standard of conduct, 101
   structure of support, 87–88, 94, 96, 103, 106, 108–109
   Sunday services, 71–74, 92, 97
   U.S. branch, 100
   website, 74
   as Western, 93
   worship music, 94
Ewe people, 13–16, 17*f,* 83, 147, 201n5
Ewe Association, 21, 50
exploitation, 115–116

F-1 student visas, 40
Facebook, 42, 57–58
faith, 155–179
faith-healing, 142–143
false prophecy, 142
familial relations
   church family, 113–114
   strained, 39–43
family reunification visas, 62
fellowships, 87
feminism, 192
Ferguson, Missouri, 58, 148–149
financial issues, 85–86, 115–116
   credit, 63
   education funding, 137
   immigration for, 141–146
Fisher, Alison, 200n16
food trucks, 39
foreignness, 26
Fowers, Blaine, 22, 203n1

France, 14
friendliness, 106, 121
friendships, 150
fufu, 55–56

Ga people, 13–16, 17*f*
Garfeld Park (Chicago, IL), 53
geographical dispersion, 21
Germany, 5, 14
Ghana, 2–3, 12–16
   Ashanti Region, 37, 147
   British rule, 47
   Charismatic churches, 30–31, 34, 82, 187–188, 198n22, 200n2, 201n8
   Christianity, 6, 66, 74–78, 90
   congregation characters, ix, x
   demographics, 81
   economy, 16, 37, 199n2
   education, 137, 150–151
   ethno-linguistic groups, 16, 17*f*
   GINI coefficient, 18
   gross domestic product (GDP), 18
   history, 46–48
   independence, 15, 36, 47
   leaving, 36–39
   migration trends, 16–18, 199n6
   Pentecostal churches, 187
   postcolonial, 197n8
   religious practices, 66, 74–75, 90, 183
   Second Coming, 36
   social conflict, 16
   social welfare, 15–16
   Tourism Board, 37–38
Ghanafest, 21, 49–52, 50*f*, 146–147, 189
Ghanaian Council of Churches, 142
Ghanaian restaurants, 39, 61*f*
Ghanaians, 64–65
   associational patterns, 20
   Chicago community, 18–22, 33, 146
   diaspora, 144
   education, 138
   geographical dispersion, 21, 144
   identity, 131–154
   legal status, 20
   migrant experience, 36–65, 131–154
   as model minority, 144
   non-attenders, 121–126
   professions, 19–20, 133–135
   residential patterns, 20–21
   socioeconomic status, 19
   taxi drivers, 133–135
   transatlantic life, 44–46
   transnational, 4–5, 8, 44–45, 138, 156, 181–182, 184–185
   US immigrants, 7, 19–21, 30–65, 131–154, 198n13
   US visas, 38
Ghanaian Student's Union, 19
Ghana National Council (GNC), 19, 21, 49, 144–146
Gifford, Paul, 75
GINI coefficients, 18
Glick Schiller, Nina, 30
globalization, 30, 81
glossolalia (speaking in tongues), 75, 110
GNC (Ghana National Council), 21, 49, 144–146
gold, 13
Gold Coast, 14–15
Gold Coast Taxi, 133, 134*f*
good churches, 118–121
gossip, 42–43, 93, 144
Great Britain, 13–14, 36
Great Migration, 52, 200n15
green card lottery, 162
group competition, 36–65

habitus, 25–26, 64–65
Hansen, Emmanuel, 199n3
Harrist Church, 75–76
Harris, William Wade, 75
Harvard University, 196n8

Hausa-Fulani people, 15–16
healing and health care, 75, 143, 145–146
Herberg, Will, 5, 28
higher education, 3, 40, 138–139
Hinduism, 5, 29, 182
history, 46–48, 52–53, 74–78
Hochschild, Adam, 14
housing projects, 57

I-20 form, 40
ICE (Immigration and Customs Enforcement agency), 16–18
identity, 131–154
    categories of, 172–177
    ethno-linguistic, 147–148
    expansion of, 177–179
    master status, 138
    national, 148
    religious, 172–177
    turning points, 139–141
idleness, 122
idol worship, 84–85
"immigrant" (label), 131
immigrants and immigration, 2, 28–30, 195n1, 195nn4–5
    anti-immigrant sentiment, 26, 197n10
    immigrant identity, 131–154
    integrative effects of, 198n20
    migration narratives, 160–165
    rationale for, 141–146
    risks, 36–65
    separatist effects of, 198n20
    transnationals, 4, 8, 44–45, 138, 156, 181–182, 184–185
    trends, 16–18
    undocumented immigrants, 131
Immigration and Customs Enforcement agency (ICE), 16–18
Immigration and Naturalization Service (INS), 16–17
imperialism, 13–14

impersonal trust, 23
inclusivity, 176
Indian American Christians, 30
indirect rule, 15
individualism, religious, 30–31
inequality, 48–52
INS (Immigration and Naturalization Service), 16–17
integration, 180–186
intentionality, 70, 120, 177–178
International Central Gospel Church Chicago, 32f
International House, 95–96
International Prayer Conference Line, 142
Internet, 81
intersectionality, 64–65
Iowa, 21
Irish immigrants, 195n1
Isichei, Elizabeth, 201n5
Islam, 5, 12–14, 16, 28–29
isolation, 122–123
"I Surrender All," 73
"I, Too, Am Harvard" movement, 196n8

Jackson, Michael, 73
Jews, 201n4
John, 82
Joyous Victory Ministries, 31, 32f

Katz, Jack, 192–193
kelliwelli, 51
kente cloth, 50, 200n13
Kofi (name), 147
Kurien, Prema, 30
Kwasi Enin (student), 3

Latin America, 30
law enforcement, 57–58, 148–149
leadership, 99–100
    church leaders, 142, 165–172, 183–184

leaving the community, 127–130
Levitt, Peggy, 29
Lexington, Kentucky, 21
literacy, 15, 85
localism, religiocultural, 28
loneliness, 122
Luhrmann, Tanya, 155
Lutherans, 123

Malawi, 8, 200n2
Malawi Longitudinal Study of Families and Health, 187
Malawi Religion Project, 187
marginalization, 33–35
maritime trade, 13
marriage, 45
Marti, Gerardo, 110
Massachusetts, 21
Massey, Douglas, 18
master status, 138
materialism, 170–171
media coverage, 3
mediocrity, 170
mega-churches, 34, 170
Methodists, 28, 74–75
Meyer, Birgit, 83, 201n5
migration, 2–4, 12–35, 160–165, 195n1, 195nn4–5. *See also* immigrants and immigration
   culture of, 199n6
   out-migration, 197n7
   rationale for, 141–146
   risks, 36–65
   trends, 16–18
Minneapolis, Minnesota, 21
minority groups, 144
missionaries, 15, 47, 75
mixed-race congregations, 33
Mole-Dagbani people, 15–16, 17*f*
Mount Zion Anglican Church, 31, 32*f*
multiculturalism, 34, 99–100, 175–176

multiracial diversity, 33
Murids, 182
Muslims, 16, 29, 182

names, 147
Nashville, Tennessee, 21
National Democratic Convention (NDC), 46
national identity, 148
nationality, 146–153, 174
NDC (National Democratic Convention), 46
negotiations, 131–154
the Netherlands, 13
New Covenant Cherubim & Seraphim Church of Christ, 32*f*
New Immigrant Survey, 202n7
New York, New York, 20
New York Times, 183–184
Nigeria, 2–3, 43, 134, 138, 170
   Charismatic Evangelical churches, 34, 82
   Pentecostal churches, 187
Noguchi Memorial Institute, 188
non-attenders, 121–126
North Kenwood (Chicago, IL), 53

Oakland (Chicago, IL), 53
Obama, Barack, 58
occultic traditions, 86–87
occupational detours, 42–43
occupational paths, 19–20
offerings, 110
"one-man churches", 75–76, 98, 142, 183
organized religion, 121
Orthodox Jews, 201n4
out-migration, 197n7
Oxford University, 196n8

pastors, 142, 165–172, 183–184
Paul, Anju, 131

Pentecostal-Charismatic Christianity, 30, 110–111, 201n7
Pentecostalism, 30, 73, 75, 183–184, 187, 198n22, 200n2, 201nn7–9
personal appearance and decorum, 73, 93–94, 102, 173
personal names, 147
personal transformation, Charismatic, 82–87, 157–160
personal trust, 12, 22–27, 65, 115–117, 127, 178–180, 185–186, 203n1
philanthropy, 145
poetics of refusal, 122
police brutality, 148–149
politics of reform, 197n8
population growth, 19
Portes, Alejandro, 4
Portugal, 13–14
prayer, 102
prejudice, 54–55
Presbyterians and Presbyterianism, 15, 31, 68, 74–75
professions and professionalism, 19–20, 93–94, 136, 165, 169
Protestant Christianity, 198n22
Protestant Evangelical Christianity. *See* Evangelical Christianity
purpose, 168

race relations, 26, 146–153, 174, 195n1
  racial order, 36–65, 195n1
  racial segregation, 33–35, 52–58
  reconciliation, 177–178
Rawlings, J. J., 36, 47
reflexivity, 192
Regional Institute of Population Studies (RIPS), 71, 188
relationship building, 39–43, 111, 114
relationship-driven ethnography, 192
religiocultural localism, 28
religion, 12–35. *See also specific religions*
  accessibility of, 66–89
  church choice, 30–35, 120–121, 126, 183
  churches of the moment, 78–82
  definition of, 29, 181–182
  draw of, 66–89
  good churches, 118–121
  immigrant, 2, 28–30, 198n20
  multicultural, 175–176
  organized, 121
  portability of, 82
  promise of, 66–89
  strange man of religion, 183–184
religiosity, 90
religious association, 132, 177–178, 185
  as basis for trust, 129–130, 156, 179–186
  as journey, 160–165
religious community, 5–6
religious diversity, 33–34
religious faith, 155–179
religious identity, 172–177
religious individualism, 30–31
religious practices, 90–130, 181, 183
religious revivalism, 75
research
  congregational studies, 108–109, 184–185
  methodology, 187–193
residential patterns, 20
revisions, 131–154
revivalism, 75
RIPS (Regional Institute of Population Studies), 71, 188
risk, 36–65
rituals, 110–111
Robert Taylor homes (Chicago, IL), 53
Roman Catholic Church, 15, 74–75, 84–85, 143, 183
rule, indirect, 15
Rumbaut, Ruben, 4

Sacramento, California, 21
schools. *See* education
segregation, racial, 33–35, 52–58
Sembène (project), 122
Sembène, Ousmane, 202n9
Senegal, 182
Seymour, William, 75
Simmel, Georg, 24, 155, 180, 203n1
singing, 110
single-parent households, 150–151
slavery, 13
Small, Mario, 24–25, 203n1
soccer, 150–151, 170
sociability, 104–105, 111, 118
social capital theory, 198n15
social class, 98
social cues, 94
social justice, 177–178
social media, 42
social relations, 41–42, 48–52, 80
   culture of connection, 90–130
   religious bases of, 180–186
   trust networks, 23, 65, 126, 129–130, 154, 179
social trust, 7, 22–23
socioeconomics, 19
South Side (Chicago, IL), 53
speaking in tongues *(glossolalia)*, 75, 110
sponsors, 62
standards of conduct, 101
standpoint theory, 192
Stanley, Henry M., 196n10
stereotypes, 183–184
storefront churches, 54–55
strange man of religion, 183–184
student loans, 40
students, 152–153, 191, 196n8
sub-Saharan Africa, 138
success, 132–136
Sunday School (Evangel Ministries), 92

Sunday services, 71–74, 97, 100–104, 107–110, 160
superstition, 170
Sweden, 13

Taiwanese immigrants, 30
taxi drivers, 133–135
technology, 74
terminology, 187
terrorism, 16–17
third cinema, 122
Thornton, Jonathan, 13
Tilly, Charles, 23, 154, 203n1
Togo, 83, 86
trade, 13–15
transatlantic life, 44–46
transcendence, ethnic, 172–177
transformation, 82–87, 157–160, 184
transnational Ghanaians, 4–5, 8, 44–45, 138, 156, 181–182, 184–185
tro-tros, 71–72
trust, 58–64, 198n16
   choosing to trust, 27
   as imaginative and symbolic activity, 117, 155, 180
   impersonal, 23
   personal, 12, 22–27, 65, 115–117, 127, 178–180, 185–186, 203n1
   problems of distrust, 25–26
   religious bases of, 180–186, 203n2
   social, 7, 22–23
trust networks, 23, 65, 126, 154, 179
   basis of, 129–130
Tutu, Osei, 13
Twi, 62, 147, 172

United Kingdom, 75
United States
   African-born population, 2–3, 6, 198n13
   anti-immigrant sentiment, 197n10
   congregational culture, 104–111

United States (*cont.*)
  Department of Homeland Security (DHS), 16–18
  diversity visa, 38
  immigrants, 2–6, 16–18, 28–30, 36–65, 141–146, 195n1, 195nn4–5
  Immigration and Customs Enforcement agency (ICE), 16–18
  immigration policy, 16–17, 38
  religious communities, 5–6
  Taiwanese immigrants, 30
  trust, 58–64
  university education, 139
United States Census Bureau, 19
United States Evangel Ministries, 100
University College of the Gold Coast, 15
university education, 139
University of Ghana, 8, 71, 79, 86, 188
University of London, 15
University of Notre Dame, 191, 196n8
University of Texas at Austin, 188
university or higher education, 3, 40, 138–139
university students, 3
Uptown (Chicago, IL), 58–59, 61*f*
  Gold Coast Taxi, 133, 134*f*
  residential housing, 59, 60*of*
urbanization, 81

values, 169
violence against blacks, 57–58
visas, 38, 40, 62, 162
visions, 75, 131–154, 165

waakye, 10, 39
Warner, Steve, 28, 105
Washington, D.C., 20
Weber, Max, 5, 28
Wednesday services, 103
West Africa
  Christianity, 30, 74–78
  immigrants from, 31–32, 32*f,* 182, 195n4
  Pentecostal churches, 187
West Indians, 26
white civilization, 169
Willowcreek Community Church, 34
Winner's Chapel, 187
women, 45
World Bank, 137
worship nights, 164
woven textiles, 13
Wuthnow, Robert, 90

xenophobia, 26

Yoido Full Gospel Church, 30, 87